READER'S DIGEST

THE PC PROBLEM SOLVER

Reader's
Digest

PUBLISHED BY THE READER'S DIGEST ASSOCIATION LIMITED
LONDON • NEW YORK • MONTREAL • SYDNEY

A READER'S DIGEST BOOK

Published by The Reader's Digest Association Limited
11 Westferry Circus
Canary Wharf
London E14 4HE
www.readersdigest.co.uk

Copyright © Eaglemoss Publications Ltd 2000
Reprinted 2001

ISBN 0 276 42496 4

A CIP data record for this book is available from the British Library

This book was designed, edited and produced by Eaglemoss Publications Ltd
in association with VNU Business Publications Ltd,
based on the partwork *PC KnowHow*

Printed in Singapore

410-005

10 9 8 7 6 5 4 3

Contents

1

Getting Started

Buying a PC

Before you even start looking for a PC you should decide which type of shop fits your needs.

There are more places than ever to buy a PC. They all have advantages and disadvantages, depending on what you need. You can find places where you'll get a rock bottom price – as long as you know what you're looking for. Other places offer better service at a premium. You can pick up the phone and order a computer by credit card from a magazine, or buy one over the Internet, made to your exact specification. Follow these guidelines to see what's best for you.

The high street

High street electrical stores and department stores are easy places to buy a PC, and you'll find well-known brands like Compaq and Packard Bell. However, often the prices are not competitive, and the models may not be the latest ones. In smaller stores, there may not be anyone to answer your questions.

The supermarket

Although there aren't many supermarkets selling computers yet, those that do are offering very good value for money. However, you'll probably find that there isn't a choice of models, and there may not be anyone to demonstrate the system or answer questions. It really will be just the same as buying anything else from your local supermarket.

PC superstores

If you want to try out a PC before buying it, a PC superstore, such as PC World, is the best place to shop. You'll find a wide range of PCs, and plenty of staff to answer questions. If you decide to buy, you'll be able to take whatever you've chosen with you right away.

You may be able to arrange a credit deal to save you paying for everything in one go. But as with high-street stores, the prices aren't as competitive as those of mail-order companies.

Mail order

Pick up a PC magazine and you could be forgiven for thinking that it's all adverts. Ordering a PC off a magazine page is one of the best ways to do it. You'll find the latest technologies, and at the keenest prices. In many cases, the PC will be put together to order.

You won't be able to try before you buy, and you'll have to wait. It's unlikely that there will be any sort of credit facilities available and you'll need a credit card.

Online shopping

Large companies such as Dell offer online shopping, as do smaller mail-order PC makers. You can't try before you buy, but there will often be lots of information about different systems. The disadvantages are much the same as for mail order, and you'll need a credit card.

Second hand

You can buy PCs second hand, but remember you'll be without a warranty, and you could end up with a PC that isn't powerful enough to run the latest programs. Unless you're on a really tight budget, it's not recommended.

Which PC?

Choosing a new PC is not easy. Follow these steps to simplify the process.

Buying a new PC can be hard, particularly if you have never owned or used one before. Here are four sample configurations. Just follow the questions and you'll have a better idea of the sort of system that will suit you best.

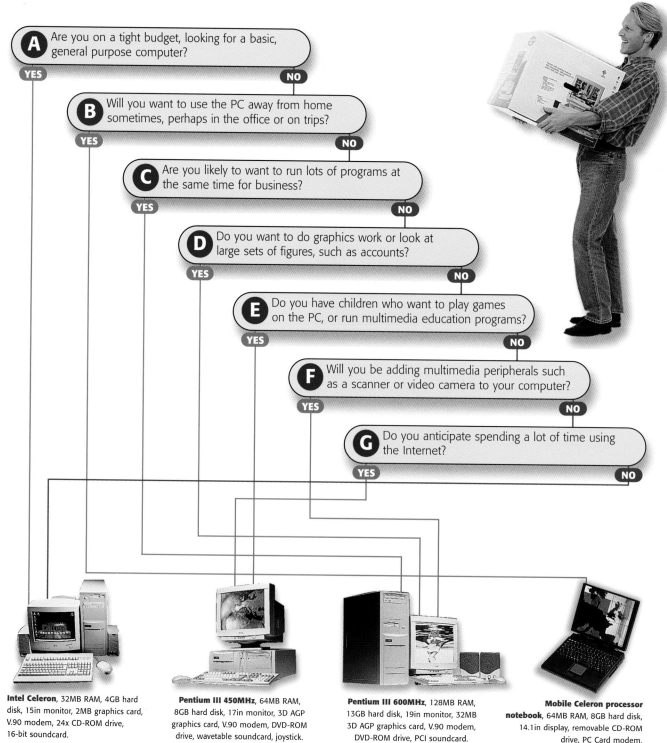

A Are you on a tight budget, looking for a basic, general purpose computer?
YES   NO

B Will you want to use the PC away from home sometimes, perhaps in the office or on trips?
YES   NO

C Are you likely to want to run lots of programs at the same time for business?
YES   NO

D Do you want to do graphics work or look at large sets of figures, such as accounts?
YES   NO

E Do you have children who want to play games on the PC, or run multimedia education programs?
YES   NO

F Will you be adding multimedia peripherals such as a scanner or video camera to your computer?
YES   NO

G Do you anticipate spending a lot of time using the Internet?
YES   NO

Intel Celeron, 32MB RAM, 4GB hard disk, 15in monitor, 2MB graphics card, V.90 modem, 24x CD-ROM drive, 16-bit soundcard.

Pentium III 450MHz, 64MB RAM, 8GB hard disk, 17in monitor, 3D AGP graphics card, V.90 modem, DVD-ROM drive, wavetable soundcard, joystick.

Pentium III 600MHz, 128MB RAM, 13GB hard disk, 19in monitor, 32MB 3D AGP graphics card, V.90 modem, DVD-ROM drive, PCI soundcard.

Mobile Celeron processor notebook, 64MB RAM, 8GB hard disk, 14.1in display, removable CD-ROM drive, PC Card modem.

Read the label

Learn to recognise the parts that make up a PC before a salesman tries to blind you with science.

A PC is the sum of many parts, and each one has a specific purpose. Knowing what they do, and why, means you can make more sense of the different options you'll be bombarded with when you go to buy one.

You may see a package that looks great and seems to include everything, but by cutting out the things you don't need and spending more money on those you do, you will end up with a system better suited to your needs.

If you're not too bothered about playing games, why have about a 3D graphics card, or special speakers? You might be better off opting for a faster modem to give you a better connection to the Internet; or you might want the best possible quality when you print out letters, even if it does take a little longer, and opt for a different type of printer, rather than a bigger screen.

To help you make the right choices, here are what some of the parts of a modern computer do, and what you might need to consider when you're choosing your system.

Graphics card
Graphics cards produce the picture on your PC's display. A card with more memory built into it will display more colours and more information at the same time. If you want to play games, look out for a card with 3D facilities. But 3D isn't necessary if you'll be mostly running word processors or other business type programs. You can add a separate 3D card later if you like.

Soundcard
Soundcards are used to play back music and sound effects. A wavetable card is the most realistic; it has samples of real instruments used to create music, rather than a synthesiser.

Modem
A modem links your PC to the phone line, so you can send and receive e-mail, surf the Internet or exchange faxes with other people. An internal modem fits inside your PC, while an external one sits on your desk and has lights to let you know what's happening. A modem's speed is measured in bits per second (bps). The faster the speed, the better.

Speakers
Some PCs rely on a speaker inside the case, but for better quality look for external ones. See if you can find some that clip on to the side of your monitor. A sub-woofer is an extra speaker which enhances bass sounds.

CD-ROM or DVD drive
Many programs come on CD-ROMs so you can install them quickly and easily; you can also use a CD drive to play music. Faster CD drives mean you can install programs quicker. The latest PCs have DVD drives. These can read CDs as well as DVD discs, which means, with the right software, you could even watch feature films on your PC.

Processor
The processor is the heart of a PC. It does all the work. The speed is measured in Megahertz (MHz) and the bigger the number, the faster the PC. A Pentium III chip is faster than a Pentium II, which in turn is faster than the Celeron.

Memory
The memory (or RAM) chips are where your computer stores the information it's working on at the moment. More memory helps it run faster, and a system with less than 32 megabytes (MB) is underpowered.

Hard disk
Computer programs and the documents you create are stored on the hard disk. The size varies from 4 gigabytes (GB) to 40GB, but under 10GB is not enough.

Look and feel

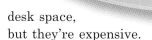

If you are going to spend a lot of time using your PC, it's important to feel comfortable with it.

PCs aren't just uniform boxes. That may have been true a few years ago, but now they come in lots of shapes and sizes, and with different add-ons. You can spend almost as much time thinking about what you want your PC to look like as you can deciding what type of system it should be.

The PC
There are, with the rare exception of all-in-one boxes that include the monitor as well, only two types of PC – the tower case and the desktop case. As the name suggests, a tower case is tall and narrow, while a desktop case sits on top of your desk, usually with the monitor on top of it. A tower case has to go either on the floor or beside the monitor. Sometimes, you'll find that a tower case has more space to add extra expansion cards or disk drives than a desktop but, on the whole, you can make your choice based on which is the more convenient shape. It might also be worth looking for a case that's easy to open if you think you might want to upgrade later – with some you have to undo dozens of screws; others come apart at the flick of a lever.

The monitor
The monitor is the face of your computer, so it's worth making sure you get a good one. Although you'll find some systems with a 14in monitor, a 15in one isn't much more expensive and will give you a much better display. If you want to do lots of graphical work or often use large spreadsheets, consider a 17in model.

You can also buy monitors that have speakers built in, which will save you having to clutter up your desk. For the ultimate in size, flat-panel liquid crystal displays (LCDs) take up very little

desk space, but they're expensive.

A key thing to look for when choosing a monitor is the refresh rate, that is how many times a second the picture is updated. Look for a rating of at least 75Hz; the higher the number the better, especially if you're going to be using the computer a lot.

The keyboard
If you buy a cheap PC, it'll come with a cheap keyboard. That may be fine for occasional use but it's a false economy for anyone planning to use the computer regularly. A bad keyboard, together with a bad seat, can end up causing you lots of problems, including RSI (repetitive strain injury).

It's worth spending a little extra for an ergonomic keyboard. These usually include a wrist rest to help you keep the right position. With some, the keyboard is split in two, which makes typing even more natural though it feels awkward if you can't touch type. If cables are a problem, you can buy a cordless keyboard; you just have to point it at the computer.

The mouse
There are different types of mouse and there are also alternatives. With most PCs you get a standard two-button mouse, but you can buy a cordless mouse or one with more buttons. The third button can be configured to do whatever you want. There's also a mouse with a wheel between the buttons. The wheel can be used to scroll through documents without having to move to the side of the screen. Or how about a pad? It's a small plastic sheet that you write on with a special pen, so you can draw on screen just as easily as you would on a piece of paper.

Software bundles

Think carefully about software bundled with a new computer: will it do exactly what you want?

Without software PCs can't do anything useful. Windows usually comes with new PCs but the software with it only enables you to write basic documents, send e-mail and connect to the Internet. To do anything else, you need extra software. The best solution is a software bundle, a collection of programs sold as a package or included free with a new PC. Free software is enticing, but what appears to be a

great deal because it includes so many programs might be a bit of a con. The first thing to consider is what you want to do with your PC. For most people a word processor is essential; plus a spreadsheet that can be used to do calculations or organise information. You might also want a personal organiser and a program to create pages on the Internet. If you're planning to use your PC for business, a database program is useful too.

Office suites

These are the most common bundles. Office suites usually contain a spreadsheet, a word processor, a personal organiser and sometimes extra programs like a Web page editor. The most popular suites are Microsoft Office, Lotus SmartSuite and Corel WordPerfect Suite.

If you're planning to buy one of these suites, shop around. Prices vary, and you may be able to upgrade the software that came with your PC at a discount.

Integrated software

Cheaper PCs are likely to come bundled with an integrated package – a single program that incorporates a word processor, spreadsheet, database and so on. The most popular integrated packages are Microsoft Works and Claris Works. They are more than adequate for most home computing.

But if you plan to bring work home from the office, find out whether you can save files in a format that is compatible with your home system. There's no point bringing work home to find your computer can't read it.

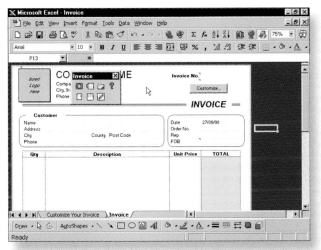

Excel is one of the most popular programs. It's a spreadsheet, which means it can be set up to perform calculations on numbers, and even turn them into instant graphs.

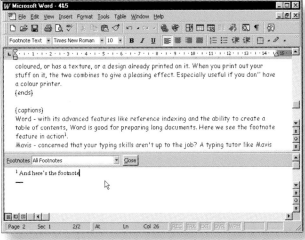

A word processor such as Microsoft Word is essential for business tasks such as letter writing or desktop publishing.

Buyer beware

Know your rights and you should be able to avoid being cheated by an unscrupulous supplier.

Understandably, people can be apprehensive when they are thinking of spending a lot of money on something like a PC. What if it goes wrong? What if it's not delivered? How should you pay? Who can help solve problems?

Fortunately, there are straightforward answers to all these questions, and the list on the next page will help you to compare PCs from different suppliers without too much difficulty. Fill in the details of different systems as you go.

Don't forget

It's easy to compare basic specifications such as the amount of memory, the size of the hard disk and so on, but you can forget other things that are just as important. For instance, will you have to take the PC back to the manufacturer if it goes wrong or will someone come to your home to repair it? If you work from home, that could be vital. Check the warranty (see pages 42–3). Fill in all the spaces on the list for each PC you're considering, and if the answer isn't obvious, don't be afraid to ask. It's your money; you're entitled to know what you'll be spending it on.

There is no final answer to which computer to buy because everyone's answers will be different. You'll have to weigh up the different factors yourself.

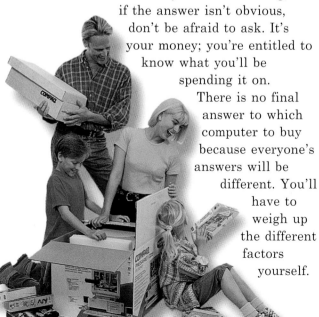

Watch out!

It can sometimes seem like the odds are stacked against you when you're faced with a computer salesperson who seems to know it all, but here are some points to bear in mind:

BEFORE YOU BUY

● If you can, pay by credit card, especially for telephone and mail-order purchases. The credit-card company is legally liable as well as the supplier, so if the PC doesn't arrive, you will get your money back.

● Always write down the names of people you deal with in person or on the phone. If there are any problems later, it'll make them easier to sort out.

● If you need a computer by a certain date, write 'Time Is Of The Essence' on the order form; otherwise you won't have any grounds for complaint if it doesn't arrive on time or turns up months late.

● If you need to do a specific task with your computer, make that clear to the salesperson. Whatever you end up buying must be fit for any task you told the salesperson you wanted to do with it.

● Remember to confirm that a price includes taxes, delivery and all the options you want with the computer.

● In-store credit agreements can seem attractive, but read the small print carefully. Buy now, pay later, interest-free credit can turn out to be expensive if you miss the payment date. A store must give you a written quotation for credit if you ask. Compare it with a bank loan or credit-card loan for the same amount.

WHEN YOU'VE BOUGHT YOUR COMPUTER

● Don't just sign for a delivery without checking the boxes to make sure that the contents are undamaged. If there is damage to the packaging, you should note that clearly on the courier's receipt, and contact the supplier immediately.

● Check all the parts of your system as soon as you can. If you don't use your scanner for a month, and then discover it doesn't work, you'll have a harder time having it replaced.

● If something goes wrong, complain promptly, but stay calm. You won't win any support by being rude to people.

● You are entitled to demand your money back within a reasonable time if the PC doesn't work. You don't have to accept a credit note or a replacement from the supplier.

● If a supplier isn't dealing with your complaint properly, contact your local Citizens' Advice Bureau for help. If you still can't get your money back and you feel you're entitled to it, contact the credit-card company that you used to buy the computer.

Shopping list

Fill in a list like the one below as you look around, to help you compare computer systems.

	Computer 1	Computer 2	Computer 3
Supplier			
Brand and model			
Sales telephone number			
Contact name			
Quote reference			
Processor type and speed			
Memory			
Disk size			
CD-ROM speed			
DVD-ROM	£*	£	£
Video card type and memory			
Soundcard			
Speakers	£	£	£
Modem	£	£	£
Mouse type			
Keyboard type			
Monitor size			
Desktop or tower case?			
Windows 98 or 2000?			
Software included			
Type of warranty			
Will someone come out to repair?			
Who pays for returning PC for repair?			
Length of warranty			
Cost to extend warranty			
Is telephone support included?			
Can the system be set up for you?	£	£	£
Total cost of system (incl. tax or VAT)	£	£	£
Delivery charges			
Time to deliver system			
Payment method			
APR if credit is being offered			
Total cost of credit	£	£	£
Length of credit period			

* Some add-ons are optional and will increase
the price of your system. Fill in the extra cost here.

Buying a printer

After your PC itself, a printer is probably the most important piece of equipment you can buy.

Sooner or later you'll need to print things out, which means, of course, you'll need a printer. Not so long ago there was really only one type of printer you could buy: the dot matrix (see page 16). Anything that offered high-quality printing was far too expensive for a home user. Nowadays, any computer store will stock several printers to suit a variety of needs at a range of accessible prices.

The most popular type of printer is an inkjet (below). It works by firing dots of ink at a sheet of paper – a bit like squeezing the cartridge in a fountain pen but more precise. Basic inkjet printers cost very little but top-of-the-range models can cost much

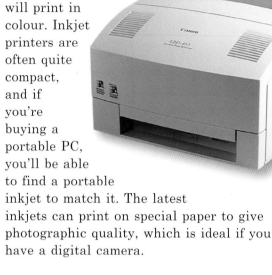

more. Nearly all will print in colour. Inkjet printers are often quite compact, and if you're buying a portable PC, you'll be able to find a portable inkjet to match it. The latest inkjets can print on special paper to give photographic quality, which is ideal if you have a digital camera.

See the light

The second common type of printer is a laser (above), which works in a similar way to photocopiers, using a fine black powder called toner to make up the images. They rely on your PC to do a lot of the work of transferring the page onto paper, so a slow PC will print slowly. Personal laser printers are compact and not too expensive (though more than inkjets). They usually print in black and white. Colour laser printers are very expensive.

Jargon buster

Cartridge The part of the printer that you replace when it runs out of ink or toner. Find out how many pages you can expect from each cartridge. More pages and a cheap cartridge means the printer is cheaper to run.

CMYK Cyan magenta yellow and key (or black), the four colours used in an inkjet printer to make up any other colour.

Dpi This stands for dots per inch, the number of dots the printer puts on the page in each inch. High numbers mean better quality.

GDI printer Sometimes called a Windows printer, this is the type of printer that uses your computer to do most of the work of creating the page.

Gsm This stands for grammes per square metre and is often used to refer to the thickness of paper a printer can handle. Bigger numbers mean thicker paper or card; typical photocopier paper is 80gsm, while a business card is about 120gsm.

Parallel port The usual way of connecting a printer to a computer. Some newer printers connect via the USB port. It's faster and the printer can be connected or disconnected without switching off the PC.

Photo-realistic This describes a printer that can produce near-photo-quality prints, but you'll need a special ink cartridge and special paper for the best results.

Ppm Pages per minute, the speed at which a printer prints. Colour printers may quote one speed for colour and another for black and white.

Sheet feeder A device or part of the printer that takes a sheet of paper from a stack and feeds it through. On printers without this facility (usually portable, or very cheap ones) you'll have to put each sheet in yourself at the right time.

Toner The fine powder used by a laser printer.

Which printer?

Follow the simple steps below to discover which kind of printer would be best for you.

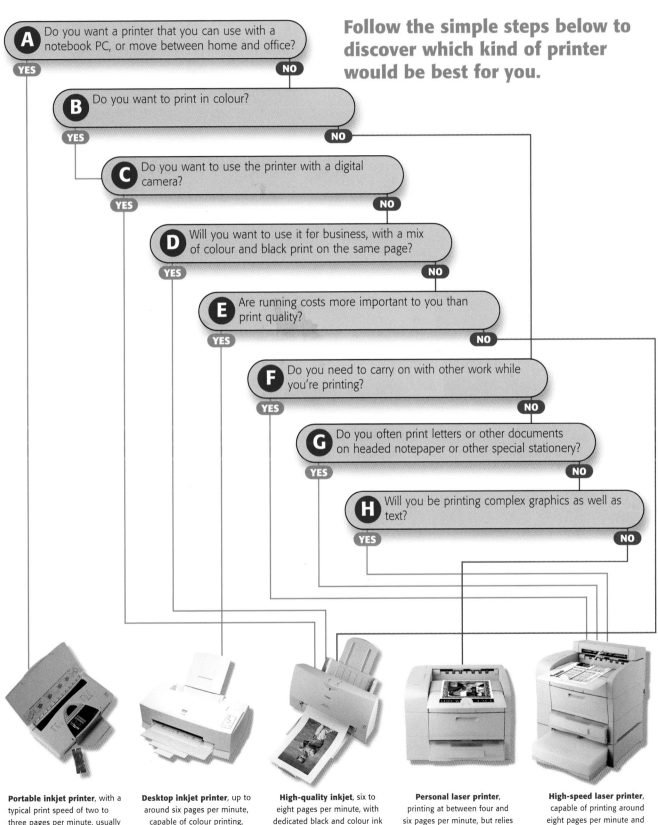

A Do you want a printer that you can use with a notebook PC, or move between home and office?
YES — NO

B Do you want to print in colour?
YES — NO

C Do you want to use the printer with a digital camera?
YES — NO

D Will you want to use it for business, with a mix of colour and black print on the same page?
YES — NO

E Are running costs more important to you than print quality?
YES — NO

F Do you need to carry on with other work while you're printing?
YES — NO

G Do you often print letters or other documents on headed notepaper or other special stationery?
YES — NO

H Will you be printing complex graphics as well as text?
YES — NO

Portable inkjet printer, with a typical print speed of two to three pages per minute, usually black printing only with a manual paper feed.

Desktop inkjet printer, up to around six pages per minute, capable of colour printing, although you may have to change cartridges for colour.

High-quality inkjet, six to eight pages per minute, with dedicated black and colour ink cartridges, and photo printing with suitable ink and paper.

Personal laser printer, printing at between four and six pages per minute, but relies on your computer to do a lot of the work.

High-speed laser printer, capable of printing around eight pages per minute and holding more than one type of paper simultaneously.

Choosing a printer

Most people opt for an inkjet printer, but for special needs consider a laser or dot matrix.

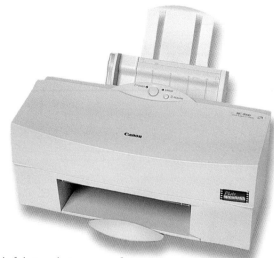

Understanding more about the different types of printer will help you make the right decision.

Dot-matrix printers

These are the cheapest type of printer, but they are hard to find. Dot-matrix printers (below) work just like the printer in a cash register, making letters up out of dots created by pins fired against a ribbon. The more pins, the better the quality of its printing. Look for a 24-pin printer if you want to buy one. Most models can also print in colour, using a multicoloured ribbon.

There's really just one reason to buy a dot-matrix printer: they're the only type that can print on carbon paper. So if you want carbon copies, or you have special stationery that has carbon in it – invoice forms, for instance – you'll need one of these. For anything else, they're too old-fashioned and not of good enough quality. You can buy an inkjet printer much more easily, so unless you see a tremendous bargain, you should not consider buying a dot-matrix printer.

Many inkjet printers work much more slowly when printing in colour, and the colour resolution may also be less than in black and white. Most inkjet printers rely on your computer to do most of the work, and so you may find the PC goes slowly when you're printing.

To get the best from an inkjet printer you need to be careful about the paper that you use. While almost all will print on cheap photocopier paper, look closely and you'll see the difference between brands of paper. Since the printer works by firing wet ink at each sheet, if the paper's too absorbent, images smudge. For the best results, you need special paper, which can be expensive. Some printers claim to give photo-quality output, but for those you may need to buy a special ink cartridge as well as the paper, making it expensive. Stick with ordinary paper and ink for all your day-to-day printing.

Inkjet printers

For most home users, this is the best sort of printer to buy. An inkjet (top right) can produce both colour and black and white printing, and the quality is very good. A modern inkjet will produce print-outs with a resolution of 600 dots per inch (dpi). It will also typically be able to print out pages of text at between four and six pages per minute (ppm). Some larger models can print on paper as big as A3, while for people on the move, there are printers small enough to fit in a briefcase.

Laser printers

These are also sometimes called page printers or LED printers. Unlike inkjets, which create the image of a page one row of dots at a time, lasers build up an image of a whole page on a special drum, just like a photocopier.

Once the whole page is created the image is transferred to paper using toner, again like a photocopier. The only difference is that instead of being scanned with a bright light, the image is made by a computer controlling a laser, or a series of LEDs (light-emitting diodes).

To create an image of a page, laser printers need memory, just like your PC. A printer with more memory can create more complicated pages. You can program some to do things like add your own letterhead to each page that's printed.

Low-cost laser printers generally have a resolution of 300dpi, although more and more models manage 600dpi at a reasonable price. Bear in mind that, because many printers have some form of enhancement, a salesperson may claim a resolution of 600dpi (with enhancement). A real resolution is more important than an enhanced one.

Laser printers usually come with more sophisticated options for handling paper than other types of printer. You may be able to have two stacks of paper so you can have headed notepaper and ordinary paper in it at the same time, saving you having to swap over.

Laser printers can be fast. If you're prepared to pay, you can buy one that will print out up to 12 pages per minute, but very detailed pages print more slowly. Unless you spend a lot of money, you won't be able to find a colour laser, or one that prints on paper larger than A4.

Specialist printers

Colour laser printers are faster than colour inkjets, but the quality of the colour printing is often not as good. Lasers use four toner colours – cyan, magenta, yellow and black – and mix other colours from these. Although they're becoming more popular, they're still not common and as a result they're expensive to run. They are best suited to producing documents on which it's not crucial that the colours are accurate.

For high-quality results you should consider other types of colour printing. The most accurate colours are achieved by printers that use a process called dye sublimation, but these are not for the casual user. These printers cost much more than a computer, the running costs are substantial and special paper is required.

Another type of colour printer is the hot wax printer. As the name suggests, blocks of coloured wax are heated and used to print on the paper. The advantage is that any paper the wax will stick to, including photocopier paper, can be used, making them much cheaper to run than dye sublimation printers. However, they are very expensive to buy and are not easily available.

Thermal transfer printers use a special ribbon and produce good-quality prints. The printers cost very little but don't be fooled into thinking they're cheap. The ribbons can be used just once, and you could find each sheet of paper costing a fortune in ribbon alone.

Consumables

When you buy a printer, remember that you're making a commitment to continue paying out money. You will need to keep your printer stocked with paper and ink or toner.

Choose the wrong model and you could end up spending a fortune, so check out how much it will cost you to run before making your decision. The first thing is to find out how easily you can obtain supplies. If the printer's not a well-known make, or it's an end-of-line special, will you be able to get supplies for much longer? Will you have to go back to just one shop, or can you shop around?

With inkjet printers, remember that most of your printing is likely to be in black, so can you replace the black ink on its own, or will you have to throw away perfectly good colour ink just because the black section of a cartridge is worn out? Remember that the stunning printouts in the shop may well have been done on expensive paper. Ask to see colour printing on ordinary paper.

With a laser printer, find out how much toner cartridges cost and be prepared for a shock. On some models, it could be more than a cheap inkjet – and you need to multiply that by four for colour. You can buy recycled units more cheaply, but find out first whether or not that will invalidate your warranty.

Back-up & storage

Give yourself more room for storing files and back up the precious data on your PC.

Your PC has a hard disk (right), which stores the programs you use as well as the work you create. In order to keep your computer working smoothly, you should always have a minimum of 100MB free on your hard disk. No matter how much free space you think you have, you will soon find that you're running short, and that's the time to think about storage.

There are other good reasons to add storage to your PC. It's a good idea to keep a copy of vital information away from your computer, in case the computer is stolen or destroyed by fire, or your data is accidentally deleted. You might want to take work to and from your office or school – and the floppy disk drive fitted to most PCs can't hold enough information, not to mention that you'd need over 1,000 floppy disks to make a copy of the typical PC's hard disk drive.

What types of storage are there, and when should you use them? How easy is it to integrate them with your PC? There are three main storage systems: expansion, to allow you to add space to your PC; removable, which you can unload and swap round easily; and back-up, for keeping information safe. Adding storage to your PC is not difficult. Sometimes, you'll need to take the PC's case off and plug in a new disk drive, but it's usually straightforward, and you'll soon be up and running with much more capacity than before.

Expansion storage

The main type of expansion storage is an extra hard disk drive; your computer will already have a main disk drive referred to as drive C. Add an extra one and it becomes drive D. If you want to experiment with editing videos on your PC, it's worth having a drive just for that; you should consider a fast SCSI audiovisual drive, which is designed to save information quickly enough for video. A slower drive just means jerky pictures.

Most PCs have a hard drive and a CD drive fitted, which means you are limited to two more hard drives using the EIDE connectors built into the PC. If you want to add anything more, you'll have to look for one of the other types of connector. If you just need more space, an extra hard disk is the cheapest option.

Removable storage

Removable storage consists of larger versions of your floppy disk drive. With a removable drive, you can eject one disk, and load another one. If you can afford more disks, you have an effectively unlimited amount of storage space.

Removable storage drives start with the Iomega Zip drive, which is available in 100MB and 250MB versions. The costlier Iomega Jaz drives are available in 1GB and 2GB versions and they perform almost as quickly as a hard disk. In all cases, the storage drives that connect to a SCSI card are faster than those that connect to your computer's parallel port, although they are not quite as versatile.

If you use your computer for a variety of tasks, a removable drive could be a good choice. You could have, for instance, one with all your office work on it, and another full of games, and just swap them over when you need to. But remember that if you want things from the different disks at the same time, you'll have problems.

Bear in mind, too, that although removable disks give you unlimited amounts of storage, you'll have to pay a lot of money for disks, and it may often be cheaper to buy a single large hard disk drive. However, if you need to move large files from one computer to another, or you can easily separate out different types of information that you don't need at the same time, then a removable drive is a great option.

You can also use the disks to back up information that you want to keep safely somewhere else.

There are, of course, removable storage devices that you can't save information on, such as CD-ROM and DVD (Digital Versatile Disc). These are used to give you access to information prepared by someone else. A DVD drive can hold the equivalent of several CDs and can even play back feature films, although you need a decoder card for that.

Back-up storage

Computers are pretty reliable, but things do go wrong with them. You might, for example, lose the data that you've just been working on. It's important, therefore, to have a back-up copy.

Back-up storage is available in a number of forms. You can use Zip or Jaz disks to save information, although it's not a cheap option. The cheapest way to back up your data is with a tape drive. This is a unit that connects to your computer and takes a small cassette of tape, copying all the information from your hard drive to the tape. If something goes wrong, you can copy it back, but make sure you have a copy of the disks you need to access the tape drive.

There are many kinds of tape drive available, ranging from units that can store a couple of hundred megabytes per tape and plug into your computer's EIDE connector, just like a new disk, to high-capacity models that use DAT (Digital Audio Tape) and can store the contents of a few hard disks on a single tape. Tapes are fairly cheap, so it's easy to buy enough to keep lots of copies of your important information.

On the down side, however, if you want just one thing from a tape, you'll have the same problem as when you want to watch a single program in the middle of a video tape; it may take some time to find it. As a result, many people also use some type of removable storage to back up information that they might want to access quickly.

You can use special versions of CD and DVD drives to back up information; CD-R (Recordable) and CD-RW (Re-writable) both allow you to save information on blank CDs, and DVD-R does the same for DVD. You can even record your own music CDs with the right programs. The disadvantage is that with a CD, it will still take a few blank discs to copy everything from your computer's hard drive, and it's much slower than other ways of backing up.

Jargon buster

ATA A common interface for storage devices which is also sometimes known as EIDE.

CD-R This stands for CD-Recordable – a CD that you can save information on once. You can't erase things that you've already copied to the disc.

CD-RW This stands for CD-Re-writable. This type of CD can be used just like an ordinary disc; you can delete and re-record data.

DVD-R A re-writable form of DVD, that holds up to 5.4GB of information.

DVD-ROM Read only DVDs, similar to CD-ROMs, but with a much higher capacity.

EIDE The standard way of connecting hard disks and CD-ROMs in modern PCs. Most computers can have up to four EIDE devices installed, including removable disks, tapes and CDs.

FireWire This is a type of high-speed connector, also called 1394, that is starting to appear on digital camcorders and may also crop up on some hard disks designed for multimedia use. It's faster than USB, but don't expect to find it on cheap PCs just yet.

IDE The standard way of connecting hard disks on PCs. Now superseded by EIDE, but the terms are often interchanged.

SCSI One of the older standards for connecting disk drives and other storage devices to a computer. You'll usually need a special SCSI controller (also called an adapter card) to add SCSI to your computer. SCSI drives can be very fast, but are more expensive than EIDE types.

USB This stands for universal serial bus, a type of connector found on most new PCs. It can be used for a number of things, including some external storage devices such as Zip drives.

Peripherals

You can get more from your computer if you buy specialised add-ons or peripherals.

Peripherals are extra goodies you can buy to make your PC more versatile and more powerful. For some people they're just gadgets, but for others they are the factor that makes it worth buying a computer.

Before you buy, find out what connectors you have on your PC. A modern PC will have one or more USB ports, and most of the gadgets listed here are available in versions to plug into them. USB versions are straightforward to set up – you just plug the new peripheral into the socket of the last one and the PC will install the software for you. If you don't have USB connectors, you can still buy peripherals, but setting them up will be harder. You may have to fit extra parts in the PC.

Joystick
PCs can be great for playing games, but if you want fast shooting action, using a keyboard and mouse lacks a certain something. The odds are better against the aliens and you will have a more realistic experience of flying that jet plane with a joystick or some other type of game controller.

Digital camera
With a digital camera you can take pictures and transfer them to your computer in minutes. Send a picture of the new baby via e-mail to relatives in Australia, or add snaps to a Web page. With a good colour printer, you can make proper prints.

Almost any camera will do if you just want to e-mail pictures or put them on the Internet. But if you want to print them, spend more money on a 'mega-pixel' camera, which takes higher quality pictures; otherwise snaps will always look grainy. And remember that while a screen built into the camera looks good, it uses batteries quickly, so choose one with an old-fashioned viewfinder too.

Scanner
A scanner lets you turn anything on paper into a computer document. With a modem, your PC becomes a fax machine. With a printer, it can be used as a copier.

A flatbed scanner looks like a small photocopier and takes up a lot of space, but you can scan almost anything with it. Other options are hand scanners, such as the Visioneer Paperport, that pull a sheet of paper through automatically. They're compact, but you can't scan a book unless you cut it up. Photo enthusiasts can buy special film scanners that give high quality.

Video camera
Add a video camera to your PC, hook up to the Internet, and you have an instant video phone. With appropriate software, the computer will save pictures of everyone who comes into the room!

Cameras come in two types. USB cameras plug in to the USB port, while others come with a capture card which can also be used with a video recorder or camcorder, allowing you to save holiday clips, or other videos on your hard disk.

For serious video work, like editing films, buy a dedicated capture card and use your camcorder. If it's just chatting to people online, a USB camera will give hours of fun.

Art pad
An art pad is the best way to create PC art. You can draw as if you are using a pen and paper on a plastic tablet. They come in different sizes, so you can find one that's the right size for your desk and the type of drawings you want to do. Check whether the pad replaces your mouse or can be used alongside it. You may have to keep swapping connectors if the pad's not convenient to use when you're not drawing.

Portables

Notebook computers offer all the functions of desktop computers in a portable case.

Notebook computers – older terms like laptop are rarely used any more – can do pretty much anything desktop computers can do. However, their small size means they don't use many off-the-shelf components and this makes them more expensive than desktop PCs of a similar specification. Consider your requirements carefully before you buy. It's essential to choose the notebook that's right for you because you can't change the screen, keyboard or pointing device if you don't like them.

Notebook PCs come in all shapes and sizes, from tiny sub-notebooks to briefcase-size models with big screens. All of them run Windows and have the same set of applications as a desktop PC. If the licence permits it, you can install your desktop applications on a notebook, to avoid having to buy two copies of everything.

One of the most important features of a notebook is its keyboard. Some keyboards are near full-size while others are compressed with small keys. Unlike a normal keyboard, there won't be a separate numeric keypad.

Most notebooks use a touch-sensitive pad as a mouse replacement. These take some getting used to and you might prefer the keyboard nipple used by some manufacturers. In either case, you can always plug in a standard mouse if you want to.

A notebook has a smaller selection of ports than a desktop PC but you can still plug in devices such as a printer, mouse and keyboard.

Some notebooks come with both floppy and CD-ROM drives fitted, others have one drive that must be swapped when you want to use the other. Some smaller notebooks have no internal drives and instead use external ones that connect with a cable.

All notebooks can be powered by the mains or an internal rechargeable battery. The battery lets you use a notebook on the move. Lithium-ion batteries give longest use but cheaper notebooks often use Nickel Metal Hydride batteries.

All notebooks have a flat-panel colour LCD screen. Screen quality varies a lot between notebooks, so look at it closely before buying.

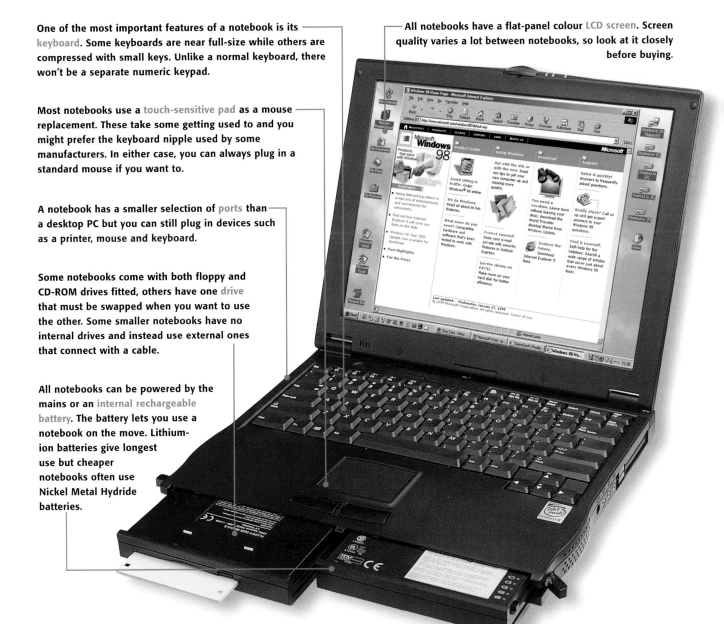

Starting up

Take a quick look at all the bits and pieces that make up a computer system.

A PC depends on software to function. Most PC software comes on CD-ROMs, which look like audio CDs but contain encyclopaedias, games, accounts programs, word processors and so on. The software programs are displayed on a monitor and controlled via a keyboard and mouse, both of which are used to send commands to the main system.

Thus far a PC has something in common with a video recorder with its cassettes, TV screen and remote control. Where a PC is different is that its processor – its brain – is not pre-programmed for the specific tasks of recording and playing tapes. It's adaptable. Among other things, it can calculate taxes, answer the phone and check your spelling.

You don't need to know about engines to drive a car, and you don't need to know how a PC works to use it effectively. However, you do need to be familiar with the controls and accessories described here.

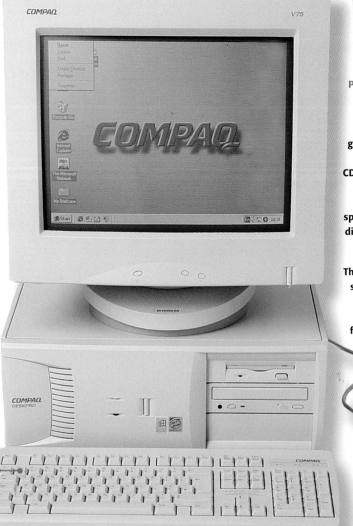

The monitor displays what a PC is doing and it does so in millions of vivid colours. Screen sizes range from 14in, which is rather small, to 21in, which is excessively generous. Most are 15in or 17in. The larger models are not only expensive, they're too bulky for the average desk. Some monitors incorporate speakers and microphones and a small number have built-in cameras for video conferencing.

The standard computer keyboard uses the Qwerty layout, a name derived from the first six letters on the top row. A rectangular keyboard is suitable for learners but some may prefer a moulded keyboard that uses the same layout in a more ergonomic case. Non-Qwerty layouts, including Braille, are also available.

PC speakers come in all shapes and sizes. Some are internal, others external. They have to be able to generate all the sounds that a PC is capable of producing, including CD-quality stereo, speech, telephone messages and exploding space ships. The best way of judging speakers is to listen to them playing different kinds of sound at different levels of volume.

The mouse controls a pointer on the screen. As you move the mouse on the mouse mat, it moves the pointer accordingly: push it away from you and pointer moves to the top of screen; pull it towards you and the pointer moves down. You may also move it from side to side and in any direction in between. The buttons on the mouse determine whether the pointer is used to draw objects, access pull-down menus or to select and move items.

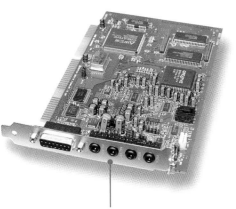

An internal modem is a device that turns computer signals into a form that can be sent down an ordinary telephone line. It must have a socket for a phone cable and may also have jacks for a telephone handset, microphone and speaker. External modems are also available.

The soundcard, which processes sound and music, plugs into a socket inside the PC. Its connectors are on the back panel. The small jack plugs are for speakers, microphone and line connections to other equipment. The larger socket accepts either a joystick or a MIDI instrument.

Joysticks are for playing games. The buttons can be programmed according to the game being played, and may be used to fire guns, launch missiles or operate the brakes of a car.

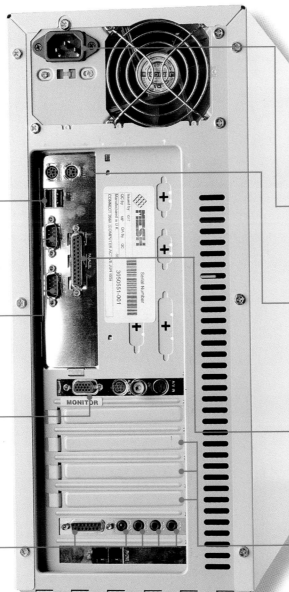

USB ports are a recent innovation. They can be used like parallel and serial ports but really come into their own when used with more complicated equipment, such as scanners and digital video cameras, where a lot of information has to be transferred very quickly.

Your computer's power lead and the socket it plugs into are identical to the lead you use to power a kettle or other domestic appliances.

This PC has two almost identical PS2 ports. One is for a keyboard and the other for a mouse. Not all PCs have these ports, in which case there'll be a DIN socket for the keyboard and the mouse has to be plugged into a serial port.

Serial ports are for connecting mice, external modems and some types of printer. You can also connect two PCs by a cable between their serial ports.

The monitor port connects your PC to a monitor so you can see what it is doing.

The parallel port was originally designed for printers, but other devices, such as a scanner or Zip drive, can be connected at the same time as a printer using a piggy-back arrangement called a pass-through adapter.

If you plan to play games with your PC you will need to connect a joystick to the joystick port which is connected to a soundcard. The soundcard will also have sockets for external speakers and a microphone.

Your computer should incorporate several expansion slots for devices such as an internal modem or a soundcard (see above).

Inside your PC

Lift the lid off your computer and you should find that it is not as complicated as you thought.

The inside of a PC looks complicated, but the modular design means that most parts are easy to change; just a question of unplugging one component and slotting in another.

Computers generally come in two types of case: desktops and towers. Although there are some slight internal differences, a tower case is essentially no more than a desktop case turned on its side. There is usually more room inside a tower case. Removing a computer's case is usually a matter of undoing a few screws or bolts and sliding off the cover. Make sure that the computer is turned off when you do it and take care not to snag any loose wires.

The **power supply** is a transformer that converts the 240V mains supply into a voltage that the PC can use. The red and yellow cables supply power to all parts of the system.

Random Access Memory (RAM) is a PC's short-term memory. When a PC is switched on, it stores parts of the operating system, running applications and any work you are doing. The more RAM a PC has, the faster it will be. RAM loses its contents when a PC is switched off.

The **graphics card** is responsible for displaying images on the monitor. Special graphics cards called 3D accelerators can speed up sophisticated three-dimensional graphics, making games look better and play more smoothly.

The chips on a PC's motherboard (main circuit board) are called the **chipset**. These control some of the most important parts of a PC and allow the processor to communicate with the other components.

Sometimes called the CPU (central processing unit), the **processor** is the brain of any PC. The faster and more powerful it is, the faster and more powerful the PC. Most PCs have processors made by Intel, but there are other types made by companies such as AMD and Cyrix.

The **hard disk** provides long-term storage for software and your work. It looks like a metal box but inside are several magnetic disks rotating at very high speeds. Hard disks store data even when a PC is switched off unlike RAM.

Expansion slots are narrow plastic slots with electrical connectors that let you add expansion cards to a PC. Some expansion cards are essential like the graphics cards, while others are useful extras like a modem. Most new PCs have several PCI expansion slots and a single AGP slot. Some older PCs may also have ISA slots (see Glossary).

A **modem** lets a computer communicate with another computer over the telephone line, for such things as accessing the Internet and sending e-mail. Most modern PCs come with an internal modem (on an expansion card) but external modems are also available.

A **soundcard** is essential if you want your PC to make noises. Some soundcards are built onto the motherboard, some fit into an expansion slot but all convert computer data into sound that you hear through your speakers.

Starting out

The online Help systems that come with the latest versions of Windows make it easy to get up and running.

In the past, when you bought an operating system for your PC, it came with copious documentation – much more than is typically supplied with today's software. However, while software and operating systems were accompanied by huge manuals, their content wasn't particularly easy to digest. They were often written by experts for experts, and so were not much help for first-time users.

Times have changed and both software and operating systems are more complex. Even compared with their immediate predecessor, Windows 3.1, Windows 95 and 98 are much more complicated operating systems. Most new PCs come with the latest version of Windows – Windows 98 SE

(Second Edition). Windows 95 and 98 (both editions) can do more but, paradoxically, are easier to use than earlier operating systems, in part because they have a more consistent intuitive user interface. Also, they can perform tricky operations, such as installing and configuring soundcards, without requiring any technical knowledge on the part of the user. In short, you should get far fewer problems with them.

When you buy Windows these days, the only manual supplied with it is the slimline *Getting Started* book. This does not attempt to tell you everything there is to know about Windows, just enough to get you up and running. It covers the basics like

Books on Windows 2000, as well as on Windows 98, are available. Go to Microsoft Press's Web site for information.

Get started with Windows 98

1 As well as the *Getting Started* book supplied with Windows 98, there's plenty of other learning material for novices. All the other material is supplied on disk, which makes it much easier to use – it's always available while you are using your PC; it's searchable, which means you don't have to dip into an index to find things; and it's also interactive, so you can click on buttons or text in the online material to launch a program or a troubleshooter wizard.

Windows online Help is your first port of call whenever you want more information on a particular Windows 98 feature. This is always available, no matter what you're doing. Simply click on Start, Help, to bring up the main **Windows 98 Help** index. Note that applications, such as Word or Excel, have their own Help system, brought up by hitting the F1 key.

using and customising your desktop, controlling a mouse and using the Internet. It also covers the changes between Windows 95 and 98. If you want more detail, you'll have to buy a book. Most good bookshops have numerous titles on Windows 98, at various prices.

If you have Internet access, pay a visit to http://computer-manuals.co.uk or www.amazon.co.uk to buy your books online.

Microsoft Press has a Web site at http://mspress.microsoft.com/ which has a comprehensive list of Windows 98 titles and other Microsoft books.

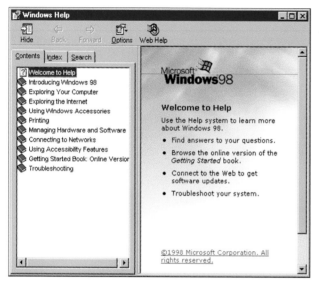

2 Help is organised into various topics indicated by tiny purple book icons. To open that book, simply click on the book icon. The book's contents are displayed on the right. If you want to browse the index, click on the Index tab. If you want to find something not listed in the Index, click on the Search tab. The *Getting Started* book is also reproduced here, in Help format. Another important source of Windows 98 learning material is the **Discover Windows 98** online tutorial. To run this, place your Windows 98 CD-ROM in the CD-ROM drive and click on Start, Run. In the Open dialogue box, type in TOUR98 and click on OK.

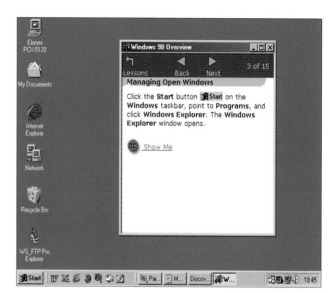

4 If you're not sure how to carry out an on-screen instruction, a **Show Me button** shows you how. Another nice touch with the Discover Windows 98 tutorial is that the interactive portions are not simulations. You manipulate your version of Windows 98 and not an imitation of the real thing.

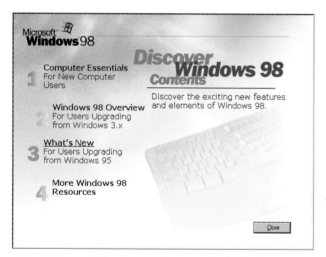

3 This tutorial has three sections, catering for absolute beginners to computing as well as those upgrading from earlier versions of Windows. The lessons are in **multimedia** form, so as well as animated graphics you get spoken instructions. And because it's a multimedia lesson, you'll find it much easier to absorb than reading it off a page.

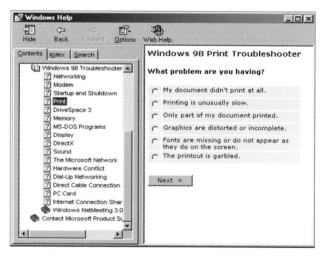

5 Also included with Windows 98 as standard are a number of **Troubleshooter programs**, which can help to solve common problems. For example, Print Troubleshooter can take you through the steps needed to determine why your printer isn't working. You can access troubleshooters from the Windows 98 Help system as well as from the Microsoft Web site at www.microsoft.com/. They take the form of a number of questions that you have to answer before you can proceed to the next question. By a process of elimination, the possible cause of the problem can be isolated and a course of action to fix it suggested.

Windows

Windows is the software that allows all your other applications and hardware to work together.

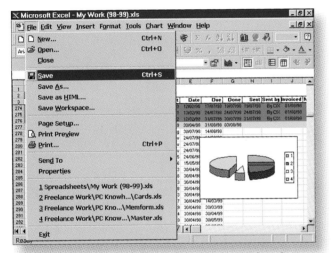

Like all good Windows programs, the Excel spreadsheet has a Save command on its File menu.

Programs have to work with the hardware in a PC and the devices plugged into it. They have to respond to instructions from the mouse and keyboard; they have to be able to generate pictures on any monitor; and they have to be able to produce text and pictures on different types of printer.

Some years ago, Microsoft came up with a program called Windows that simplified these activities. It provides background services for all other programs. It understands how a PC's monitor, mouse, keyboard and printer work, so that the other programs don't have to.

There's a parallel with how companies work. Whatever a firm's main activity is, it needs administrative and office services to do the mundane tasks like running the switchboard and providing cleaning, maintenance and security. Windows does the equivalent for PCs.

The technical name for a computer's supporting software is its operating system. Windows is not the only operating system for PCs, but it's the most popular one. When you buy a piece of software, whether it's a business tool or a game, it's written for a particular combination of computer and operating system.

The majority of programs are written for Windows, so if you don't use Windows you limit your choice of programs.

The popularity of Windows is thus self-perpetuating. Because it's so popular, software designers write programs for it, which increases the range of programs for Windows and makes it more popular. Microsoft continues to develop and improve Windows despite its virtual monopoly. Windows 98 SE (Second Edition) is an updated version of the original Windows 98, which in turn replaced Windows 95. Before 1995 there were several versions of Windows that were not identified by their year of release and some are still in use on older PCs. Windows 98, in both its editions, introduced new features – wizards, programs and utilities – to improve both the speed and reliability of the operating system. It is also designed to integrate your desktop with the wonders of the Web more closely.

Consistent system

Each version of Windows is consistent. For instance, the Windows Print command is always in a program's File menu which is always in the same place on screen. Before Windows there was no conformity between programs and every time you bought a new one it had to be learnt from scratch.

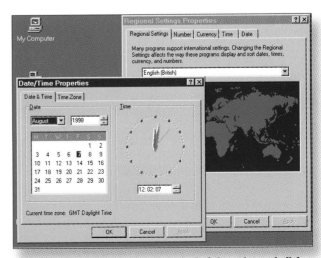

The Date/Time Properties box is typical of the point-and-click approach of Windows. Dates and times are displayed as screen clocks and calendars that look just like the real things.

Going soft

Master the art of Windows software in an instant: get to grips with GUIs, identify with icons and wise up to WYSIWYG.

Software programs, the collective name for all types of computer programs, are simply a huge set of instructions which make your PC do something useful. They tell your PC what to do with the information you are feeding into it, what to show on screen and what to print. There's no point in having a PC without any software. It would be like having a television that didn't receive any channels, buying a CD player but no CDs, or refitting your kitchen but not bothering to buy any food to cook in it. One without the other is no use to anybody.

Software is supplied on a set of floppy disks or CD-ROM discs, from which you transfer it onto your PC's hard disk. When you buy a PC, you should find the operating system, usually Windows, has already been loaded onto it. Once on your PC's hard disk, programs are represented by a small picture or icon on the screen. When selected, the PC finds the program on the hard disk, loads it into the PC's memory bank and gets it ready for you to use.

Windows operating system

This book concentrates on software that works with Microsoft Windows because, as already discussed, this is the operating system used by most PCs today. Windows presents you with graphics, images, icons and lists of choices called menus, which make it easy to use.

Windows is called a graphical user interface or GUI (pronounced gooey). It's also an example of what's become known as a WYSIWYG program because 'what you see (on the screen) is what you get' when you start printing.

Once you have mastered the way Windows works, you can work your way around any Windows-compatible program, no matter how new it is to you.

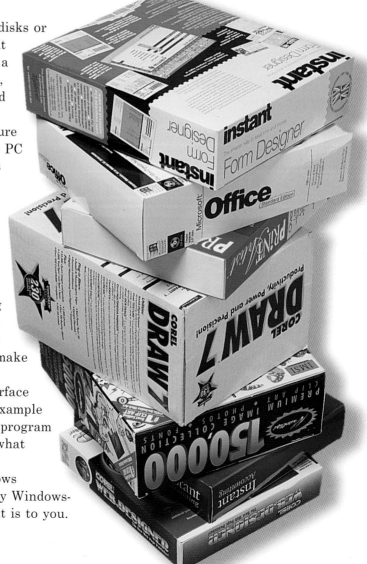

Choosing software

Whatever you want to do with your computer, you'll probably find a software package to suit.

Software programs are divided up into separate categories, depending on what they are being used to do. System software (the operating system) controls how the computer works. It incorporates utilities, such as ScanDisk and Disk Defragmenter, to help improve the speed and reliability of your PC. Applications are used to produce something such as word processing programs for writing a letter, a graphics program for designing a poster, or a spreadsheet for calculating how much your computer has cost you!

Another category you may come across is network software which enables groups of computers to communicate with each other and share peripherals, such as a printer.

CD-ROMs

Nearly all PC software comes on CD-ROMs. They store the instructions that make a program work. When you buy a new program you have to install it, that is copy it onto your PC, before you can use it. Usually all you have to do is put the disc in the CD-ROM drive and it will automatically start its installation program. Then you simply follow the instructions that appear on the screen.

The range of available software is extraordinary. The chances are you'll be able to find a program that will help you do anything you want to do. There are programs for writing letters, drawing pictures, making music, sending faxes, designing room interiors, laying out gardens, running household accounts, budgeting for a loan repayment, keeping lists, planning meals, creating a family tree, designing greetings cards, learning a foreign language, planning a journey and so on.

Software for free

New PCs usually come with several programs (sometimes dozens) to get you started.

Typically these will include popular programs such as a word processor, a spreadsheet, perhaps a home-finance program, a multimedia encyclopaedia and a few games. You can buy new software from a high-street computer shop or by mail order. One may be cheaper than the other, so it pays to compare prices.

Cover discs

There are several ways in which you can check out a program before you buy it. Many computer magazines include a free CD-ROM containing demonstrations of a number of programs – it's rare for them to include the full version of a particular program – and you can download demonstrations from the Internet, but there will be restrictions. They may stop working after a number of days, for example, or they won't let you save anything you've done. Visiting a computer exhibition is another way of getting a look at new software.

When you buy a program, fill in and return the registration card that comes with it. When you register you become eligible for extra information about the program, free updates when small changes are made to it, and news of new versions.
Registration is free.

Office and business

Check your cash flow, draft your correspondence and keep up with contacts – all from your PC.

Using a PC to run a business, no matter how small, makes good sense but software is only worth buying if it saves you time and lets you conduct your business more professionally.

Word processing

If all you ever do is scribble the odd letter, you don't need to buy any software at all, just use WordPad or Notepad which come with Windows. For anything more sophisticated, you need a word processor. Word processors can handle different sizes of text as well as coloured, underlined, bold and italic text. You can count how many words you've written, get the program to check your grammar and so on.

Spreadsheets

Spreadsheets act rather like a sophisticated calculator. They look like large grids made up of rows and columns; the numbers you want to calculate are typed into the grids. Spreadsheets use various formulae to make complex calculations and are perfect for analysing cash flow, working out repayments or setting up a family budget.

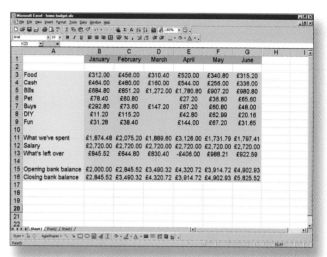

Spreadsheets **like this one in Excel are useful for keeping track of your household expenses.**

Databases

Databases are used to store information in such a way that you can find it again quickly. In an address database for example, you simply go to the search feature, type in the name you want and the details appear on screen.

Organisers

PC organisers usually include a calendar program for appointments, a to-do list of tasks, a name and address list, a notepad and sometimes an expenses manager. You can set audible alarms to remind you to do something.

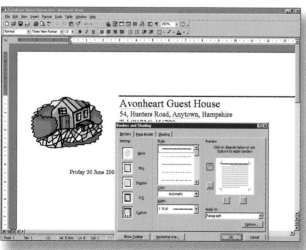

Because word processors **can also display and print out pictures, they're useful for creating letterheads. This is being designed with Microsoft Word.**

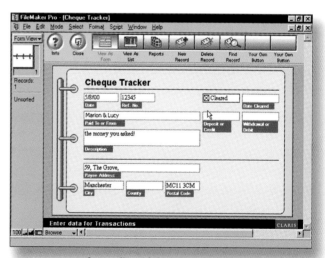

Databases **sound complicated, but they needn't be. This is one created in FileMaker Pro that lets you keep a record of the cheques you're writing.**

software

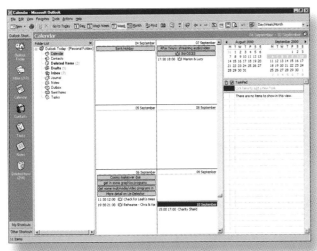

Organisers, such as the calendar in Outlook 2000, are a good way of keeping track of appointments and lists of things to do.

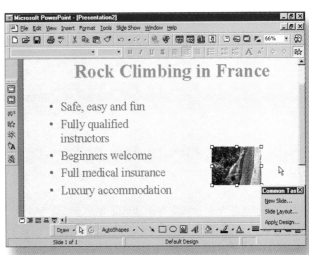

Presentation programs like Microsoft PowerPoint can be used to create compelling slide shows.

Desktop publishing

These programs are excellent for creating club newsletters, invitations, cards, adverts, business cards, stationery, posters and so on. You can incorporate colour pictures and photos and use many of the same layout techniques that you see in magazines and newspapers.

Presentation software

Remember the school overhead projector? Presentation programs are their modern equivalent. Use them to assemble slide shows, creating each slide with colourful graphics, text, and perhaps some background music, or a

short video clip that will also play on the computer screen. These programs are great for presenting to any kind of group, whether it's a club or society, or a parents' evening.

Suites

The office suite is a collection of programs (usually a word processor, a spreadsheet and a database) designed to go together. When you've worked out the basic functions (saving, printing, copying, moving and so on) in one, you know how the others will work. The programs in office suites are also good at swapping information between each other.

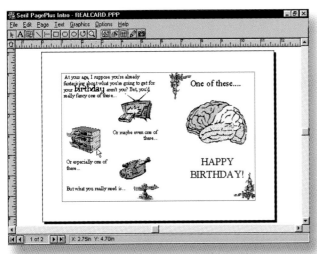

Desktop publishing programs, such as Serif PagePlus 6.0, can produce effective results such as this birthday card.

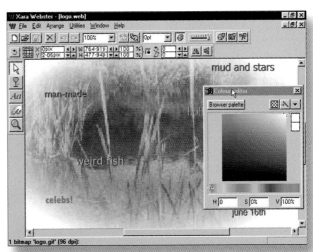

There are many kinds of graphics program. Here Corel Xara Webster is used to produce images for display on a Web site.

Getting hooked

Before you can explore the Net you need to buy a modem and link up with a service provider.

A modem is simply a piece of hardware that plugs into your PC and connects you to the Internet. There's no magic, no messing about and no hi-tech wizardry needed.

There are two types of modem – external and internal. As the names suggest, the external one plugs into a socket at the back of your computer and sits on your desk, while the internal one is a small card that fits into a slot inside your computer. If you don't have an internal modem already fitted, an external one is the easier option because you don't have to fiddle around inside the computer to get started. It really is just a matter of plugging it in. However, internal modems are cheaper.

How it works

The modem connects your computer to the Internet by way of the telephone line. It converts the information sent out by a computer, which comes in digital code, into a form that can be sent over the phone – beeps, whistles and other noises. If you listen to a modem making a connection and a fax machine dialling a line, you'll notice they sound similar.

When you make a connection to the Internet, for example to send a message to your grandmother in America, your computer software lets you type 'Hello Granny' as a message. This simple message is made up in digital code in the computer. When you send the e-mail, your modem converts the code into noise. The noises are packaged and sent out along the telephone line until they reach your Internet service provider (the company, a bit like the phone company, which provides you with your Internet connection). The service provider has a number of modems and these convert the noise back into computer code and send it across the Internet until it reaches its destination, your grandmother's Internet service provider in the United States.

Mail box

When Granny next collects her e-mail, the message will be waiting for her in her mailbox with her service provider. Its modems convert it back into beeps and whistles, pump it down the telephone line, through Granny's modem where it is put back together as computer code again and it appears as 'Hello Granny' on her computer screen. So, all a modem really does is turn your information into noise.

Cable and satellite

The Internet can be a bit slow, but it doesn't have to be. A few years ago, the standard modem used to connect to the Internet ran at only a quarter of the speed of the latest models. However, modems simply can't go much faster over an ordinary phone line.

That doesn't mean you'll be stuck in the slow lane for ever, though. Cable and satellite television are available to most homes now, and they can deliver the Internet at much higher speeds than a telephone line. Over the next couple of years, you'll be able to buy boxes that will let you access the Internet via your cable link, or even satellite.

In fact, you can already join up to the Internet using cable or satellite links in some areas – although in the case of satellite links, you still need a modem to request the information you want, which is then beamed to you via your satellite dish. At the moment it's not a cheap option, since different cable television companies use different, incompatible equipment. But once there's a standard you should be able to buy a high-speed connection as easily and almost as cheaply as you can buy a modem today.

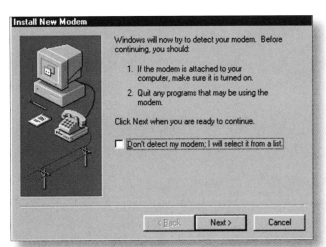

Windows makes it easy to install your new modem. Not only does it ask you questions in plain English, but it will even quiz the modem itself to find out exactly which model you have got, and ensure it is installed correctly.

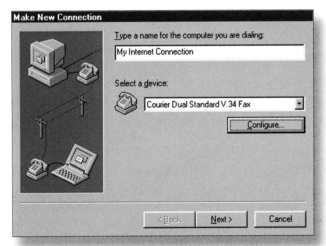

When you come to make your first connection to the Internet, you'll find that the modem you have installed is there to use, even though Windows calls it a device instead of a modem.

Buy the modem that offers the best value, taking into account its speed. The speed of your connection with the Internet is decided by the speed of the modem together with the quality of the phone connection and the amount of traffic through your ISP.

The modem's speed is shown on the box – 28.8, 33.6 or 56. The fastest modems for an ordinary dial-up connection are 56K, that is 56,000 bits per second (bps). In fact, they can only receive data at that speed; the maximum speed for sending information is 36,600bps.

Some modems are flash upgradeable, which means they have a special type of memory that can be upgraded to the latest, or standard, version by downloading a program from the manufacturer's Web site. This was how many people using the two different versions of 56K modems – x2 and K56flex – were able to switch to the new standard, V.90.

Internet consoles

You don't have to have a computer to connect to the Internet. You can use a special Internet console, which plugs into your TV and lets you access the Web and e-mail. They're much cheaper than a PC and there's no complicated setting up to do. But there are drawbacks.

A console can't be used to do tasks such as word processing or household accounts for which you could use a computer; nor is it able to cope with the latest Internet features, such as live video, which are usually written for PCs.

If you want basic access to the Internet, a console is a good idea, but if you have a computer already, you're better off buying a modem for it instead.

Most modems can also be used to send and receive faxes, although generally at slower speeds (up to 14.4 bps). If the modem has voice features, it can be used for setting up your PC as an answering machine or with a voicemail system.

The faster the modem the better, as the quicker it can move information between your PC and the Net, the less time you will spend waiting for pages to appear on screen, and the cheaper your telephone bills will be (because you won't be connected for so long).

Some software, including a start-up program, comes with the modem. Load this onto your PC as instructed, plug in the modem, and the next time you turn on your PC it will notice that there is a new modem attached and install it for you. In just a few minutes you will be ready to get connected.

Jargon buster

Dial-Up The method by which you connect to the Internet. You dial your Internet service provider using a modem attached to a phone.

Download To transfer information – a picture or message, for example – from the Internet onto your PC. Sending data from your computer onto the Internet is known as uploading.

Handshake The noise you hear modems and fax machines making when they connect with each other.

ISDN An alternative method of connecting to the Internet. It stands for Integrated Services Digital Network and can be quite a lot faster than an ordinary modem.

Kbps Kilobits per second, the speed at which information is sent using your modem.

Login The act of connecting to your Internet service provider when you want to use the Internet.

Modem The box that connects your computer to the Internet. The name comes from MOdulator/DEModulator.

Serving up the Net

Choose an Internet service provider that will give you exactly what you want from the Internet.

Internet service providers, or ISPs, are the vital link between you, your PC, your modem and the rest of the Internet.

Get connected

An ISP uses the phone lines to connect your PC, via the modem, to its modems at the nearest ISP exchange point, which is nearly always a local phone call away. From here you get connected directly to the ISP's computer network which has a permanent link to the Internet.

Choosing an ISP depends on what you want to do on the Net. Competition is fierce to get your business, and everybody's at it – banks, stores, publishers, supermarkets. As a result the services they offer, and the cost, are changing all the time. Some ISPs, such as Which or CompuServe, use their exclusive content to encourage you to choose them. Others, such as UUNET or Demon, emphasise the quality and reliability of their service. So what to look for?

Free Internet Access – this used to mean no monthly subscription fee, but you still had to pay telephone charges. Now there are unmetered access schemes with no subs and no

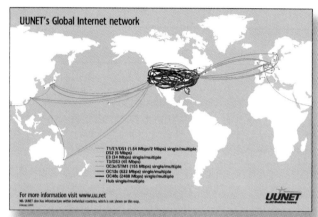

UUNET's Global Internet network

For more information visit www.uu.net

UUNET **covers the globe. It is one of the world's biggest ISPs, and has a presence in most countries.**

phone charges. Beware though, not all of these 'free' offers are totally free. Some involve an upfront administration charge. With others you may have to use a specified telephone service and guarantee a minimum monthly amount in non-Internet phone calls.

Broadband Access – this uses recently developed technology that operates at a different frequency from voice calls, so enabling you to access the Internet over your existing phone lines but at speeds of up to 50 times faster. It's always open – no lengthy dial-up to connect to the Internet – for which there's a monthly flat-rate charge. So it's useful if you want a video piped to your PC in a flash.

MSN Australia **is just one of the global services offered by Microsoft's ISP, the Microsoft Network.**

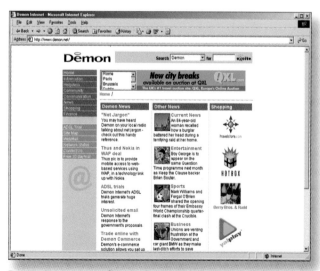

Demon Internet **was first in the UK to bring access to home users and now it is established as one of the UK's biggest ISPs.**

WAP – Wireless Application Protocol-enabled services allow you to access Web sites or send information and e-mail via your mobile phone. This is useful if you need to trade shares or book a restaurant while on the move. Several ISPs are now offering WAP-enabled services.

Well-known brands are now starting to appear as ISPs, such as Richard Branson's VirginNet, for example.

Dixons' FreeServe was the first of the free UK Internet service providers and is also the biggest.

AOL, the world's biggest ISP by quite a large margin, is easy to use and offers all kinds of extras before you even start exploring the Internet.

Ask about technical support. If things go wrong, you need to know your ISP will be there to help. Is it free, 24 hours a day, seven days a week? Test the phone number it gives.

Every ISP should offer a number of e-mail addresses and Web space where you can create your own site. In addition each ISP has its own particular services (see below). Ask about software. Your ISP should provide everything you need, for free and in a package that makes it easy to install and get started.

If you choose a free ISP, you have nothing to lose if you don't like the service, and most of the ISPs that charge let you try out the service for a month before you commit yourself.

The top ten providers

● **AOL** This is an online service rather than just an ISP, which means you get extras like member-only chat areas, magazine areas and so on. AOL is the world's biggest Internet service provider, with millions of customers.

● **BT Internet** An ISP operated by British Telecom. It is easy to set up and get running, with straightforward software.

● **CompuServe** This is another online service provider, and one of the longest established. As well as Internet access there are long-running forums where members can discuss issues such as politics, gardening or sport.

● **Demon** The first Internet service provider to bring Internet access to the home in the United Kingdom, and one of the UK's largest. No fancy extras are offered, just simple Internet access, without hassle, for a low monthly cost.

● **FreeServe** FreeServe was the first ISP to offer access to the Net for free. All the user pays for is the phone call. The service compares well with other ISPs. The 24-hour technical support is on a premium rate line, however.

● **LineOne** A newcomer to the scene, this offers extra value in access to its online publications, newspapers and special family entertainment areas, as well as Internet access itself.

● **MSN** Microsoft Network is Microsoft's online service provider. There's plenty to see and do here, with possibly the widest range of online entertainment, including live chats with celebrities, news services, magazine areas and more.

● **UUNET** UUNET is a giant in the world of the ISP, with a global presence that few others can rival. Its Pipex Dial service is a popular choice for home users.

● **VirginNet** Richard Branson's Virgin brand has extended into the Internet access market. VirginNet trades on its ease of use, for even the most inexperienced of computer users.

● **Which? Online** A relative newcomer that has picked up an impressive number of members. This is the online service provider arm of the British Consumer Association, so it offers added value in its reports and magazine content.

World Wide Web

The World Wide Web is your window onto the Internet and all the information it contains.

An Internet without pictures, lacking in links and requiring you to master a whole host of obscure commands to get anything done would be no use to anyone. But that's what it was like until the early 1990s when the World Wide Web burst into the picture.

Hyperactive

The Net can trace its origins back to the 1960s, but the Web was only conceived in 1989 when a British scientist at a nuclear physics laboratory came up with the idea of linking pages on the Net. The idea was that you could be reading one page, say about Elvis Presley, and if there were any highlighted words (hyperlinks), you could click on them to open another page that delved further into the subject. Clicking on the word Graceland, for example, would open a document about Elvis's home.

The clever bit is that these documents don't need to be stored in the same place. They can be stored on any computer connected to the Internet. The main thing is that when you click on a highlighted link on a Web page the

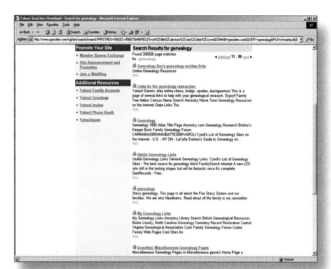

Web page communities have started to grow. The biggest of all is Yahoo! GeoCities, made up of thousands of individuals with Web pages. Like-minded people get together to form streets and avenues that have Web pages covering similar topics.

information you request appears on your screen. It doesn't matter where it comes from.

At first the World Wide Web consisted of pages of plain text but it didn't take long for pictures and sound to appear. Now few people would dream of using anything but the Web to get what they want from the Internet.

Anyone can have a home page on the Web. ISPs give free Web space when you join, that is

The Web is composed of links. Almost everything on this page for kids is a hyperlink. If you move your mouse pointer over it and the pointer changes into a hand shape, you can click on that link and get more information.

You can even do your shopping using the Web. Amazon.com is one of the world's biggest bookshops, but it only exists on the Web. Ask it to find the book or CD you are interested in and order with your credit card.

Resources like ZyWeb make creating a Web page as simple as making a few selections from the screen, and that includes fancy graphics, buttons and fonts.

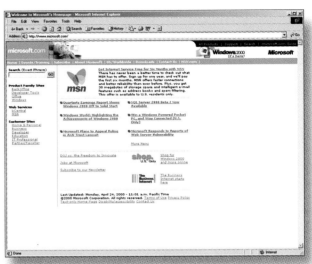

The Microsoft Homepage, viewed using Microsoft's Internet Explorer Web browser. If you've used any Microsoft product, you'll feel at home with Internet Explorer.

from 5–50MB on a hard disk connected to the Net on a Web server – a computer that stores Web pages. Designing a Web page isn't difficult. Your ISP will give you software to turn it into a simple question and answer session.

Room for everyone
Schoolchildren, housewives and business people are all on the Web these days. Web pages are used as an outlet for your writing or artistic talents; to tell the world about your hobby; to sell handicrafts; or as an online fan club for your favourite pop star.

Browsing

The Web is not much use unless you have a way of viewing it, which is where Web browsers come in. Browsers are programs that enable you to use the Web easily.

Choosing a Web browser isn't difficult. There are two that lead the field by a margin: Netscape and Microsoft. Netscape has its Navigator browser and Microsoft has Internet Explorer. They are both big, fully functional programs, and they are free.

Internet Explorer integrates well with your operating system, because Microsoft make Windows as well. Netscape has been making Web browsers longer than anyone, and pioneered the whole Web browser software industry.

Stick with the browser your ISP supplies. It will offer technical support if you have problems, and it will be installed on your computer as part of the ISP package. This is likely to mean you will use Microsoft Internet Explorer, as more ISPs seem to be doing deals to distribute this rather than Navigator.

Finding stuff

Nothing on the Web is any good unless you know where to find it. The answer is search engines. These are like phone books. If you want to find a site, let a search engine look for it. Type in a word that describes what you want and the search engine will scan its directory and return a list of sites that contain relevant information.

TOP THREE SEARCH ENGINES
● **Yahoo! (www.yahoo.com)** The first Web search engine, and one of the biggest. Search by entering a keyword, or just browse through categorised directory listings.

● **AltaVista (www.altavista.com)** One of the most powerful search engines. It's easy to use and works quickly.

● **Ask Jeeves! (www.askjeeves.com)** Rather than suggesting you enter a single word to start a search, Ask Jeeves (below) insists you ask in plain English.

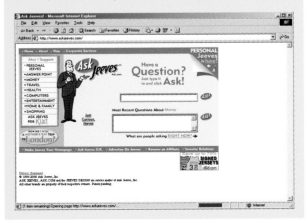

Games

Enjoy your hard-earned free time with a quick shoot 'em up, a murder mystery or a whist drive.

Avoid the bloodthirsty games and those in poor taste by checking the box for the ELSPA rating; it's like a film certificate. Most games can be played with the mouse and/or keyboard, although some need a joystick, which is like a pilot's flightstick.

Action

The range is enormous. There are realistic flight simulators and first person shoot 'em ups, where your character hurtles down corridors, shooting everything that moves. There are some good car-racing games (often using real circuit layouts), platform games (in the style of Sonic the Hedgehog) and space fighting games; plus games for most sports.

Strategy

These games, often with themes of trade and conquest, are more thought-provoking than their action counterparts. Typically the game will give you an aerial view of a city, a country or the ocean floor, and your job is to make your side prosper. Detective games are fun too, where you solve a crime by interviewing suspects and gathering clues.

Aliens vs Predator **adds a new twist to the first person shoot 'em up by letting you play as an alien, predator or marine.**

Card and board

There are loads of these games, from the two that come free with Windows to curious hybrids like Star Wars Monopoly which is the original game reworked with Star Wars locations and characters. Versions of Chinese games are popular, as are bridge and chess, jigsaws, solitaire, poker and whist.

Online

On the Internet, you can play games against other people. You both connect at the same time and instead of playing against the PC, you race against each other, or try to defeat each other's armies, or test your chess skills.

You control a dungeon full of monsters in Dungeon Keeper 2 **and it take lots of planning to keep adventurers out.**

This amazingly realistic game is Microsoft's International Football 2000. **It's a demanding program that requires a powerful computer to run properly.**

2

Solving Problems

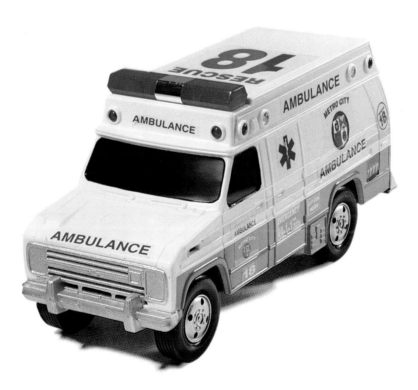

Getting help

When things go wrong with your computer the most important thing is to know where to go for help.

Everyone needs a little help with their computer from time to time – not just total beginners and those who want to learn more, but also the most experienced power users. The hardware and software inside a computer are far too complex for any one person to have a complete mastery of them, and of course not all computers and certainly not all software are alike.

Hard even for the experts

It's a rare person who can take a car to pieces and put it back together again. It's rarer still to find someone who can do it with a PC. In both cases even the experts need to resort to product manuals and installation guides. The same goes for you. But thankfully there is no need to have years of expertise behind you before you know where to look for assistance. One great feature of the computer business is that you never have to look very far to find sources of help.

A culture of support, technical helplines and online advice has grown up around computers. Even if you sometimes feel that you're out on your own with your PC, nothing could be further from the truth. PCs, peripherals and software go wrong for even the most experienced users – usually at the worst time. So read on to learn how to prepare yourself for the worst. When PC illness strikes, knowing who to call for help is as important as understanding how to administer the remedy.

You will need

ESSENTIAL

Software Current software versions. Few software vendors and publishers offer technical help with obsolete software. An upgrade to the latest version may solve your problem anyway.
Hardware A modern PC. As with cars, it gets increasingly difficult and expensive to obtain assistance as the age of your kit increases.

PC warranties

Warranty tip

When you first buy a computer product, check to see whether there are circumstances under which the warranty is rendered void. Many manufacturers will not fix a broken peripheral device, for example, if they think you have been fiddling unnecessarily with the internals. Watch out for labels that read Warranty Void If Removed.

Jargon buster

E&OE Many adverts for PCs and peripherals carry this expression in the small print. It stands for Errors and Omissions Excepted. It's a standard disclaimer to cover the advertiser in case there are printing mistakes in the advert, which means it's up to you to ensure that generous warranty promises are not one of the errors.

The law is on your side if any computer kit you buy breaks down – but only for a limited period.

Whenever you buy a non-consumable product in the UK the law covers you for a limited period in case your purchase turns out to be faulty. The rules are particularly strict in the case of electrical goods, which the law expects to work well for up to a year as proof that they were manufactured properly and sold honestly. If a product breaks down within a year, the law regards it as a faulty product and expects the manufacturer to fix or replace it. If it breaks down a year after purchase the law regards it as bad luck.

Return to base

There is every reason to take PC warranties seriously. If your PC or peripheral is covered by a standard one-year warranty and anything goes wrong, you will have to return the PC in its huge packing box. This is known as a return to base warranty: you return it at your expense, and the manufacturer fixes it and sends it back to you at its expense.

Save time

If you live within driving distance of the place where you bought the product, you can save time and expense by delivering it in person rather than arranging couriers or parcel collection. Naturally, if the product is small, you should be able to send it back in the post as long as it is well padded and marked Fragile in huge lettering. Just remember that in all cases, and without exception, it is essential that you call up the company first to tell it that the product is faulty. The company will issue you with a returns number which must be printed clearly on the outer packaging and on a covering letter inside. This will speed up the process considerably.

Collect and return

If having to foot the return bill on a faulty product irritates you – as it should – buy from companies which offer enhanced warranties. A popular alternative is a collect and return warranty, which is basically the same as return to base except that the company arranges and pays for all transport or postal costs involved in returning the product for fixing. Better still is an on-site warranty, which means that a representative from the company will come to your home or office to fix the product in situ. This person should be a qualified PC engineer, but if the faulty product is a printer, monitor or other peripheral device, what usually happens is that a delivery person turns up with a replacement and simply takes your broken one back with them. This system is known as on-site swap out.

Mechanical faults

You also need to consider how warranties affect software, because the situation can be very different. The floppy disks or CD-ROMs provided in a software package will be covered for mechanical faults, but only for a short period such as 90 days. This is considered to be enough time for you to discover that the disks aren't working. However, trying to convince a software company that the software itself does not work will be futile. There may be internal conflicts and other rare reasons why a software package might not function properly on your PC but these are not normally considered in law as the fault of the software seller. You cannot return a software product for an instant refund once you break the seal.

Online support

You may be offered assistance by phone or online. Many PC manufacturers take a holistic view of computing and offer hotline support for their PCs and the software installed on them. Take time to find out if the company you are buying from is going to provide this kind of help. When you are buying kit, it is easy to get carried away with slick advertising. Keep reminding yourself that computer products can go wrong unexpectedly, no matter who you buy them from, so it's up to you to make sure you obtain the best warranty cover available.

Watch out for E&OE disclaimers when you buy computer equipment from mail-order adverts.

Watch out!

When looking at warranties, be sure to check the small print. Many manufacturers offer generous sounding five-year warranties, but this may cover replacement parts only: after the first year or two, you might have to pay for the labour charge which can be high. Look for genuine parts and labour cover. Also, with collect and on-site warranties, find out how quickly the company will respond to your call for help. Will you get a replacement the next day, the next week or when?

Extended support

Jargon buster

Remote diagnostics Some support companies may offer this as a hi-tech method of providing help inexpensively without having to send an engineer to your doorstep. With your permission, they will call up your PC over the phone line and use specialist software tools back at their office to work out what the problem is and identify corrupt files, missing drivers and so on. You may need to install some remote diagnostic software as part of the deal, and you will certainly need a modem.

For real peace of mind it is worth extending the short-term warranties offered by most manufacturers.

Long, generous warranties are a new phenomenon in the UK. When you buy computer kit you are much more likely to get a simple or short-term warranty included in the product price, with the option of extending the cover as required. This is the same kind of deal offered to consumers when they buy hi-fi equipment or kitchen appliances. But TVs, hi-fis and microwave ovens are much less likely to go wrong over time than a computer, and much less expensive to fix or replace when they do.

Buy early

There is a lot to be said for extending a warranty on PCs and peripherals – depending on the cost, of course. Often the price of upgrading a standard warranty to an on-site warranty or extending an on-site warranty by an extra year is very little. Such upgrades will always be cheapest if you pay for them when you buy the product to start with, and will increase exponentially each year if you put them off until later.

A useful alternative to consider is employing a third-party support company to look after your kit. When you purchase on-site warranty extensions from PC manufacturers, you may well find that this cover is provided by a specially appointed third-party support company anyway. This arrangement is cheaper for a manufacturer than having to staff its own in-house support team, and offers good service to buyers because they get expert help from a dedicated support engineer every time.

Piecemeal

As with any service and support deal, you need to compare the cost with that of getting something fixed yourself. If your PC's power supply fails, for example, it can cost a fair amount for a new one and you will have to fit it yourself or pay someone to do it for you. Then you will probably start wishing you had paid for one year's on-site support, covering all parts and labour.

It is worth calling a few companies to check prices and coverage deals. Some companies require a small monthly retainer and then offer cut-price call-out charges in an emergency. Third-party support companies offer a sliding scale of prices according to response time, whether you want an engineer at your door in two or four hours, or whether you are happy to wait until the next day or the day after.

Call-out charge
Smaller companies, such as local PC shops, simply charge for each call-out just like a plumber or electrician. You might even be able to find someone who can fix small problems cheaply and who knows where to turn if there is a major problem.

Two other support methods worth considering are training and PC audits. By attending a training course run by experts you will learn to head off and resolve many non-critical PC errors yourself, so you can save a lot of money. An audit is rather like a car service or health check. It's worth having one to keep your PC in top form.

Hotlines
You can find numbers for support companies in PC magazines, on the Internet and at the library. As well as checking out what they have to offer, you might want to try their emergency hotlines for size if you can get hold of the telephone number. If it turns out to be permanently engaged, consider yourself warned off. This goes for manufacturers offering extended warranties too: if you can't get through to the support line, the warranty is worthless.

Manufacturers often say that if a piece of hardware is going to go wrong, it will do so within the first three months after purchase, but things can go wrong at any time. If you rely on your computer for work, an extended support deal is well worth the money.

Ten per cent rule
When trying to gauge the value of extended and third-party support, apply the ten per cent rule. For full on-site support, many companies charge an annual fee of ten per cent of the purchase price of the products being covered. Naturally this charge depends on the quantity and age of the equipment, but it gives you an idea of prices. If you don't need fast response call-out, the cost will be much less.

Internet tip
To get the most from the Internet it helps if you can see exactly how fast data is being transferred between the Internet and your PC, and if any errors are getting in the way. Use software that will monitor your connection, such as DUN Monitor, which is available free on the Net. Connect to the Net and use your browser to find www.southdown.co.uk/users/jgrieve. Select the link that says Dial Up Networking Monitor and download the software as instructed.

You can configure DUN Monitor to run as you want it to. You can change the colours used on the graphing feature, and choose when and how the DUN Monitor window should appear. Setting it to show statistics when a call is established and hiding them when you disconnect is the best bet.

Now every time you connect to the Internet a window will pop up that shows you exactly how fast data is being sent and received. As you tweak your PC and modem configurations you should be able to monitor the improvements. The higher the figure next to Current, the faster your Internet connection is running. If this figure slows down considerably you know there is a bad connection and maybe you should try again later.

Online support

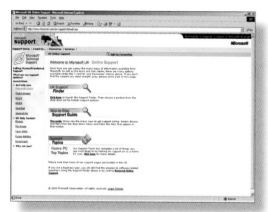

All the major software companies offer technical assistance on their Web sites, from simple lists of common problems all the way to interactive Help databases like Microsoft's dedicated support site.

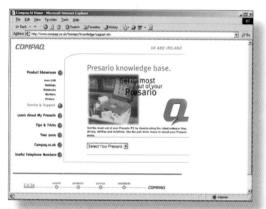

Instead of wasting time being put on hold on a telephone support hotline, browse your hardware manufacturer's Web site. It may have the driver, update or fix you need for immediate download.

Netiquette tip

When asking for advice in an Internet newsgroup or online forum, bear in mind that these areas are not always run by the company which manufactured the product you are having trouble with. Those most likely to come to your aid are people like you who just happen to own the same product, and are offering their knowledge for free. For this reason, be polite in your request. Simple netiquette phrases like please and thank you, and not typing your message in capital letters will increase your chances of a speedy and equally polite response.

The Internet is an enormous and valuable resource for anyone having trouble with their PC or peripherals.

One of the biggest benefits the Internet has brought to the everyday PC user is instant support. When you go online, you don't have to wait in a queue or answer a set of predetermined, irrelevant questions to find what you want. The volume of information and advice that can be obtained online often goes well beyond the scope of mere product manuals, and can go into far greater detail than an operator on a telephone help desk.

Weak link

The weak link in the chain is that you need a working PC and modem plus an online service provider to get online to start with. If you are having problems with any one of these three, you will have to resort to other sources of help. But if the problem is with another peripheral, a software application or a non-critical PC component, you will be surprised at how much support information is available to you for free.

Hardware and software companies all over the world have established sites on the Web and with online services such as AOL and CompuServe for this purpose. It is, after all, cheaper for them to provide support this way too. In the first instance, if you are having trouble with a product, a quick visit to the company's Web site may reveal the answer in the form of an FAQ (frequently asked questions) or troubleshooting page. It could well be that other users are having the same problem as you, so the company may have published the solution on its site for all to read.

Available for download

Many hardware problems are caused by drivers, the little software utilities which enable each computer component to work with each other. Hardware manufacturers generally ensure that their latest drivers are always available for download from their online sites. Perhaps you have recently upgraded your operating system or are reinstalling the components (graphics card, soundcard, Zip

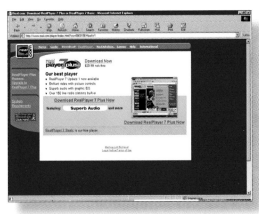

Check the company Web site to see if any free upgrades are available. If so, take advantage of them because it may be that the problem you are having has been solved in the upgraded version.

Netscape's SmartUpdate Web site allows you to access the latest versions of relevant software quickly and easily.

drive for instance) in another machine, but have lost your original driver disks. All you need to do is go to the company's online site, locate its support section and download the drivers you want.

Software works in much the same way. Many companies provide free updates to their programs between major upgrades, and make them available for immediate download. If you are having trouble with a brand new product version 1, always check the relevant site for an update to version 1.01 or 1.02. It will often be the answer to your troubles.

Up to date

Some software products will update automatically, providing a menu command or a button which accesses an Internet site and checks to see if a newer version of the program is available, downloading it as necessary. Many anti-virus programs let you do this, ensuring that you always have an up-to-date list of viruses. Windows 98 owners can also ensure that they have the latest updates by running the Windows Update program near the top of the Start menu.

Forums

You can take advantage of more interactive online help by posting your questions in specific Internet newsgroups and relevant forums hosted by online services (see pages 57–8). Post a cry for help one day and by the next day you should have at least half a dozen responses, any of which may have the right answer. The respondents will generally be people with some measure of expertise in – or at least experience with – the product you are having difficulty with. And the clever solutions they give might not even be known to the manufacturers.

Favourites tip

When you first visit an Internet site run by the manufacturer of a product you own, or a user organisation associated with it, remember to add the site to your Bookmarks (Netscape) or Favorites (Internet Explorer). Even if you only discovered the site by accident, you never know when you will need to hunt it down again to obtain help or contact information. Keep a portfolio of these sites ready for emergencies.

Jargon buster

Patch This is a small piece of software which fixes errors or bugs in a program that were discovered after it was put on the market. These days, the sticking-plaster imagery of the term is considered unfortunate and most software companies now refer to patches as updates. This new term implies that you are getting extra value for no expense, but updates are generally devised for fixing errors and bugs just the same.

Jargon buster

FAQ Stands for frequently asked questions. An FAQ is a list of common problems raised by PC users about a particular product, along with the solution. It's always worth checking an FAQ for an answer before taking your support query further up the ladder.

User groups and

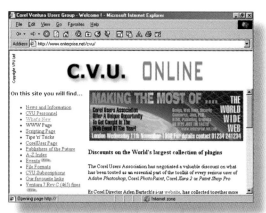

Some software applications are so complex yet so popular that they encourage the formation of self-help associations online, such as the Corel Ventura User Group which organises training courses, seminars and competitions.

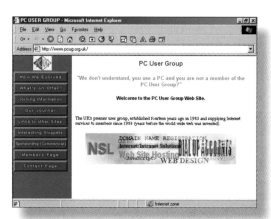

Hardware-specific user groups are less common than software clubs and more regional. But they can still be a valuable source of hands-on help when it really matters – and inexpensive too.

Think small

Often the biggest problems are caused by the smallest things. The term bug was originally coined when an insect flew into the valves of an early computer and caused an entire program to go wrong. Recurrent serious PC crashes may be due to nothing more than a corrupt driver file (easily reinstalled), a broken processor fan (very cheap to replace) or a badly seated memory chip (just press it back in). Only when you have checked the small items should you concentrate on the bigger suspects.

Often the best place to look for help with hardware or software is an online group of fellow users.

Once you have obtained help from an online source, such as a fellow PC user in an Internet newsgroup, you will appreciate the potential of these users' knowledge when pooled. Even the best products have been known to be indifferently or expensively supported by their manufacturers at times, and this has led to the creation of user groups. These are self-help organisations which specialise in a specific product area, from something as general as computers to individual software programs.

Members benefit

The essence of a user group is to distil the expert knowledge from dedicated users of a product to benefit all its members. Typical groups organise training courses, negotiate discounts on computer products, and provide a pool of support resources for those in need of help. Software user groups are generally national or international, and may even obtain a little bit of funding from the software company itself. Hardware user groups, especially those focusing on PCs rather than peripherals, tend to be regional and meet up on a regular basis.

User groups were much more popular in the 1980s when desktop computing was still new. Since then, manufacturers have a better understanding of what buyers expect and offer their own support services. People these days do not perceive such a great need for organised self help. However, a user group has no compulsion to toe a corporate line: if it has discovered a problem in its chosen product, it is hardly going to keep quiet about it. As a user group member, you will hear about problems before anyone else, and also be party to the first solutions.

Geeks galore?

User groups have a public image of being populated by geeky fan-club types. Ignore the image. If you take your computing seriously, getting involved in a user group could well save your neck one day, and will almost certainly help you achieve more with your PC. Even if you're not keen on joining

utilities

clubs, a local user group get-together twice a year is no great effort considering what can be obtained in return. User groups can be located by searching the Web or checking at your local library.

Utilities

Getting organised is not the only self-help option open to those in need of expert support. In addition to the various disk and file utilities on the market, there is a wealth of problem solving and disaster prevention software available shrink-wrapped on the shelves. These range from anti-virus programs to full hardware troubleshooting utilities. In principle, everyone should own an anti-virus package, especially if they are connected to the Net. For the sake of a cheap utility, it would be a foolish way to lose your files.

Useful utilities

Another popular type of software troubleshooting utility is the kind designed to identify the cause of a PC problem rather than promise a solution for it. For example, if your PC keeps crashing and you don't know why, these utilities will try to analyse your PC components and perhaps prompt you with a series of interactive tasks before identifying the problem. With this knowledge, you can confidently fix the problem yourself, go out and buy a new component, call up a support company or do whatever is necessary. It may not save you money, but it will save time by accelerating the process of getting things fixed.

Some utility software, such as Network Associates McAfee's FirstAid 2000, will attempt to check your hardware and software components for problems and suggest appropriate solutions, ending the uncertainty of what's gone wrong.

Jargon buster

UGNETs User groups use the product's initial followed by UG (user group). If the user group is online, it often tags the word NET on the end. WUGNET is the Windows User Group.

Watch out!

No-one is infallible in their judgement and it can happen that interference with the internal workings of your PC, peripherals or software can cause more problems rather than solve the original fault. When you call in a support engineer there will at least be some kind of guarantee that if it all goes wrong, the company will make every attempt to put things right at its own expense. But if you are on your own or taking advice from a user group, you have no-one to put the blame on.

This isn't a reason for not trying to solve computer problems yourself, but a warning that fiddling can do more damage than good unless you know exactly what you are doing, or at least know how to restore everything to its original state. Take notes when offered help by a user group and read them back to the helper to check you have understood the method and not missed anything. When reconfiguring or reinstalling hardware or software, take a note of each step you have completed, along with sketches and listings. This way, it'll be easy to retrace your steps if necessary. These notes may also be invaluable if the problem ever crops up again, or if someone else asks you for help.

Consult the manual

Hunt the .pdf

An increasing number of hardware and software companies provide simple installation manuals on paper, but supply the complete product guides as electronic documentation on a disk or CD. Invariably it will be in Adobe Acrobat .pdf format, which can be opened and printed only by the Acrobat Reader program. This can be downloaded for free from Adobe's Web site at www.adobe.co.uk.

When something goes wrong with your PC, you could always try reading the manual.

There is an old curse in the computing world which is often quoted in its short form: RTFM. It stands for 'read the friendly manual' – or close enough – and is intended to remind PC users that the answers they are looking for are right at their fingertips. This is more applicable now than ever, as intuitive software and plug and play hardware give the impression that any lack of instant functionality is an insurmountable problem that can be solved only by contacting product support staff.

Keep the manual safe

Most PC kit can be installed and used without wasting time poring over the instructions, but make sure you keep the manual safe just in case. One day you may need to move a hardware device from one PC to another, and will appreciate having the instructions. Dull and obscure documents like a motherboard manual suddenly become valuable the day you decide to upgrade your processor or RAM. Net forums are full of queries about motherboards, posted by people who threw away their manuals.

Software manuals are fat and off-putting, but if you look, the solution to your problems could be in there. Some software companies help by providing troubleshooting chapters, and many products come with separate user and reference manuals. The first gets you up and running, while the second contains details if you ever get stuck.

Look at books

Check out the computing shelves at your local book store or an online bookshop. Flicking through hundreds of pages of paperback books is probably not the best method of obtaining a solution to your computer hassles, but it remains the most convenient way of training yourself on a topic in far greater depth than a product manual ever could. If you come to rely heavily upon a particular product, especially software, having a huge tome of detailed documentation at hand is as practical as it is reassuring.

Fault finders

Even if your PC is displaying no obvious symptoms, it's still a good idea to give it a regular checkup.

It's rare for a PC to develop a mechanical fault. When a computer goes wrong it's often because an item of software has been added or removed, disturbing an otherwise stable system. It is less likely that a hardware component has worn out or broken down. Usually the first indication of a problem is that a file won't load properly or a procedure that used to work perfectly now produces unpredictable results.

Fault finders and fixers

Diagnostic software should be able to do more than simply find faults. It should determine whether the PC's hardware is working properly and identify any problems with the applications software or operating system. And it should correct or repair the faults it finds, except where the problem is a hardware malfunction.

It's quite easy for a computer to carry out the second and third tasks of putting its own software system in order, but working out whether a fault is caused by hardware or software can be problematic. Take, for example, not being able to send or receive e-mail. If you have a hardware fault, it could be that the modem is broken or that the phone line itself is dead. Perhaps the modem is working fine,

To test any component in a PC using FirstAid 2000, all you have to do is click on the relevant item on the virtual Desktop. You may also instruct FirstAid to run an automated full system check, as here.

Fact file

● **Crash protection** Provided by a small program which remains permanently in memory and intervenes whenever a situation occurs which could cause a PC to crash. Preventing a crash doesn't fix the underlying problem, but it preserves your data and gives you a chance to correct things yourself.

● **Background monitoring** Differs from crash protection in that it doesn't assume responsibility for your PC, it merely warns when potentially dangerous situations occur. Most warnings are about low memory, shortage of disk space or overburdened system resources. If you ignore the warnings, your computer might crash.

● **Recovery disk** A floppy disk containing enough MS-DOS to start your PC plus copies of key system files from the hard disk and some simple recovery tools to get Windows working again. It's an advanced version of the basic Startup disk you can make using the Add/Remove Programs dialogue box in Windows.

● **Smart disk** A type of hard disk which can warn you before it fails if its condition is deteriorating. Don't dispose of your existing hard disk just to fit a Smart one, but do make sure you ask for a Smart disk on your next computer. The acronym stands for Self-Monitoring, Analysis and Reporting Technology.

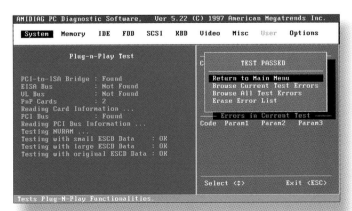

The tests in AMIDiag can be run as separate programs or through this DOS-based control panel.

Buying tips

● AMIDiag, Micro-Scope and Eurosoft's PC-Check don't pretend to fix problems, simply to identify them. They don't work within Windows and two of them don't even insist on the presence of MS-DOS. Programs like these are for people who build and test PCs for a living.

● Network Associates McAfee's First Aid 2000 and Symantec's Norton Utilities are typical of Windows-based diagnostic programs suitable for casual users. Both programs include preventive modules to monitor a PC and detect problems before they develop. FirstAid 2000 is the best choice for absolute technophobes but the Norton Utilities offer more features for those with the expertise to use them.

● Don't buy any diagnostic tools until you've looked at what's already on your PC. There are several diagnostic and maintenance utilities in Windows 95 including the invaluable ScanDisk, which can fix many minor disk errors. Windows 98 has even more to offer with System File Checker and Registry Cleaner, which maintain the integrity of Windows and prevent problems arising.

● Two powerful companies have recently been busy acquiring many of the smaller utility vendors. If you can't find products for sale with McAfee, CyberMedia, Dr Solomon, QuarterDeck and Norton labels try looking for them under the Network Associates or Symantec banners.

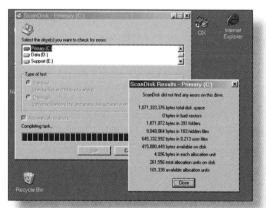

Under some versions of Windows, ScanDisk runs automatically whenever it is needed, but it may also be started on demand.

Top five brands

● **AMI** 020 8848 8686
● **Eurosoft** 01202 297315
● **Network Associates** 01753 827500
● **Scope Diagnostics** 01438 747424
● **Symantec** 020 7616 5600

but it has come loose in its mounting slot. Maybe the family pet has chewed the phone cable between the socket and the back of the PC.

Diagnostic software can tell you if your e-mail software isn't getting a signal from the modem, but it can't tell you why there's no signal. For this reason, the most appropriate diagnostic software for non-technical users is interactive – at least to the extent that when it can't diagnose a problem by itself it enlists your help rather than giving up.

Disaster recovery

Software designed to run under Windows is the easiest to use. But what do you do if your computer is so badly damaged that Windows won't even start? Some Windows diagnostic programs, such as Norton Utilities, are supplied with emergency floppy disks to boot a PC to MS-DOS. From here further repairs can be made, but don't expect an MS-DOS program to be as easy to use as its Windows counterpart. (See pages 89–92 for starting up your computer in MS-DOS.)

Early warning systems

The ideal diagnostic software for non-professional users should work in both Windows and MS-DOS. It should include preventive maintenance and background monitoring. And it should be able to back up important Windows system files and reinstate them when required. Look for a graphical program that can run a system test automatically. And bearing in mind that there will always be situations which require human intervention, it's worth choosing a program that can show you what it expects you to do using explanatory video clips.

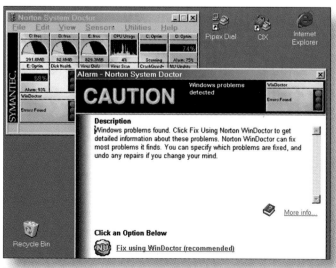

Norton's System Doctor runs in the background. If it identifies any problems there's a good chance they can be fixed by a companion program called WinDoctor.

Windows Help

With Help on your side it's easy for anyone to get to grips with Windows in next to no time.

Windows is a sophisticated operating system with an enormous number of features. It's easy to use, but that doesn't mean that when you want to do something the way to do it is going to be obvious. It's not realistic to expect to learn or remember everything you will ever need to know. Even experts sometimes have to think twice about how to go about a task, so don't be discouraged if you have to as well. The secret is to know where to find the answers and the first place to look is in the online Help.

Getting Windows to help you

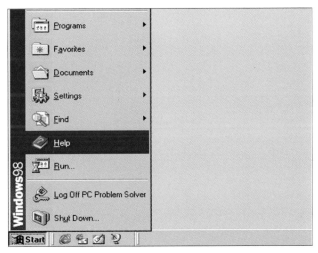

1 You can get to the online Help for Windows from the Help option on the Start menu. Click on this and you'll see the Help Topics dialogue box. Another way to start **Windows Help** is to click on the Desktop and press the F1 key. Pressing F1 will nearly always load the Help file of whatever program you're working in.

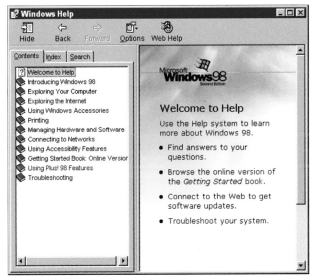

2 The **Contents page** of the Help Topics shows the topics on the left and a welcome message on the right. Each topic contains more topics and when you click on one, they will appear. Some topics are nested several layers deep, but at the bottom level there is always a subject with a question mark icon next to it giving access to the relevant information.

Depending on how complex the Help file is, you might have to navigate several levels of book icons to get to the Help pages that you need, or you might get to them after opening a book at the first level.

Help tip

Windows lets you add your own notes to help files. Click on the Options menu and then on Annotate. Type your notes into the Annotate box, then click on Save when you've finished. A tiny paper clip appears to remind you that you've made additions to that Help page. To see the notes, just click on the paper clip next to the name of the topic.

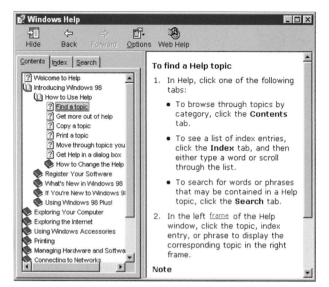

3 Click on one of the subjects and its contents appear in the right of the window. Most help pages make extensive use of **hyperlinks** – words or phrases that are underlined – to link together pages containing related data. Hyperlinks are usually shown in green. If the underlining is solid, clicking on the hyperlink will take you to another page. If it is broken, a small pop-up window will appear above the page to give you further information.

4 Contents pages are useful for browsing through a book or a Help file, but if you're looking for something specific it's better to use an index. If you click on the Index tab, Help Topics shows you the **index** page for the Help file. Scroll through the list of keywords until you find what you want and double-click on it. Alternatively you can type the word you are interested in and the list will automatically select an entry.

Help tip

Sometimes the Windows Help program can tell you exactly how to solve a problem. However, sometimes, you may need to load a different program to get you out of trouble. If you click on the curved arrow ↵ in Help, it will automatically take you to that program.

5 The **Search tab** lets you do a search on the whole of the text in the help file, not just keywords. Some versions of Windows Help ask you to create a database of words to be searched. Other versions handle this automatically and perform a database search as soon as you click on the List Topics button.

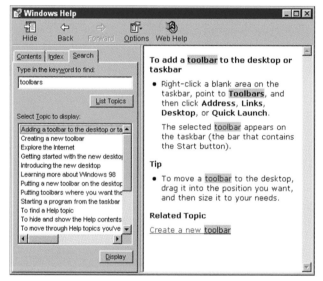

6 Type a **phrase** that describes what you want to find, click on List Topics and Help displays the relevant list. Double-click on a topic and its contents are displayed in the right of the window with the matched words highlighted. Windows may not always use the same terms as you, so if a text search doesn't locate the data you want, try using different words.

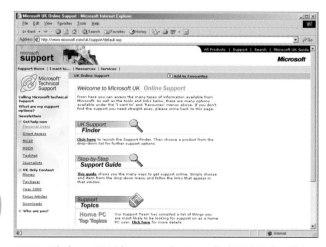

7 Windows 98 SE has a new feature called **Web Help**. Click on this button and if you're connected to the Internet, your Web browser will display Microsoft's online Help site. This may contain more comprehensive and up-to-date information on the subject you're looking for (see pages 55–6).

KnowledgeBase

You can find answers to even the most obscure questions about Windows on the Internet.

Your first stop, the online Help that comes with Windows (as described on pages 53–4), has answers to common questions. But if you have a more advanced question or a more unusual problem, it probably won't have the solution. However, there are other sources of information that you can access via the Internet. One of the most valuable is provided by Microsoft. Its Web site contains a searchable KnowledgeBase covering known problems with all Microsoft applications, not just Windows, plus troubleshooting wizards and downloadable files. If you have a problem with your computer, don't waste time trying to guess the answer – consult the KnowledgeBase.

Accessing the KnowledgeBase

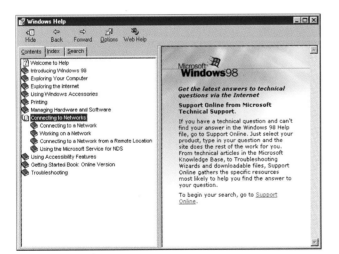

1 If you want to know how to do something in Windows, or need help with a Windows problem, the first place you should look is the **online Help pages**. After all, you don't want to spend time searching the Net for an answer that is already on your computer. Online Help includes a Troubleshooting section that can help you solve common problems. See pages 25–6 and 53–4 for more information.

If you can't find the answer you are looking for in online Help, try Microsoft Support Online. To get there, click on the Web Help button at the top of the Help window. When the Support Online page appears, click on the link at the bottom marked Support Online.

2 This link will take you to the home page of **Microsoft Product Support**. From the links on the left, or by picking an option from the list, you can get information on how to use the support site, and also obtain information about what support you are entitled to as a user of a Microsoft product and what other support services you can receive if you are prepared to pay for them.

If you want help with a technical matter, click on Online Support Requests or Custom Support, or select FAQs by product. If this is your first visit to the support site you will be taken to a registration form which you must complete before you can get access to the support areas. In future you will be asked for your e-mail address and password in order to access the site.

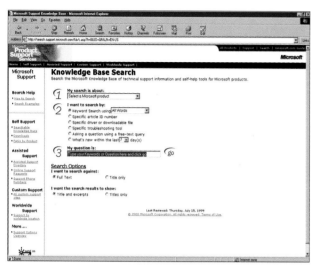

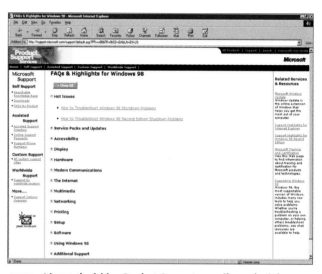

3 If you click on Searchable Knowledge Base, you'll find the search engine. You can narrow the search to a specific Microsoft product by selecting one from the dropdown list at the top, then typing keywords or a question in simple English to help the search engine find what you want. Click on **Go** to start the search. It can sometimes take a minute or two to get an answer: KnowledgeBase is a big service and it's heavily used.

5 It's worth visiting Product Support even if you don't have a technical problem. The site has useful tips that can save you time by showing you easier ways of doing things or forewarning you of problems. If you click on the **Frequently Asked Questions by Product** link on the search page, you will be taken to a new page containing a list of general topics. Click on one to get more information. You can also access lists of common questions about popular Microsoft products and there's a good chance that you will find something useful here.

4 If you are lucky, your question will result in a number of articles being returned. The search engine will show you the title of the article and a short extract that gives a more detailed description of what it relates to. To view the complete text of any article of interest click on the **hyperlink**.

If the article is relevant, print it from your browser. You'll almost certainly want to refer back to it later. Before closing your browser, skim through the article to see if it contains links to other, related articles that might also be relevant to your problem.

6 If you click on **Download Center**, you will be able to see if there are any upgrades for Microsoft products you have. It's worth checking here, even if you aren't experiencing a problem, because there may be improved versions of utilities and fixes for bugs that you haven't yet hit.

As a registered user of Product Support, you can sign up to receive regular news bulletins about products or areas of interest. For example, the Support News Watch will keep you posted about the latest support issues and product fixes. These bulletins are free, and they will help you get more from your software.

Search tip

Don't use product names such as Windows 98 in KnowledgeBase searches: it makes the search take longer. To search for

articles that relate to a specific product, select it from the dropdown list.

Online newsgroups

If you run into trouble using Windows, there are millions of other users online who would be happy to help you.

The biggest problem for the home PC user is knowing where to go for help. A knowledgeable friend can be a huge asset. But if you don't know any PC experts, or you don't want to annoy your pals by constantly asking questions, there are other ways to get help. The Net is a link to millions of Windows users. If you have a query, someone out there knows the answer.

There are several sources of help you can try. Online services such as AOL and CIX are good places to ask questions if you have access to them. If you don't, Internet news is a great resource, and the Web itself is a mine of information. It's disconcerting if you have a problem with your PC and don't know what to do. But if you're on the Net you're never alone.

Getting help from other users

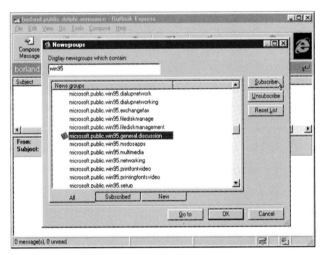

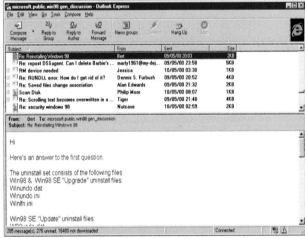

1 **Newsgroups** are the most popular discussion forums on the Internet and they are some of the best places to go to seek help and advice. If you have an Internet connection your ISP should provide access to a news server. To read and post messages in newsgroups you can use Microsoft Outlook Express.

There are thousands of newsgroups. In order to participate in a newsgroup you must subscribe to it. To choose the best ones to subscribe to, look at the newsgroup list (Tools, Newsgroups). If you type keywords, Outlook Express filters the list so that only the groups whose names contain those words are displayed.

Newsgroups devoted to discussion of Windows 95 and Windows 98 usually have names that contain win95 or win98. The microsoft.public newsgroups are the premier forums for getting help with problems as they are monitored by Microsoft. There are newsgroups for specific topics like disk management or printing, so you should subscribe to the most appropriate one for your problem.

2 Most of the newsgroups devoted to Windows issues are busy, so when you connect to the news server it's best to download only the **message headers**, not all the messages. Right-click on the newsgroup name and select Mark for Retrieval, New Headers. When this action has completed you will have a list showing the subject headings of each message, which will provide a clue to the question that was asked. To see the text of a message just select it from the list and Outlook Express will download the message body.

It's considered bad form to ask a question without first checking to see if the same question has been asked recently, so spend a few minutes browsing the list of headers. Messages that have replies to them are shown with a plus sign alongside. Quite often these replies will be useful answers.

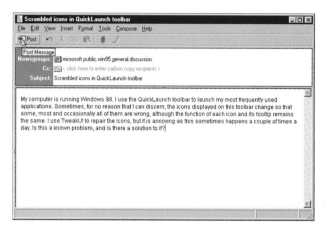

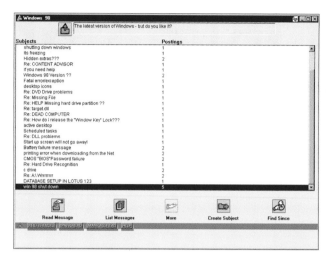

3 If you can't see any messages that answer your question, you'll have to post a message yourself. It's much like sending an e-mail. Click on the **Compose Message** button to open a window into which you can type your message. When you have finished, click on the Post button to send it.

The newsgroups are busy so you must do everything you can to help the person who has the answer to your question find your message. First, choose the most appropriate newsgroup to post your message. Make the subject header (which is all anyone who downloads headers only will read) a succinct description of your problem. Subject headers like Windows Problem or Help Needed aren't very useful. In the message body keep to the point. Ask your question or describe your problem as clearly as you can. You should also make sure you provide any technical information that might be relevant, such as the version of Windows, the type of graphics card, how much memory your computer has, what other programs are running when the problem occurs and so on.

5 If you subscribe to AOL or CIX these services have their own **online forums** which are available only to subscribers. The number of participants is thus restricted so there is a better chance your question will be read and answered than in some of the busier Internet newsgroups; and if you want to see what topics have been discussed before you won't have to plough through quite so many messages.

Although it is less well known than AOL, CIX is a valuable resource for computer users in the UK because it is the only online service that is UK-specific. With only around 15,000 subscribers it has more of a community feel and offers a better chance that you will receive the help you want. CIX is unique in that the software used to access its conferences (which are similar to Internet newsgroups) is designed to be used offline, so you won't run up a large phone bill while participating. For more information about CIX in the UK call 020 8255 5000.

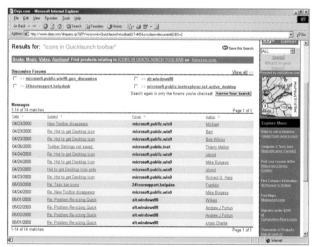

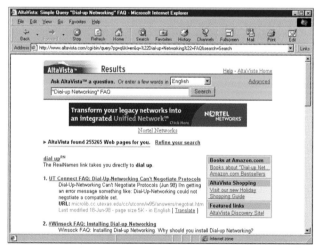

4 The AOL forums provide a valuable resource for computer users. Most forums are led by hosts who will help out with problems or questions you have. You can either chat to them live (at certain published times) or post a message through the message board. The computing forums themselves cover a variety of topics from building Web sites to PC maintenance to other operating systems including Linux and Macintosh. If it's all too much there are forums for more general topics such as camping and caravanning or comic books. There is a monthly subscription fee to join AOL, which also covers Internet access and other exclusive editorial content.

6 Web sites are another invaluable source of help and information. **FAQs** (compilations of frequently asked questions and answers relating to a particular topic) are usually created by individuals with a particular interest in that topic. A simple way to locate them is to include the keyword FAQ in your query when using a Web search engine like AltaVista. If you're interested in productivity tips and shortcuts rather than problem solutions, try searching for hints and tips instead.

Visit the Web site of your favourite computer magazine. Most magazine sites carry a wealth of information, including how-to articles and advice from the readers' help pages. Some sites even have online message boards where you can post your questions in the hope of receiving a reply.

Troubleshooting basics

Skilled computer engineers are thin on the ground, but DIY computer maintenance is an alternative.

The twin themes of troubleshooting and disaster recovery make computing at home sound much more dangerous than it really is. The dictionary defines a troubleshooter as an expert detector and mender of any trouble, mechanical or otherwise, but it's also true to say that a good troubleshooter should be able to anticipate and prevent disasters as well as recover from them.

Never fails

Most PC failures have nothing to do with mechanical problems, so if you're unlucky enough to have bought defective equipment there's little you can do apart from claiming a repair under warranty or paying for a replacement. Most manufacturing defects come to light when a PC is almost new, and if a computer doesn't fail in the first three months of intensive use the chances are it never will.

In order to keep your PC working properly you must be sure to install its software correctly, follow the rules about starting and closing it down safely, and run regular maintenance checks. Nevertheless, faults are bound to occur.

Do it yourself

If it's a software or configuration problem you can fix it yourself. If it's a hardware problem you might prefer not to open up your PC to replace the defective component, especially if the system is still under warranty. But being able to identify a hardware fault means you can request repairs knowing exactly what you're letting yourself in for and what they should cost.

You will need

ESSENTIAL

Software Windows includes a number of diagnostic and repair tools, but those from third parties such as McAfee and Symantec offer additional features and ease of use. Two programs everyone should have are a better back-up utility than the one included with Windows and an up-to-date anti-virus program.

Hardware Some form of removable storage with a capacity of at least 100MB and preferably more. This could be a Zip, LS-120, Jaz, SparQ or similar disk-based drive or a tape unit designed specifically for backing up hard disks.

Other Basic household cleaning materials such as lint-free rags or dusters and an all-surface cleaning spray.

Use back-up

Microsoft Backup can be installed from the Add/Remove Programs icon in Control Panel. It lets you make full and incremental back-ups of an entire disk or of selected files and folders. Unfortunately, it doesn't work with many popular types of drive, including Travan.

Installation tips

● Install one piece of software or hardware at a time.

● Make a full back-up (or a copy of your system configuration files) before installing new software.

● Make a note of everything you do, while you're doing it. Don't rely on your memory.

● If, when installing software or drivers you get a warning that existing files on your hard disk are newer than those being installed, do not replace them with older versions.

When changing hardware or software, making a back-up first can save time and trouble.

When it comes to keeping your PC in first-class order, prevention really is better than cure, if only because when your computer goes down it always seems to do so at the most inconvenient time. Keeping your PC in good shape needn't take more than a few minutes a week, but do remember to find extra time to make a back-up before changing any of the software or hardware in your system.

Back up your troubles

Backing up a hard disk is boring and most people tend not to do it, even when they know they should. But while you have to be dedicated to stick to a regular back-up regime, it's not too much of a hardship to make a precautionary back-up before installing a new piece of software or hardware (1).

A new piece of software may replace existing files with more recent ones. The new program may work fine but programs you've been using without problems for years may suddenly stop working. Removing the offending software won't fix the problem because the old files have been

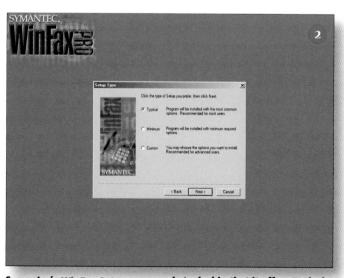

Symantec's WinFax Setup program is typical in that it offers Typical, Minimum and Custom installations. If a new program conflicts with an existing one, try a Minimum installation and, if this fixes the problem, add extra features one at a time using the Custom option.

overwritten, but after reinstating the working system from a back-up you can try reinstalling the offending software with a different set of options (2). Even if you haven't got a back-up drive you can make a copy of crucial Windows registry and configuration files on a floppy disk and use these to restore a system to good health. This isn't as good as a full disk back-up, but it doesn't require any special kit and the software you need comes free with Windows (3).

Hardware or hard luck?

Anyone unversed in the ways of Windows might think installing new hardware is foolproof – if a component doesn't work, take it out again. But it's not that simple. Every time you start Windows it identifies the components in the system, allocates resources to them and makes sure it has the correct drivers installed. This means that when you start up a PC after adding a new component, Windows might take resources from an existing device and give them to a new one. Removing the offending component doesn't restore an identical system. You need to restore your previous settings from the back-up.

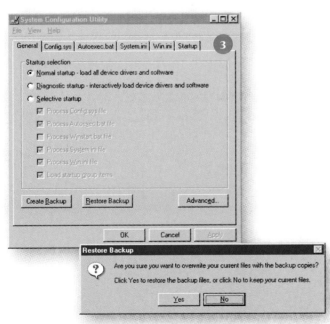

You can back up your system configuration using Windows. Go to Programs and the Accessories/System Tools folder and select System Information. On the Tools menu choose System Configuration Utility. Use this to make a copy of your system settings. If you decide not to keep the new program, uninstall it and restore the original settings by clicking Restore Backup.

Troubleshooting

When it works, plug and play is great, but when it doesn't, it's a pain. After installing a new component you should run your system thoroughly immediately afterwards to make sure that it's working properly, and you should check Device Manager (4) for conflicts. The effects of resource conflicts can be far reaching, so installing a new soundcard might prevent a seemingly unrelated item such as a network card from working. This won't be evident if you're not currently logged onto a network, which is why checking Device Manager is so important.

In **Device Manager a red cross next to a piece of kit means it has been disabled. A yellow exclamation mark means there's a problem with the device or its drivers.**

Daily essentials

● Always close down Windows before switching off your PC. Don't cheat by hitting the power switch before the message that it's safe to do so.

● Don't put any liquids near your PC. Assume that they're going to get knocked over and keep them far enough away so that if they *are* knocked over your equipment stays intact.

● Keep dust at bay. Inside your PC it clogs air vents and causes overheating. In floppy disk and CD-ROM drives it damages precision components and can lead to errors reading data.

● Spring clean your PC once a year. Vacuum the ventilation slots, make sure the external leads and cables are secure, and remove the lid of the system box to check that nothing has come loose.

First aid

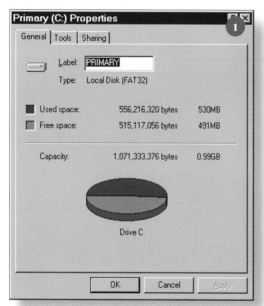

To check the amount of free space available on a hard disk, double-click on the My Computer icon on the Desktop; right-click on the drive you want to check and select Properties. You should regard 20MB of spare disk space as a minimum, but a better guide is to allow 10 per cent of the total disk space. This 1GB partition is fine because it's half empty, but when the available space is down to 100MB, old files should be ruthlessly chopped.

Before running ScanDisk, click the Advanced button and select the Delete option for Cross-linked files and the Free option for Lost file fragments. Make sure there's a tick next to Automatically Fix Errors. A Standard test checks for file corruption and a Thorough test also scans the surface of the hard disk for defects.

Here's what to do if, despite the precautions you've taken, your computer lets you down.

The usual warnings of problems with Windows are that it tries to load but crashes before finishing, or it loads smoothly but then won't work properly. In these cases the fault is almost certainly a missing driver, corrupted file or invalid system setting.

The same is true even if there is no sound from Windows and the CD-ROM drive has apparently disappeared. Just because hardware won't work doesn't mean it's broken. The only time a problem is more likely to be a hardware defect than a software problem is when your PC won't even start.

Define the problem

First ask yourself what has changed since your PC last worked. Have you installed new software? Have you installed new hardware? If the answer is yes, the chances are your problem stems from here and you can identify its source. Even if you haven't installed anything new, perhaps you've attached and subsequently removed a piece of equipment such as a borrowed printer. If your PC thinks the device is still there, it will try to use it.

It's not always possible to pin down the source of a problem, but it helps if you can find out what you have to do to make it happen. It's no good ringing a helpline with an intermittent problem. You'll spend hours on hold only to find that the problem won't manifest itself if somebody's listening.

Check your disk

When looking for the cause of a glitch, start with your hard disk. It's a common source of problems and it's easy to check and fix. There are two conditions to look for: one is a shortage of disk space and the other is a corrupted filing system.

To check the free space on a disk, double-click on My Computer on the Desktop. Right-click on the drive you want to check and select Properties. The amount of disk space you need depends on the programs you use. Many won't run without enough space for their temporary files and anything less than 20MB is a serious cause for concern (1).

The disk filing system can become damaged through no fault of your own, but it's more often the result of switching off your PC without closing Windows first. The symptom is that a program crashes during a disk access. To repair a damaged filing system, check for free disk space as described opposite, then click the Tools tab followed by the Check Now button to run ScanDisk (2).

Resolve conflicts

If the hard disk is OK and you can't pin the blame for a problem on the installation of some new piece of hardware or software, suspect a conflict between existing programs or drivers. To check for driver conflicts, try starting your PC in Safe Mode (3). This is a diagnostic mode of Windows in which it starts without loading any inessential drivers.

Turn on your PC and when you see the message Starting Windows... press F8. This brings up a menu from which you should select Safe Mode. Because the usual display drivers are not loaded in Safe Mode, the screen will revert to a 640 x 480 simple VGA format. This is normal so don't worry.

If the problem goes away when you start in Safe Mode, you know there's a driver conflict. In this case use Device Manager to disable each driver in turn until you find the one causing the problem.

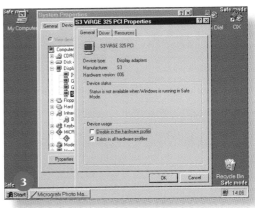

You can't forget you're in Safe Mode because there's a warning in each corner of the screen. Safe Mode can start a PC that has tangled drivers, but the information it provides is limited.

Hardware faults

Only after performing all the checks described here should you start to suspect a hardware defect. To test hardware effectively you need special equipment and training, but a viable alternative (if you have access to spare components) is to swap them one at a time until you identify the culprit.

Most people don't have convenient boxes of spare kit in the corner of their living rooms, but there is another option, which is to run the Hardware Diagnostic program (4). Initially provided with later versions of Windows 95, it can be found on the installation disk in a folder called \other\misc\hwtrack. The program itself is called Hwdiag.exe and is started by double-clicking on it.

In Windows 98 it has been renamed as the Hardware Info utility for Windows and is run by going to the Start menu and typing hwinfo/ui in the Run... box.

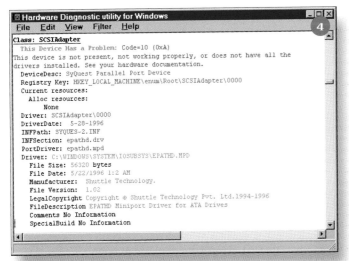

Hardware Diagnostics provides a lot of technical information which, even if it doesn't make sense to you, will help a support engineer. Fortunately, the information is colour coded so all you have to do is look out for the warnings in red.

Software tools

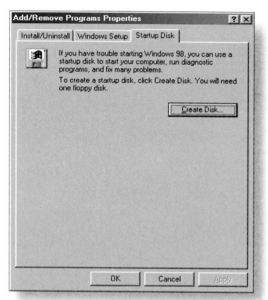

You can easily create your own boot disk if the manufacturer hasn't supplied one, through the Add/Remove Programs facility.

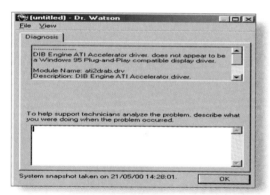

The diagnostic tool for Windows 98 is called Dr Watson. It will help you to discover the cause of any problems you may have.

Watch out!

Don't install two utility products with the same function because they might interfere with each other and cause problems. Utilities that run permanently in the background such as virus checkers, crash detectors and Recycle Bin enhancers hook themselves into Windows in order to do their jobs, and if two programs try to hang on the same hook they might pull it out altogether.

There's no shortage of software tools to help you keep your PC in order. Here's the pick of the bunch.

When your computer's sick, it's time to call the doctor. There are various utility programs which will come to the aid of your ailing PC.

The first step is to make sure your machine can boot up, even if it's not well enough to run Windows. Some manufacturers supply an emergency boot disk with a new PC. If not you should create one, when prompted, during the Windows installation process. However, you can make a boot disk at any time. Simply click on Start | Settings | Control Panel | Add/Remove Programs. Select the Startup Disk tab and click on Create Disk. There are also commercial programs which provide emergency recovery utilities.

Windows 98 comes with a useful diagnostic tool – Dr Watson (Windows 95 users have a similar program called Microsoft Diagnostics). Named after Sherlock Holmes' sidekick, Dr Watson won't fix anything but it will help track down the villain of the piece. If you have to call a helpline it will also provide answers to any awkward technical questions you may be asked about your system.

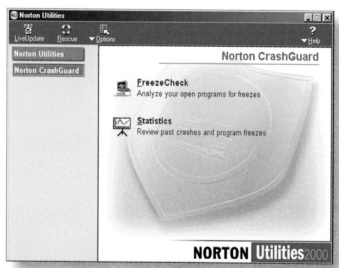

Norton CrashGuard from Symantec is supposed to detect when something is about to go wrong and give you a chance to save your work. This is a tall order and, surprisingly, it sometimes works. CrashGuard is also part of Symantec's SystemWorks.

McAfee's First Aid 2000 from Network Associates is one of the most comprehensive compilations of utility, recovery and diagnostic programs.

Commercial programs

Hundreds of commercial utilities are available to help you fix ailing PCs, but it's no good dashing out to buy one after problems have manifested themselves. The utilities operate within Windows and they must be installed when Windows is intact, not when it has started flaking away.

Some utilities are designed to perform one task thoroughly, but the trend is to bundle products together. Uninstallers are popular single-task utilities. These tools remove all traces of a program you no longer require, instead of leaving stray files to jam up the works. WinDelete, CleanSweep and Uninstaller are the most popular titles.

All in one

Other types of program that are sold separately include back-up tools, anti-virus scanners and crash preventers, but these facilities are often provided in the all-in-one products, too. Programs like First Aid, Nuts & Bolts and SystemWorks incorporate up to 40 separate utilities to diagnose and repair PC problems. Many of these are preventative and if used judiciously will stop problems occurring. But you'll also find recovery and file management tools, along with instructional videos and diagnostic procedures.

Internet tip

Several tools and utilities supplied on the Windows CD-ROM have already been mentioned. If you do not have access to these, download them from Microsoft's Web site.

The Microsoft Windows download site is at www.microsoft.com/windows/downloads.

Norton CleanSweep, also part of Symantec's SystemWorks, is one of many programs designed to uninstall Windows programs cleanly and thoroughly. It works best when it's installed early in the life of a PC and is then used to monitor the installation of the other programs.

Dead PCs

● If your PC is totally silent and there's not even a power light on the front, check the plugs and fuses and make sure the mains switch is turned on at the wall.

● Test the power cable by swapping it for another one. Most monitors use cables that are interchangeable with PCs, as do other items of household equipment including kettles.

● If the computer remains dead you have a defective power supply, which needs replacing.

● A PC that beeps when it's switched on and then locks up has a hardware fault. This may be a loose chip, expansion card or memory module, but it could also indicate a faulty motherboard. Remedies include replacing internal components.

Peripheral problems

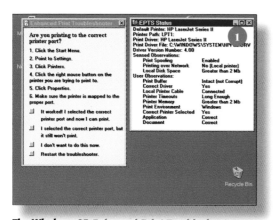

The Windows 95 Enhanced Print Troubleshooter leads you by the hand through the minefield of printer testing.

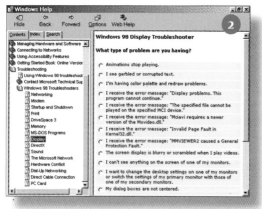

The Display Troubleshooter in Windows 98 helps you to get to grips with any monitor and graphics card problems you may have.

You should take the same care of the devices you plug into your PC as you do of those inside it.

Printer

Printers cause more problems than other peripheral devices. They are more likely to suffer a mechanical defect than the rest of the system because they have more moving parts, and they rely on a stable Windows installation and correct BIOS settings.

There are two printer troubleshooters built into Windows, but they don't tell you how to take care of your printer and the importance of checking the BIOS settings in your PC (1). Printers are designed for use by Windows and they use sophisticated printer drivers offering a number of output options. Advanced printer drivers rely on communication between the printer and the PC and can thus provide estimates of how much ink or toner is left in the printer and how long a print job will take.

For this communication to work the printer port of your PC must be set to EPP (Enhanced Parallel Port) or to ECP (Enhanced Capabilities Port) in the BIOS. Refer to your printer manual for the settings for your printer and to your PC manual for advice on changing BIOS settings. The usual method is to

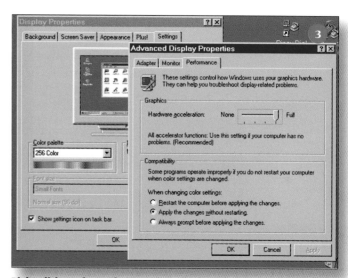

Right-click on the Desktop to view Display Properties. Assuming the monitor and graphics card are correctly identified, try adjusting the Hardware Acceleration level on the Performance tab (Advanced Options) until random corruption is eliminated.

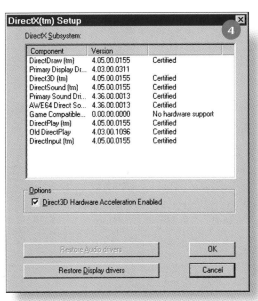

There are two simple rules to follow regarding DirectX. **If it's working, do not under any circumstances change it. If it isn't, reinstall it from the latest version you can lay your hands on.**

hold down the Delete key during the boot sequence.

Printers also need a certain amount of mechanical care. Paper disperses a fine dust that can clog up mechanisms. Every type of printer has maintenance needs related to the technology employed. Lasers have toner waste bottles to empty, fuser pads to change and corona wires to clean. Inkjets tend to sublimate vapourised ink, which must be removed. Even simple dot-matrix printers eventually require pulverised ribbon waste to be vacuumed away.

Monitor

Problems with monitors almost always stem from inappropriate Windows settings and may be caused by a poorly configured graphics card. If your monitor is inert and you have checked the cables, switches and fuses, you probably have a hardware failure on your hands, but if you've got any sort of picture at all the chances are it can be improved by tweaking the settings in Windows. There's no monitor troubleshooter to help you in Windows 95, although there is a good one in Windows 98 (2).

Most graphics problems are caused by the wrong display adapter and monitor settings in Display Properties (3). If these are OK – the settings relate to the names on the box – the problem is almost certainly related to Microsoft DirectX. This is one of Microsoft's ongoing projects to turn Windows into a games platform. In Windows 95, if you have problems with moving graphics, find DxSetup.exe (in \Program Files\DirectX\Setup) and run it.

In the resulting dialogue box, DirectDraw and Direct3D should have the word Certified next to them (4). If there is a problem, reinstall from the most recent copy of DirectX available. Look for the files on Windows games CDs, on magazine cover disks and at www.microsoft.com on the Internet.

Practical Considerations

Keep mice and keyboards clean (see page 115). If you're having problems with sound, don't blame your speakers apart from checking that they're properly connected, but do make sure you've got them plugged into the Speaker output of your soundcard. If you have amplified speakers and the output is distorted, try plugging the speakers into the Line Out instead of the speaker jack.

Troubleshooting

Windows Help includes up to 16 troubleshooters. The exact number depends on how recent a version of Windows you have. The troubleshooters are in the main part of Windows Help (accessible through the Start button) under Troubleshooters. Most people are more familiar with the Help systems built into their applications than the one in Windows, so the troubleshooters are often ignored. However, they're all good, and two of them are directly related to peripherals — one for printing and another for modems. The troubleshooters use a question and answer approach that leads you along sensible lines. There's an even better printer troubleshooter, called Enhanced Print Troubleshooter, in the \other\misc\epts folder of the Windows CD-ROM.

Whenever you have a problem with Windows, the built-in troubleshooters should be your first port of call.

Anti-virus tools

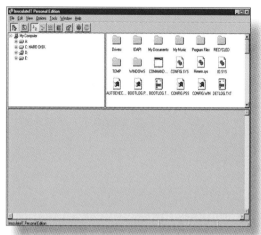

InoculateIT Personal Edition **from Computer
Associates is just one of the anti-virus programs
available.**

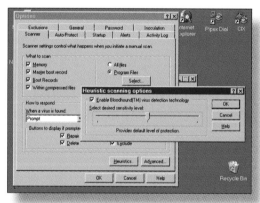

Norton **AntiVirus** **includes heuristic protection
(a method of scanning) to help it recognise
new viruses.**

Viruses pose a genuine threat to PCs, but anti-virus programs give you peace of mind.

Viruses may hit the headlines only occasionally,
but they are an ever-present threat to PC users. For
the novice, the only safe way of tackling them is
with a commercial anti-virus program.

Early anti-virus programs found a virus on your
hard disk only after you'd been attacked by one.
Current products prevent contamination in the first
place. Should a virus try to install itself on your
system, the program will warn you and help you to
deal with it. Even if you've been attacked by a
virus it's not too late. Provided you follow the
instructions of an anti-virus program scrupulously,
most can detect an infestation and remove it.

Dealing with a virus

If you have an anti-virus program installed and a
virus tries to copy itself onto your PC's hard disk,
the anti-virus program should detect the activity
and prevent the virus from attacking. In the case of
a pre-existing virus infestation, an anti-virus
program might be able to remove the virus with no
harm to the system, but there is a possibility that,
in removing the virus, some program files will be
altered. It's advisable to reinstall any software that
does not work properly after a virus clean-up.

If you have a back-up that you know to be good,
use it. Scan every removable disk you have and
contact anybody with whom you exchange disks to
get them to check theirs. For more information on
viruses see pages 99–108.

Minimise virus risks

● Most anti-virus programs can be updated free of
charge for a period of up to 12 months. Make full use of
the update service for maximum protection.

● An anti-virus program is not a substitute for regular back-ups.

● Don't use floppy disks from unknown or untrustworthy sources.

● Schedule a weekly or monthly virus scan to supplement your
anti-virus program's background protection, which may not be as
thorough as a comprehensive disk scan.

Error messages

Understanding error messages helps you sort Windows out when it goes wrong.

Nobody's perfect. We all do silly things sometimes, like trying to copy files to a floppy drive without a disk in it, or deleting a program and then trying to run it. When this happens, Windows displays an error message to inform us politely of what we have done. Usually the solution is obvious, or explained in the message.

Software isn't perfect either, and when it fails you may see error messages of a different kind. The reason for software or system errors may be harder to find, and the solution may be outside your control. But it helps to be able to distinguish problems that you can solve from those you can't. There are hundreds of different error messages that you may see when you use Windows, although many of them will appear in rare circumstances. Here, you can see a rogues' gallery of the more common ones, with explanations of what they mean and how to deal with them.

Understanding error messages

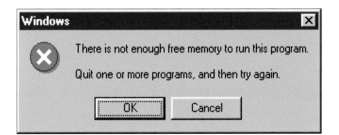

There is not enough free memory to run this program. Quit one or more programs, and then try again.

This message appears if there is not enough memory to start a program. The suggested remedy of closing one or more programs may solve the problem. If the problem occurs frequently, the virtual memory available to Windows may be restricted. From the Control Panel open the System icon, click on the Performance tab and then on the Virtual Memory button. It is usually best to let Windows manage its own virtual memory settings. In particular, there should be no maximum size for virtual memory. If no limit is specified, check how much disk space is free. If there is insufficient free space (less than 100MB) this will limit the amount of virtual memory available to Windows.

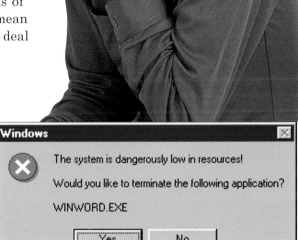

The system is dangerously low in resources! Would you like to terminate the following application? <application name>.

The cause of this message may be similar to the preceding one. It may also occur because other applications have used memory, but have not freed it after use so that Windows can let other programs use it. The error usually occurs in the middle of some work. You should try to save your work, if necessary closing other applications to try to recover sufficient memory to do so.

Once your work is saved, restart Windows before continuing what you were doing. This will allow Windows to recover any memory that has temporarily been lost.

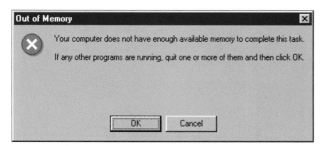

Out of memory. Your computer does not have enough available memory to complete this task. If any other programs are running, quit one or more of them and then click OK.

This message can be a little misleading. It does not necessarily mean that all the memory in the computer has been used. It usually means that Windows cannot find a suitably large block of memory, in one chunk, in the place where the program needs the memory to be. Closing other programs may free enough memory to solve the problem. If that does not work, restart Windows and repeat the operation that caused the error to occur.

Access is denied. Make sure the disk is not full or write-protected and that the file is not currently in use.

This message usually occurs if you try to delete, move or rename a file that is in use. Close any applications that may be using the file. In rare cases, this error can persist because the application that was using a file crashed while the file was still open. Windows may still think that the file is open. In this case, you may have to restart Windows before you can rename or delete the file.

The disk in the destination drive is full. Insert a new disk to continue.

This message occurs if you are copying a group of files to floppy disk, and there is insufficient space on the disk for all the files. If you insert a new floppy disk and click on Retry, Windows will copy the remainder of the files to the new disk.

The disk is write-protected. Remove the write-protection or use another disk.

This message should be self-explanatory. You are copying files to a floppy disk or disk cartridge and the write-protect tab is enabled. To allow the disk to be written to, remove it from the drive and slide the tab on the back until the hole is closed. Then reinsert the disk and click on Retry.

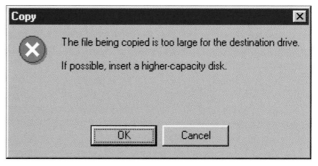

The file being copied is too large for the destination drive. If possible, insert a higher-capacity disk.

This message is fairly clear. If a file is larger than the target drive (for example, 1.4MB in the case of a floppy disk), Windows cannot copy it. It cannot split the file across two or more disks. The only solution to this problem is to use a third-party utility, for example a compression utility such as WinZip.

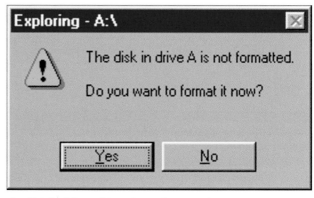

The disk in drive <drive> is not formatted. Do you want to format it now?

The drive referred to in this message is usually the floppy drive or a removable disk drive. The disk must be formatted before you can read or write to it. To format a floppy disk, right-click on the A: drive in Explorer and select Format from the menu. However, if you are sure that the disk contains data, the error could be the result of a malfunction such as a faulty floppy drive or the internal data cable coming loose. Check the disk in a different computer before formatting it, which would destroy any data.

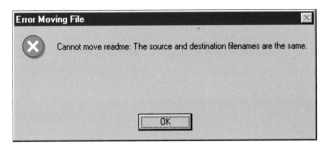

Error Moving File

Cannot move readme: The source and destination filenames are the same.

OK

Cannot move <filename>: The destination folder is the same as the source folder.
Cannot move <filename>: The source and destination filenames are the same.

These appear if you try to copy or move a file or folder to itself. It is easy to make this mistake using drag and drop in Explorer.

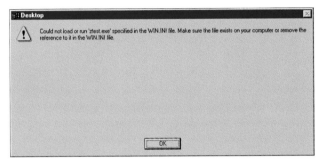

Desktop

Could not load or run 'ztest.exe' specified in the WIN.INI file. Make sure the file exists on your computer or remove the reference to it in the WIN.INI file.

OK

Could not load or run <filename> specified in the WIN.INI file. Make sure the file exists on your computer or remove the reference to it in the WIN.INI file.

This message will appear if a program has added its name to the load= or run= line in Win.ini, in order to be run automatically at startup, and the program has subsequently been moved or deleted. Either reinstall the program or run Sysedit and remove the reference to the file from Win.ini.

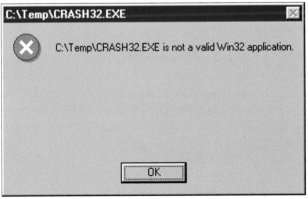

C:\Temp\CRASH32.EXE

C:\Temp\CRASH32.EXE is not a valid Win32 application.

OK

<filename> is not a valid Win32 application.
This error means that the program you are trying to run is corrupted. This could be as a result of a disk error: run ScanDisk to make sure that your hard disk is OK. Alternatively, you might have copied or renamed a non-program file to a filename with an .exe extension. Delete the file and, if it is a program that you need, restore it from a back-up or reinstall it from the original Setup disk.

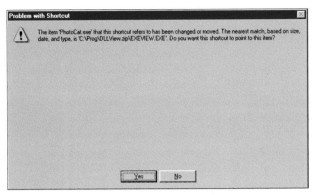

Problem with Shortcut

The item 'PhotoCat.exe' that this shortcut refers to has been changed or moved. The nearest match, based on size, date, and type, is 'C:\Prog\DLLView.zip\EXEVIEW.EXE'. Do you want this shortcut to point to this item?

Yes   No

The item <filename> that this shortcut refers to has been changed or moved. The nearest match based on size, date and type is <filename>. Do you want this shortcut to point to this item?

This message usually appears after a program has been uninstalled or deleted when the shortcut used to run the program has not been removed. Windows attempts to locate the file that the shortcut should be pointing to, but as it has usually been deleted the file it finds is unlikely to be of any use. You should either reinstall the missing application, or delete the unwanted shortcut.

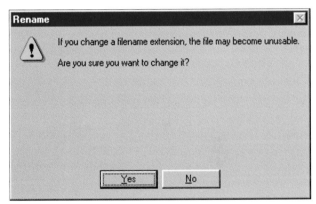

Rename

If you change a filename extension, the file may become unusable.

Are you sure you want to change it?

Yes   No

If you change a filename extension, the file may become unusable. Are you sure you want to change it?

If you try to rename a file using Explorer, Windows may display this message. The reason is usually because you are changing the extension to the filename: the three characters after the dot at the end of the filename which tell Windows what type of file it is. If you change these three characters, Windows won't know what application to use to open the file. If in doubt, click on No, so that Windows will ignore your change.

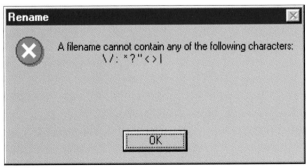

Rename

A filename cannot contain any of the following characters:
\ / : * ? " < > |

OK

A filename cannot contain any of the following characters: \ / : * ? " < > |

This message is more or less self-explanatory. You cannot use any of the characters shown when copying or renaming a file.

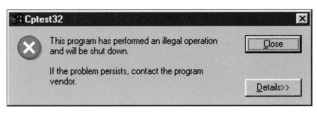

```
Cannot find a device file that may be needed to run Windows or a Windows
application.

The Windows registry or SYSTEM.INI file refers to this device file, but the
device file no longer exists.

If you deleted this file on purpose, try uninstalling the associated application
using its uninstall program or setup program.

If you still want to use the application associated with this device file, try
reinstalling that application to replace the missing file.

vnetsup.vxd
Press any key to continue
```

Cannot find a device file that may be needed to run Windows or a Windows application.

The Windows registry or SYSTEM.INI file refers to this device file, but the device file no longer exists.

If you deleted this file on purpose, try uninstalling the associated application using its uninstall program or setup program.

If you still want to use the application associated with this device file, try reinstalling that application to replace the missing file.

<filename>

Press any key to continue.

If this message appears, it will be displayed in text mode during startup. When you press a key as instructed, Windows may continue loading, and run normally. However, having to do this every time Windows starts is annoying.

This message occurs because a device driver which Windows is instructed to load in one of its configuration files has been deleted. Usually, this is the result of deleting files manually, using Explorer or an uninstaller utility instead of using Control Panel, Add/Remove Programs. If you know the identity of the program you deleted, reinstalling it should stop the error from appearing.

If Windows runs normally without this file you can try removing the instruction to load it from the configuration files. However, this can be difficult. Run Sysedit, select System.ini and search for the filename shown in the message. If it appears, delete the line containing it. If the filename does not appear in System.ini, run Regedit and search for the name there. If it appears, delete the value containing it. You must back up your configuration files before changing them just in case the change makes things worse instead of better.

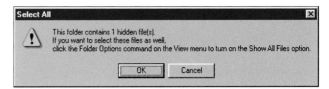

This program has performed an illegal operation and will be shut down. If the problem persists, contact the program vendor.

This error is, sadly, seen all too often. It is usually the result of a program bug. If you can make the error message occur by carrying out a specific sequence of actions, it is definitely a bug and you should report it to the software vendor. If you are lucky, you may be able to get an update to the software that doesn't have the bug.

If the error occurs frequently, seemingly at random, and if it effects a number of different programs, it could be caused by faulty memory, an overheating processor or some other system malfunction, rather than a software bug.

If you click on the Details box you will see some diagnostic information which may help to determine the cause of the problem. To make a record of the information, select it with the mouse, copy it to the Clipboard, paste it into Notepad and then print it.

This folder contains <n> hidden file(s). If you want to select these files as well, click the Folder Options command on the View menu to turn on the Show All Files option.

This is another fairly self-explanatory message. Windows allows files to have a hidden attribute, which means that by default they are not shown in Explorer file listings. Files are usually hidden because they are for use by an application, not by the user, and hiding them helps protect them from being tampered with.

If you use Edit, Select All to select all of the files in a folder so as to move or copy them to another location or to delete them, and there are hidden files in the folder which Explorer is not showing, it will display this message instead. To delete, move or copy the hidden files you must first change Explorer's Folder Options so that the files are shown and can be selected in the folder window.

Jargon buster

Illegal operation When a program performs an illegal operation it means that the program has done something that the computer thinks it shouldn't have. Examples include protection faults where a program tries to access a protected block of memory belonging to another program or Windows itself, and exceptions which are error conditions trapped by software. Stack faults occur when a program fills up the amount of space reserved for temporary data storage.

You need not worry about what type of illegal operation a program performs, but if you report the error to the software vendors they will probably want to know what you did immediately before the message appeared.

DIY fixes

Make sure you always have the latest device drivers and you can eliminate many problems with Windows 98.

Device drivers are one of the biggest causes of problems with Windows 98. These are programs whose purpose is to control hardware devices such as graphics and soundcards. It would be impossible for Windows to offer support for every device available, so modular device drivers are the best way of dealing with this problem. That's why whenever you add a new piece of hardware, Windows 98 always installs some software for it.

Few device drivers are perfect and some can cause problems. But that's not a disaster because they are easy to replace and updated drivers will solve the problem. New drivers include extra features. You might buy a 3D graphics card to enhance your games playing, then find your existing games do not support the card. Go to the game's Web site and you may find a driver that makes the game work with your new card.

How to update drivers

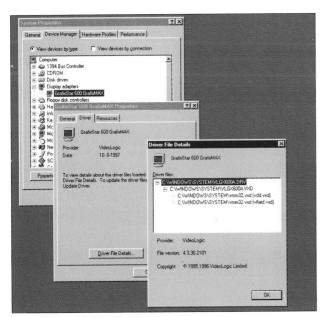

1 The first thing to do is to find out the version numbers of the device drivers your PC is presently using. It's easy to find the maker's name and version numbers of your device drivers. Open the System icon in Control Panel and click on the **Device Manager** tab. Scroll down the hardware list and open a device by clicking on the + symbol. Select the device and click on Properties. Click on the Driver tab and then the Driver File Details button. This lists the Provider and the File version. Here VideoLogic is the manufacturer, the graphics card is a GrafixStar 600 and the driver version is 4.3.30.2101, which can be condensed to 4.3.3.

2 It's a good idea to create a Notepad document, listing the device name, manufacturer and version number for each device on your system, and update this list when you install a new driver. Then you'll have all the current driver data in one place whenever you need to check it. The next step is to go to the manufacturer's Web site. If you don't know the precise address, use a search engine like Yahoo or AltaVista. Look for support, drivers or downloads to access the download area. This is the VideoLogic Web page that has the latest drivers for the GrafixStar 670. Check the version numbers. While you're there, add the address of the site to a **Favorites** sub-folder called Driver Updates to make it easier for you to return to that page to check for updates.

It's a good idea to keep your device drivers up to date if you want your PC to run smoothly, so pay regular visits to hardware manufacturers' sites. Apart from the call charges, downloading drivers is free.

Windows 98 has a Windows Update feature which is designed to keep all your software up to date with the minimum of effort. It can connect to the Internet, access the Windows Update site, analyse the software on your PC and automatically download and install any updates. But to keep your device drivers properly up to date you have to do some of the footwork yourself. It's difficult to say exactly which drivers you will need as every PC has different hardware fitted, but a good place to start would be your graphics card, 3D accelerator and soundcard drivers.

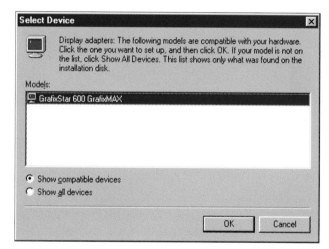

3 To download the new driver click on the filename. This causes a **File Download** dialogue box to pop up. Select the save this program to disk option and click on OK. Select a location for the file to be saved to and click on the Save button. If the page warns that you'll need an additional patch file for the driver to work under Windows 98, so you'll need to download this.

5 Open Control Panel and click on the System icon. Click on the Device Manager tab and scroll down the hardware list to find the device whose driver needs updating, in this case the GrafixStar display adapter. Click on Properties and the Driver tab. Click on the **Update Driver** button to launch Update Device Driver Wizard. Select No, Select Driver From List and click on Next. Select Display a List of Drivers, click on Next and click on the Have Disk button.

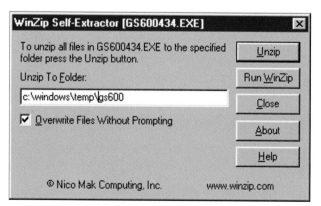

4 To simplify downloading, the various driver files are archived in a single file, which you then have to unpack at your end. Most drivers are supplied as self-unpacking executables but you might come across one or two that are supplied as compressed .zip files. To expand these sorts of files you'll need a utility program, such as **PKZip** or **WinZip**. Either way, unpack the files to a temporary folder, such as c:\windows\temp.

6 You can now specify where to **locate** the updated drivers. In this case type c:\windows\temp. Click OK and as long as the device is listed in the next window, click on Next and the driver software is installed. Click on the Finish button to close the Update Device Driver Wizard. You'll need to restart your PC at this point. If the driver isn't more recent than the one currently installed, the wizard will tell you and then allow you a second bite of the cherry by choosing other drivers from the list previously displayed.

System conflicts

Turn to Windows for help if the components of your computer system refuse to cooperate.

Computers are often called systems. They are not just boxes that you plug in, turn on and use, but collections of components that work together. Every time you install a software package or add new hardware you change your system from the standard product that has been made by the thousand to a configuration that is much rarer and perhaps unique to you.

As the combination of hardware and software on your PC is so rare, it has probably not been tested. The interfaces are standardised, so there is a good chance everything will work. But components may conflict or fail to detect each other. Windows should detect problems and report errors, giving you a chance to correct them.

Sorting out system conflicts

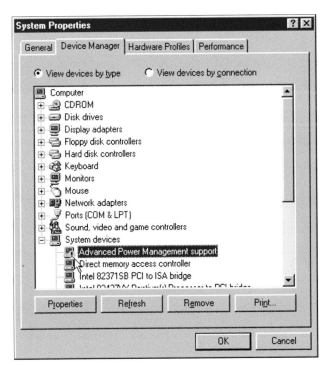

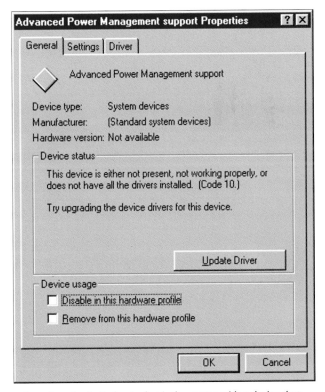

1 When Windows detects a problem with a device, such as an external piece of hardware you have added or something inside your PC, the problem is flagged in **Device Manager**. If you find that something isn't working, and you've checked obvious causes such as the connection to your PC and the power cable, look to see whether Windows has noticed a problem by opening Device Manager. The quickest way is to right-click on My Computer and select Properties. If there is a problem with a device its Device Manager icon will be marked with an exclamation mark in a circle.

2 In order to find out what is the matter with a device that Device Manager thinks has a problem, select its entry and click on the **Properties** button. The General page of the Properties dialogue box includes a Device status panel. This panel contains a brief description of the problem and an error code, together with a suggested solution. If your computer is still running Windows 95 or earlier, however, you will be given an error code only. A full list of Device Manager error codes and a description of the fault is given on the next page, with Microsoft's recommended solution in a separate panel.

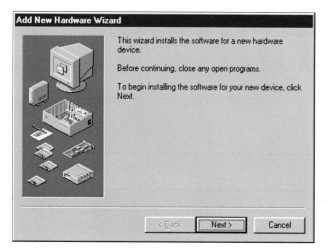

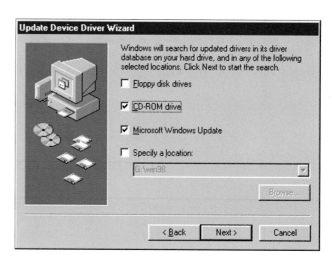

3 For most errors reported by Device Manager, Microsoft recommends that you delete the device entry from Device Manager and reinstall it. To delete a device, simply select the entry and click on **Remove**. Close Device Manager and restart Windows. If the device was a plug and play device, Windows should redetect it when it restarts and install the drivers for it automatically. If it doesn't, you will have to run the Add New Hardware Wizard from Control Panel.

4 If reinstalling the device does not help, there may be a problem with the hardware or with the software drivers for the device. To resolve hardware conflicts, see page 77. In case there are known driver problems, update to the latest drivers. This is easy if you have Windows 98 and your PC is connected to the Net: just click on the **Update Driver** button on the device properties page. Unfortunately, hardware problems can't usually be overcome except by replacing the hardware.

Device Manager error codes and how to resolve them

Code 1 The system has not had a chance to configure the device.
Code 2 The device loader failed to load a device.
Code 3 The system has run out of memory.
Code 5 A device needs something that Windows does not know how to give it.
Code 11 The device failed.
Code 18 An error occurred and the device must be reinstalled.
Code 19 The registry returned an unknown result.
Code 23 The device loader delayed the start of a device and failed to inform Windows 95 when it was ready to start the device.
Code 27 The part of the registry describing possible resources for a device is inconsistent.
● For these codes the recommended solution is as follows: remove the device from Device Manager by selecting the entry marked with the exclamation mark and clicking on Remove. Close Device Manager. Then run the Add New Hardware Wizard from Control Panel to reinstall the device.

Code 4 The setup information (.inf) file for this device is incorrect.
Code 8 The loader for a device could not be found. The setup information file for this device may refer to a missing or invalid file.
Code 9 The information in the Registry for this device is invalid.
Code 17 This is a multiple-function device and the setup information file contains invalid instructions on how to split the resources between functions.
● For these codes try removing the device and then reinstalling using the Add New Hardware Wizard. If that fails, contact the manufacturer of the device for an updated setup information file.

Code 6 There's a conflict between this device and another device.
Code 12 The device requested a resource that was not available, perhaps because it is in use by another device or because the system is out of resources.
Code 15 The device has a resource conflict with another device.
● For these codes follow the advice in Troubleshooting Conflicting Hardware in Windows Help.

Code 7 Windows cannot configure this device. If it works correctly you can ignore this error.
Code 13 The device failed due to a problem in the device driver.
Code 20 The loader for the device driver software returned an unknown result. This could be caused by a version mismatch between the device driver and the operating system.
Code 26 The device failed to load. There may be a problem with the device driver such as the file being corrupted.
Code 28 The device was not installed completely.
● For these error codes try removing the device from Device Manager and reinstalling it. If this fails, obtain an updated driver.

Code 10 The device failed to start. It may be missing or not working properly, or its drivers may be improperly installed.
Code 24 The device was not found.
● If these codes are reported for an external device, check the connections and power to the device. If you can't see why it isn't working, try removing it from Device Manager and reinstalling it.

Code 14/Code 21 Both indicate that a problem was found that might be resolved by shutting down and then restarting your PC.
Code 16 The device was not fully detected by Windows. Not all of its resources may be recorded. To resolve this problem, click on the Resources tab of the Device Properties dialogue box and enter the resource settings manually.
Code 22 The device is disabled in this configuration. You should enable it by unchecking the Disable In This Hardware Profile check box in the Device Usage panel on the property page.
Code 25 Windows 95 is in setup mode. You won't see this because it happens during the first reboot in W95 setup only.
Code 29 This device has been disabled because it does not work properly with Windows 95. If you see this error code, contact the device manufacturer for advice.
Code 30 This device needs an interrupt (IRQ) resource that is being used by a DOS driver loaded from the MS-DOS startup files Config.sys or Autoexec.bat. To solve the problem, remove the real-mode driver from the MS-DOS startup files.

Hardware conflicts

When new bits of hardware fail to work with your system, it's up to you and Windows to sort things out.

From the outset, PCs were cleverly designed to be extendable. It's very easy to add extras, such as disk drives or special expansion cards, to a PC. There is, of course, a limit to the number of additional devices you can fit to your PC. For example, there are a fixed number of expansion slots on motherboards and a fixed number of empty drive bays in system cases.

When you exhaust these that's it. You can't fit anything else. As well as these obvious limitations there are also a number of invisible limitations as well. Called hardware resources, these are as much a limitation as the physical ones. Once a PC's hardware resources are used up, it doesn't matter that you can physically install the device, it won't work properly.

Fixing hardware conflicts

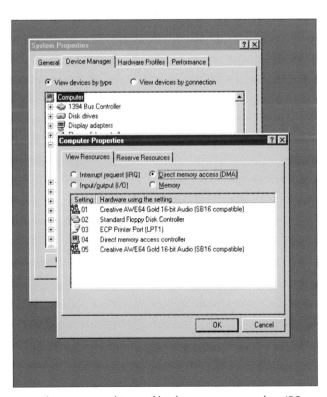

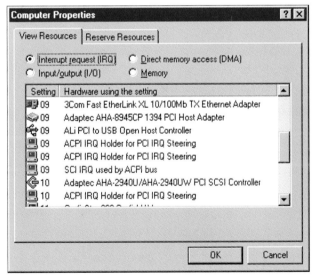

1 There are several types of hardware resources such as IRQs and DMA channels and they are listed in **Device Manager**. Just select Computer and click on Properties to list the current hardware resource settings. As a rule these resources can't be shared. If one device is using a DMA channel then another device can't use it. However, PCI cards in modern PCs can share IRQs. In the example in step 2, three devices are sharing IRQ 9.

2 If you have a modern PC and stick to **PCI cards** and **USB devices**, you should have no problems with hardware conflicts. Try to steer clear of older, ISA cards and parallel port devices, and anything you fit should plug and play easily.

Occasionally you might want to fit an older, non-plug and play card. To avoid a hardware clash, you may have to help Windows out. You'll know when you've got a clash because something will stop working. A typical example would occur if you allocated an internal modem to COM 3, which shares IRQ 4 with COM 1, which on older PCs was used by the mouse. If you did this, the mouse would stop working whenever you connected to the Internet.

Windows 95 and 98 make it easier to sort out clashes. It sounds complex but it isn't. Bring up Device Manager by right-clicking on My Computer and selecting Properties. Click on the Device Manager tab to display the tree of hardware devices. Any device that isn't working is flagged with a yellow badge with a black exclamation mark. In Step 3 there's a problem with the hard disk controller.

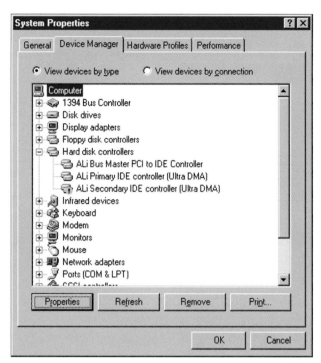

3 Select the device and click on the Properties button. Click on **Resources** and uncheck the Use Automatic Settings tick box which lets you manually adjust the various settings.

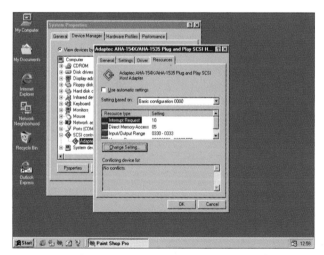

4 Next select the resources such as Interrupt Request or Input/Output Range in the **Resource Type** list in turn and look at the contents of the Conflicting device list. Most will say No Conflicts but one or two may say Device Conflicts With plus the name of the other device and the value of the resource in question. These are the resources to adjust.

Jargon buster

● **DMA** Direct Memory Access is a method whereby a device can access RAM, bypassing the CPU. There are only eight DMA channels and typically five are free.

● **IRQ** Interrupt Request is a direct link between a device and the CPU, used by the device to get the attention of the CPU. There are 16 IRQs in a PC and typically five are free. This means IRQs are scarce but IRQ sharing is possible in modern PCs.

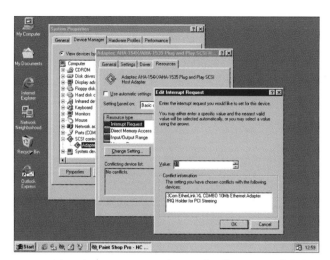

5 Select the Resource Type that needs adjustment and click on the **Change Setting** button. Another dialogue box pops up. Use the up and down arrows to adjust the resource values until the Conflict Information box tells you that No Devices Are Conflicting. Click OK. If another Resource type needs adjusting, select it and click on the Change Setting button again. Once all the Resource Types have No Conflicts, click OK one last time. You may need to restart your PC to bring these changes into effect.

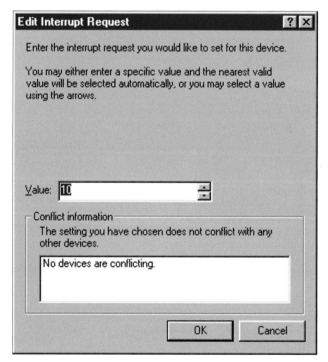

6 This method works best when you've got plug and play cards installed in your PC. These are entirely software configurable, so you can adjust them without opening up your PC. If you have non-plug and play cards fitted, all is not lost, because at least Device Manager tells you which settings will and won't work. The sequence is much as before. You adjust your hardware resources in Device Manager until every entry is labelled No Conflicts. Then make a careful note of these settings and shut your PC down. Once powered down, you can open up the PC system unit, extract any card that's causing problems and manually apply to the card the settings you've noted down. This could involve moving one or two **jumpers** or flicking a **DIP switch**. You'll have to refer to the documentation that came with the particular card for more details on how to adjust these settings.

Startup menu

Windows Startup menu can save the day if Windows refuses even to start.

Like any complex system, Windows can go wrong. When it won't even start, the reason is often connected with one of the software drivers that Windows loads at startup.

Software drivers are loaded to perform specific tasks or control an item of hardware. Often problems occur when you install new hardware or a new application. If that is the case, you can solve it by removing the hardware's drivers or uninstalling the application. If the cause isn't so clear, you may have to identify the culprit using a process of elimination.

False start

If Windows won't start, you might have to try to solve the problem using the unfriendly MS-DOS environment. But Windows' Startup menu offers a choice of options, one of which will probably succeed in getting you into Windows so you can sort the trouble out. The Startup menu is usually hidden. If you have Windows 95 you can open the menu by holding down

the F8 key when the message Starting Windows appears. This also works with some machines running Windows 98. Otherwise, hold down the Ctrl key while the PC boots and release it when the Startup menu appears.

Boot it out

First choice, Normal, is the way Windows starts up if you don't use the menu. The menu has a countdown timer. If you don't choose any option, after 30 seconds Windows will start up in the normal way.

The second menu option, Logged (Bootlog.txt), can be used to try to discover the cause of the problem. It creates a detailed log of what happens during startup in a file called Bootlog.txt in your C:\ root folder. You can view the contents of this file by opening it in Notepad. The information will be helpful to any Helpline staff you may have to call. Any problem such as Windows suddenly hanging or freezing is likely

Understanding Windows' Startup

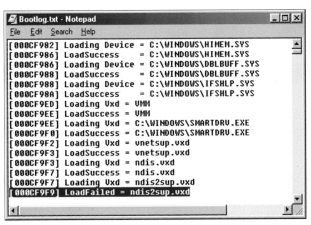

1 The Windows Startup menu lets you choose a **startup mode** for troubleshooting Windows problems.

2 A **logged startup** creates a log of everything that happens during startup in a file called Bootlog.txt.

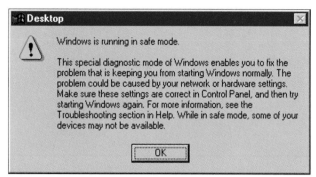

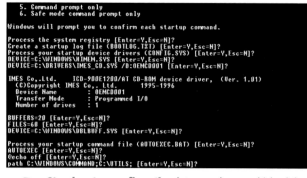

3 In **Safe Mode** essential software drivers only are loaded, allowing Windows to start so you can correct a problem.

4 **Step-by-step confirmation** lets you choose which of the commands in your startup files should be used.

to be something to do with the last entry in the Bootlog file.

The Bootlog file also keeps track during shutdown. If Windows hangs and you don't get the message 'It is now safe to turn off your computer', restart choosing a Logged startup. Shut down Windows in order for the Bootlog file to record what happens. Restart normally again and open the Bootlog.txt file. The last entry may reveal what is causing the problem.

Safety first

Starting Windows using the third option, Safe mode, is a good way of proving that the system itself is all right. In fact, if Windows hangs during startup it will start in Safe mode automatically the next time you try to start it. This gives you a chance to reconfigure the system and remove the problem that caused it to hang.

Safe mode uses the most basic configuration of Windows with the minimum of software drivers needed for it to run. The screen resolution is a basic 640 x 480 with 16 colours. Essential drivers only are loaded, so some hardware devices may not be accessible from Safe mode.

First step

The Step-by-step Confirmation option helps you to troubleshoot problems caused by the drivers and programs loaded by the startup files Config.sys and Autoexec.bat. When you choose this option, Windows will display each of the lines in your Config.sys and Autoexec.bat files, and ask you to

Jargon buster

Boot The name given to the process by which a PC loads its operating system. It has nothing to do with kicking the PC. The term is derived from 'pull yourself up by your bootstraps'.

confirm whether the line should be used or not. Press Enter to execute the command or hit Esc to ignore it.

Choose this option and execute all the commands except those that you suspect of causing trouble. If Windows will start when those commands are not run and locks up if they are, you have located the problem.

Option five, Command Prompt Only, takes you straight to an MS-DOS prompt after executing all the lines in Config.sys and Autoexec.bat. If you are an expert user you can correct a problem by removing or replacing files using MS-DOS commands, or in the worst case by re-running Windows Setup.

The Safe Mode Command Prompt Only option is for use in situations where an error in Config.sys or Autoexec.bat prevents even MS-DOS starting. It gets you to a command prompt without executing either of these files, so you can then edit them and correct the problem.

Startup tip

Starting Windows in Safe Mode resets the Taskbar to its default settings, size and position. If you accidentally lose the Taskbar by resizing it to nothing, you can use this method to restore it.

Sorting out software

Windows can come to your rescue when your computer crashes unexpectedly or displays an error message.

PCs should be like reliable domestic appliances – plug them in, turn them on and they work. But PCs can stop working even if there's nothing physically wrong with them. The trouble is software. Software can contain programming bugs that cause the computer to crash. It can also play up because it is incompatible with other software. To test every possible software combination for every software package would be a huge task and it's not done.

One source of trouble is when two or more software programs share a common component. There can be different versions of common files, and when you install software it may replace a file used by one program with an incompatible version. When you uninstall software, files may be removed that other programs still need. This is not an unusual problem.

Sorting out software problems

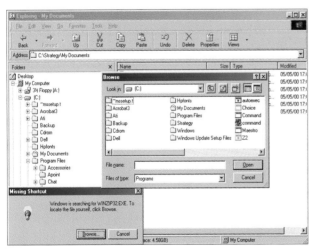

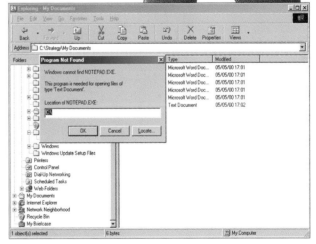

1 One problem you may experience is when an application goes missing. You click on its entry in the Start Menu, and instead of the program starting, Windows displays the **Missing Shortcut** dialogue box, with an animation of a torch swinging back and forth across a folder. This shows Windows is attempting to locate the program by looking for one with a similar name anywhere on your hard disk. If it finds a likely looking program it will ask if this is the one you want to use. It rarely is.

You can try to locate the program yourself by clicking Browse and using the Open File browser. This is a good idea if you know where the program is because you moved it to a different location.

If you deleted the program, deliberately or accidentally, click Cancel and reinstall the missing program from the original disks.

2 A similar problem will occur when you attempt to open a file that was created by an application that has gone missing, or one that needs the missing application in order to be displayed. In this event, Windows will display a **Program Not Found** dialogue box.

If this occurs and you know where the missing application has gone, you can type its location into the field in the dialogue box. Alternatively – and more easily – you can click on the Locate button and use the Open File browser to locate it.

Applications do not usually switch location of their own accord. So unless you have good reason to know where a program has gone, it has probably been deleted. You could try searching through the Recycle Bin. If you find the missing application in the Recycle Bin, you can restore it by right-clicking its icon and then choosing Restore from the menu that appears. If you can't find it in the bin then you will probably have to reinstall the program.

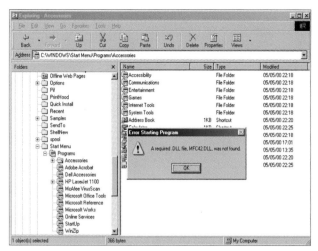

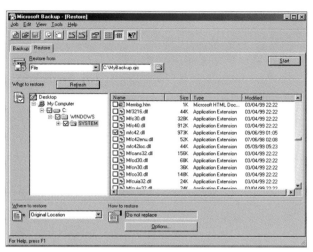

3 If an application exists but a file that the application itself needs is missing, you may see one of several different **error messages**. These may range from the clear 'A required file… was not found' to the completely misleading 'A device attached to the system is not functioning'.

One reason for files going missing is that you have uninstalled a program that you no longer want. The uninstaller removed files that were used by the unwanted program not realising that they were needed by something else. Another reason could be that you have been tidying up your hard disk and deleted some files that should not have been deleted. It is not advisable to delete anything from Windows or its System subfolder using Explorer.

5 Back-ups are the best insurance you can have against software problems. If you have a **full back-up** taken when the program was working correctly, simply restore it.

If you don't have a tape drive, but have a new computer with a big hard disk and still have lots of space free, consider backing up your Windows files to a Back-up folder on the hard disk. It won't help if your hard disk crashes, but the contents of the back-up will be very useful for recovering lost files. If you have a back-up, search for the missing file in the list of backed-up files. If you find it, place a tick against it and tell Back-up to restore the file.

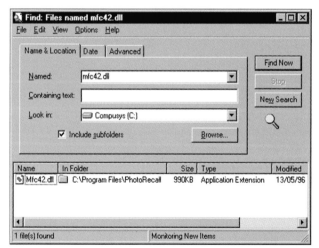

4 If the error message names the file that is missing you could try searching for it on your hard disk. The first place to start looking for the missing file is usually in Windows' **Recycle Bin**. You shouldn't hold out too much hope of finding the file there, however. Most uninstaller applications delete files completely rather than moving them to the Recycle Bin, which doesn't immediately free up any hard disk space.

If you used a utility such as Uninstaller or CleanSweep it may have created a back-up of the files it removed. If so, follow the utility's instructions for recovering the missing files.

Another thing you could try is to see if there is a copy of the file hidden anywhere else on your hard disk. Open up the Windows Find File tool, type in the name of the missing file and let Find File search through your C: drive, and any other hard drives if you have them. If you find a copy, you should copy it — or the latest version of the file if you discover more than one — to the Windows System folder using drag and drop.

6 If a program tries to use a shared file and the version it finds is not compatible with it, you may see the message 'The file… is linked to missing export…' or 'Call to undefined dynalink'. Windows Explorer will also give you the message 'A device attached to the system is not functioning'.

The usual cause of this problem is that you have installed a new application and it replaced a file used by the program you tried to run with a different, incompatible version. Another possibility is that you have different versions of the same file in different locations on your system and the wrong version gets loaded. In both cases, faulty Setup programs are to blame, although knowing the culprit won't help you solve the problem. This kind of problem is called a **version conflict**, and solving it can be quite tricky.

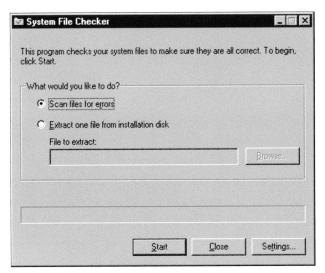

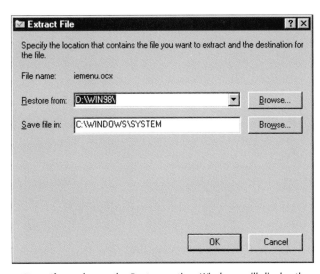

7 If the problem you are experiencing is with Windows itself or one of the standard Windows accessories, it may be that one of Windows' files has been deleted or overwritten. If you are using Windows 98, the best thing to do is to run the **System File Checker** on the Tools menu of System Information which is under System Tools on the Accessories page of the Start Menu. System File Checker can do two things. It can check the files on your system against a list of exactly what files were present when Windows 98 was first installed, and tell you which files are missing or have changed. And it can rectify problems by restoring Windows files easily from the Windows 98 CD-ROM.

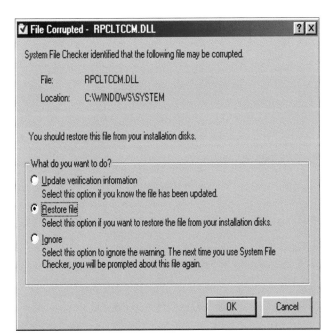

8 To check your Windows system files make sure the **Scan Files for Errors** option is selected and click on Start. System File Checker will take a couple of minutes to check your files. You will see a progress bar move across as it works.

If it finds a file has changed or is missing, System File Checker will show you some information about what it has found and ask what you want to do. You can choose to ignore the warning if you think it has nothing to do with the problem, or you can choose to restore the file from the Windows CD. The Update Verification Information option should be used only by experts who know that there is a good reason why the file has changed or been deleted and want to tell SFC to treat this as the status quo from now on.

9 If you choose the Restore option, Windows will display the **Extract File** dialogue box. Windows knows where the missing file should go, and where it should be restored from — it assumes that the CD-ROM or disks are in the same drive that was used when Windows was installed. Simply click on OK and the file should be restored.

Windows will offer you the option to create a back-up copy of the file you are replacing. This is a good idea in case restoring the original Windows file causes worse problems. In that case you could restore the other file which would be copied to the Windows Back-up folder. If you want to replace a specific Windows file the name of which you know, perhaps because you have seen a solution to a problem printed in a magazine, choose System File Checker's Extract One File option, type the name of the file you want, click on Start and the file will be restored in exactly the same way.

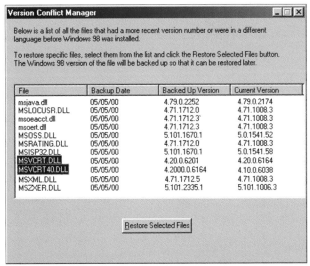

10 Another useful tool that Windows 98 offers for resolving file version conflicts is the **Version Conflict Manager**. You will find this also located on the Tools menu of System Information.

Run the Version Conflict Manager, then wait as the tool gathers information about the software it finds on your hard disk. When it has finished, the tool will display a list of all the files it finds where the current version is not the latest one.

If you see the file that was named in the error message in the list, select it and click on Restore Selected Files. Windows will replace the current version of the file with the newer one. You will have to restart Windows for the change to come into effect.

Jargon buster

Shared program files These comprise a collection of functions used by Windows. They can be the cause of problems but are generally very useful. They reduce the memory used by software because they are loaded only when they are needed and just one copy is loaded no matter how many programs share the file. They include Dynamic Link Libraries (DLLs), shown in Windows Explorer as file type Application Extension. These have a filename ending in .dll. Other shared program files include ActiveX components (.ocx) and Visual Basic Extensions (.vbx). Be wary of deleting these.

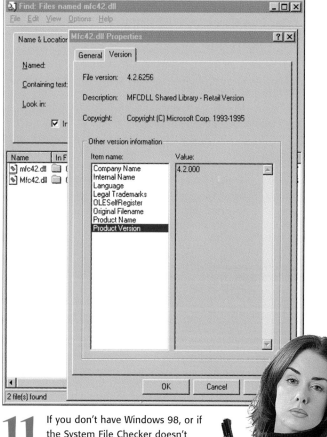

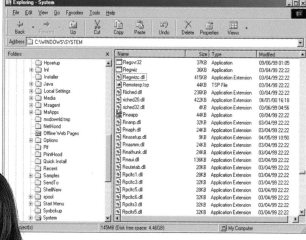

11 If you don't have Windows 98, or if the System File Checker doesn't solve the problem, you may be able to solve it yourself. Be warned, though: this is advanced stuff and you should not attempt it if you aren't confident about what you are doing. Reinstalling the problem application will often eliminate the error and is less risky.

Use the Windows **Find tool** to search for the file named in the error. If you find more than one copy of the file on your hard disk, only the latest should be accessible to Windows. To check the version number, right-click on each file, click on Properties from the menu, click the Version tab and then select Product Version from the list of items. If the file doesn't display a Version property page you will have to use the file date to determine which is the latest.

12 The latest version of a shared file should be placed in the Windows **System folder**. Windows will find it there regardless of which application wants to use it. If there is a file of the same name already there, rename it first so it is not overwritten. Select the file, press F2, move to the start of the filename and insert XX at the front. If you found other old versions of the file, rename these too. Make a note of the changes you made so that you can undo them if they don't solve the problem. Now you can drag the newer version of the file from the Find window and drop it in the System folder.

Troubleshooting tip

Many software problems of the type covered here can be resolved automatically by the troubleshooting tool First Aid 2000.

Net doctor

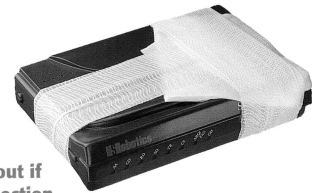

Windows Troubleshooters can help you out if things go wrong with your Internet connection.

Using the Net may seem as easy as clicking on links in your Web browser or buttons in your e-mail program. However, a lot of work goes on behind the scenes in order to bring Web pages, e-mail, downloads and other things from servers on the Internet to your PC.

Windows simplifies the process of connecting to the Internet as much as possible and your Internet software hides the nuts and bolts of how the connection is achieved. If everything works, there's no need to try to understand what is happening. But if your Net connection doesn't work, a small amount of knowledge about how your connection is set up can go a long way towards helping you identify and solve the problem.

Trouble-free surfing

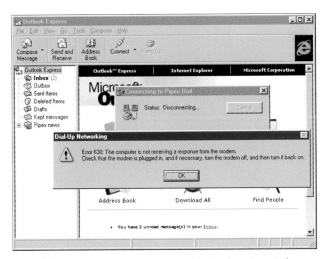

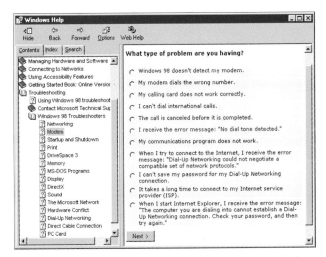

1 Before your computer can connect up to the Internet, three things have to be properly installed, set up and working. First, your **modem** has to be connected to your computer (or installed inside it if it is an internal model), and it needs to be recognised by Windows using the appropriate modem driver. Second, the **TCP/IP** communications protocol must be installed and correctly configured for your Internet service provider (or for each ISP, if you have more than one service provider). Third, the **dial-up networking software** (DUN) must be properly configured to dial in to your ISP and establish communication between your computer and the Internet.

If your Internet connection stops working, the reason might be just that your modem or the dial-up networking software needs to be reset. Shut down the PC and turn off the modem, wait a while and then try again. The problem might also be a temporary fault at your ISP. Wait a couple of hours and try again before you decide that the problem is at your end.

2 If you still can't get connected, the first place to seek help is Windows Troubleshooters. Problems with your modem and DUN are dealt with by the **Modem Troubleshooter**. Click Start, Help and open the Troubleshooting chapter of the help system. The Modem Troubleshooter can help with faults such as your modem not being detected, problems with dialling and failure to establish a connection after your modem has dialled your ISP. To use it, click the radio button next to the description of your problem, then click the Next button at the bottom of the page. Try the remedy suggested by the Troubleshooter. Then click another radio button to tell it what the result was, click Next and so on.

Modem tip

If you experience problems connecting to the Internet, a modem log (as described in step 6) will often show what is going wrong.

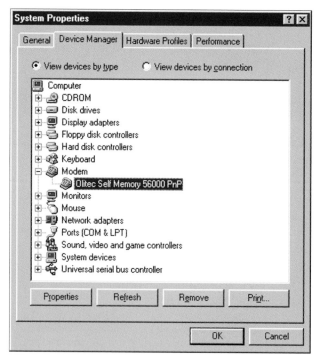

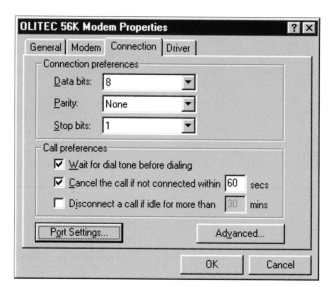

4 Poor performance can be caused by using the wrong **port settings**. You can check the settings from the Connection tab of the Modem Properties. The preferences should be Data Bits 8, Parity None and Stop Bits 1. The modem should always wait for a dial tone before dialling. ISPs usually answer the phone after a couple of rings so you can save time by selecting Cancel The Call If Not Connected Within and specifying a shorter interval. Click on Port Settings to open the Advanced Port Settings dialogue box. PCs made in the last few years have a 16550 compatible UART chip so the box at the top left of the dialogue box should be checked. If it isn't, your PC may have an old-type UART. In that case, leave the check box alone, but consider upgrading your serial port.

3 If the Modem Troubleshooter fails to solve your problem you will need to dig deeper. If you still think that your modem might be the cause of the trouble, check its entry in **Device Manager**. To get to Device Manager right-click on My Computer, click on Properties, then click on the Device Manager tab. Expand the Modem entry to show the modem device. If it is marked with a little exclamation mark then there is a problem with it, such as a hardware conflict. Click on Properties to get more information about the fault. If there is a conflict try the Hardware Conflict Troubleshooter to see if that can resolve the problem.

If Device Manager doesn't show your modem's specific make and model but shows it as a Standard Modem, then although the modem may be working you will probably not be getting the best performance from it. You will need to install a driver provided by the modem manufacturer. Consult the manual that came with the modem for instructions on how to do this.

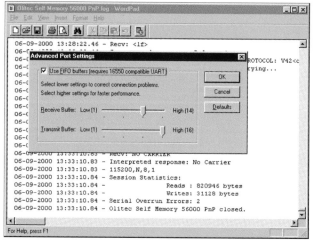

5 A 16550 UART chip can store 16 characters of data in each direction in a buffer. This improves performance by avoiding the need for the PC to fetch each character one at a time. The sliders in **Advanced Port Settings** determine how full each buffer can get before the PC must move the data out of the buffer. Set them too low and performance will suffer as the buffers will never be fully used. Set them too high and characters may be lost because the PC may not manage to empty the buffer in time to make room for the next. If this happens it is called an overrun error.

Overrun errors harm performance because the data lost has to be re-sent. You can find out if they are occurring by getting Windows to log each connection and inspecting the result. If errors occur, move the Receive Buffer slider to the left a notch. The Transmit Buffer slider can be left at maximum, but reduce the setting if you have problems uploading files. It isn't a good idea to move the Receive slider to maximum as errors are likely to occur, but you can try it.

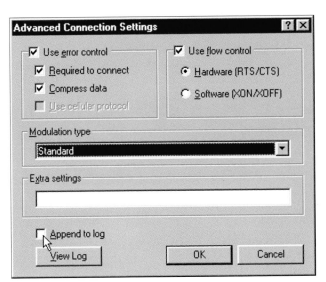

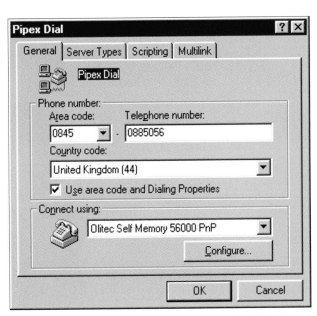

6 Click the **Advanced... button** on the Modem Properties dialogue box to bring up the Advanced Connection Settings dialogue box. You tell Windows to create a modem log by checking the Append To Log box. To view the log in WordPad, click View Log. The session statistics, including the error report, will be at the end of the log. If everything is working well you can turn logging off again. At the top of the Advanced Connection Settings dialogue box Use Error Control and Compress Data should always be checked. Check Required To Connect, too. This makes Windows drop a line rather than attempt to use a connection with no error correction. Modulation Type should be Standard. Use Flow Control must be selected, and the type of flow control must be Hardware. If you can't get a connection to work unless you disable hardware flow control, there is probably a fault in your modem cable.

8 You'll need to open the **Dial-Up Networking** folder in My Computer to check the dial-up networking and TCP/IP protocol settings. Select the icon for your ISP, right-click it and select Properties. The General page specifies the phone number to dial for this ISP. Use Area Code And Dialing Properties tells Windows to take account of the settings made using Control Panel's Telephony icon. The Telephony settings include important information for Windows such as how to disable the Call Waiting signal which can crash your Internet sessions.

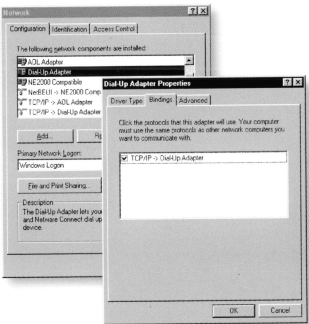

7 If nothing happens after your modem connects to your ISP the fault might be with the **communication protocols**. Open Network in Control Panel. If your PC isn't part of a network the only items you need to have in the components list on the Configuration page are a Dial-Up Adapter and TCP/IP. If you connect to the Internet using AOL, you will see an AOL Adapter instead. Select the Dial-Up Adapter and click on Properties. The only protocol that should be associated with this adapter is TCP/IP. If others are listed, their check boxes should not be checked.

9 On the **Server Types** page, ensure Type of Dial-Up Server is PPP: Internet, Windows NT Server, Windows 95 (or 98). If it isn't, you won't get connected. None of the Advanced options on this page are needed. Enable Software Compression is not required and will not speed up your connections because data is compressed by your modem. The option usually does no harm, but if you experience problems getting a connection, try disabling it.

You will often find Log On To Network is selected. This causes a delay in establishing a Net connection while your PC looks for a Windows network at the other end of the line. Additional delays can be caused by having allowed protocols other than TCP/IP. If you use Dial-Up Networking to connect to a Windows network you will need Log On To Network and other network protocols, but for Net access the only box that needs to be checked on this page is TCP/IP.

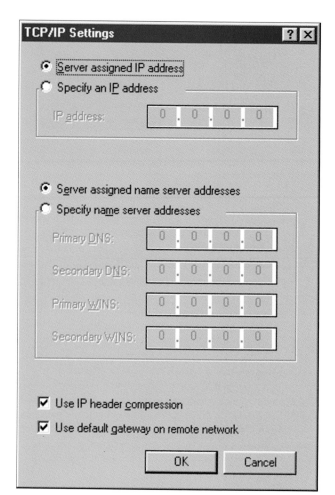

11 Some ISPs require your PC to log on to their network after dialling the number by typing your user name and password. Because this would be tiresome for you to do every time you connect, Windows will do it for you. What to type and what prompts to watch for are controlled by a script. However, many ISPs now use a different method of logging on which doesn't need a script and is simpler. If your ISP does require a scripted login click on the **Scripting tab** and check that the name of the script file appears in the File name box. If you click Edit you will be able to view and change the script in Notepad. You shouldn't need to write or modify the script yourself; your ISP should provide one.

The Step Through Script box should not be checked. Start Terminal Screen Minimized is usually checked. If it isn't, when you dial the Internet a small window will pop up showing the prompts from your ISP's server and the replies that Windows types back.

10 Click on the **TCP/IP Settings button** on the Server Types property page to check the protocol settings for your Internet connection. The settings to use in this dialogue box are dependent upon your particular Internet service provider. However, most ISPs nowadays assign you an IP address — a group of four three-digit numbers that uniquely identifies your computer on the Internet — each time you log on instead of allocating a fixed one. This simplifies setting up, because you don't have to type in an address. If you have been given an IP address, however, you should click on Specify An IP Address and type the numbers into the boxes below. The same applies to the Name Server addresses in the group below.

IP header compression can make things work a little quicker, but if your ISP doesn't support it you won't get connected at all. If you can't get connected, try deselecting this option. Use Default Gateway must be checked.

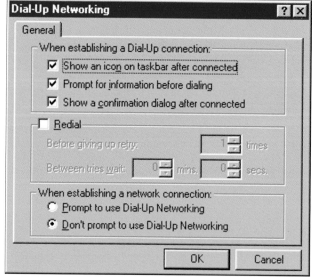

Jargon buster

UART Stands for Universal Asynchronous Receiver/Transmitter. It's a chip that receives data from the modem whenever it arrives and stores it ready for access by your computer's processor. It does the same thing for data going from the computer to the modem.

TCP/IP Stands for Transmission Control Protocol/Internet Protocol. Used to send information over the Internet, it states how this must be packaged and addressed so that it reaches the right destination and the computer can understand it.

12 Some Dial-Up Networking settings are accessed from the Dial-Up Networking folder. Click **Connections** on the menu bar, then Settings. A dialogue box appears. The first panel determines what happens when you make a connection. Show An Icon On Taskbar causes an icon showing two connected PCs to appear in the Taskbar's system tray. The screens flash to show data transfers. Shut the connection by right-clicking on this icon and choosing Disconnect. Prompt For Information Before Dialing controls whether Windows displays the Connect To dialogue box so you can enter your user name and password before dialling. If you don't choose this option, Windows will go ahead and do it using previously stored values. At the bottom, Prompt To Use Dial-Up Networking will make Windows ask if you want to connect to the Internet each time you start an Internet application.

Running MS-DOS

With a few tweaks Windows should be able to run most MS-DOS applications and games.

Most software available today is written to run with Windows. But you may have older programs, particularly games, that are written to run with the MS-DOS system.

Before Windows became popular, most PC software was written for MS-DOS. Games are often still written for MS-DOS because they use the full screen and don't need resizable windows, a title bar, menus and so on. They can also achieve better performance by controlling the PC hardware directly instead of getting Windows to do it for them.

Most MS-DOS programs, particularly those with a text-based display, run well under Windows, but some have difficulty and a few programs refuse to run at all. The easiest way to avoid problems is not to buy MS-DOS programs, or at least not those that don't claim to be Windows-compatible. However, if you have an MS-DOS program that won't run under Windows you can often get it to do so by changing some program property settings.

Running DOS applications

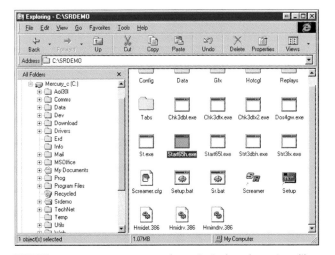

 MS-DOS programs are shown in Explorer by an icon like an empty window frame. They can have a file type of .exe or .com. In an Explorer Details view, .exe files are shown as type Application. Windows programs are also Application files, so the presence of an icon is the only easy way to distinguish MS-DOS programs from Windows programs. You can run MS-DOS in the same way as Windows applications, by double-clicking on their icons. Windows-compatible MS-DOS programs may come with shortcut files. The shortcuts may have pictorial icons and will contain special configuration information for Windows. If shortcuts are present you should use them to run the program from Windows.

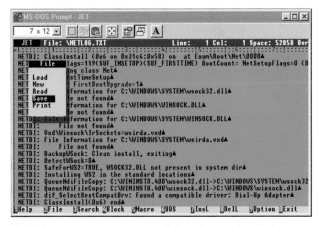

 MS-DOS programs were designed to use the whole screen. However, programs that have text-based or low resolution graphics output can be displayed under Windows in their own **window**. This allows you to switch between MS-DOS and Windows programs with ease, and even to copy and paste information from one to the other.

An MS-DOS window can have a toolbar which allows you to quickly change some of its settings. The buttons have tool tips to tell you what their function is. At the left of the toolbar is a dropdown list for selecting the character size (width multiplied by height in pixels.) If you choose Auto from the dropdown list you can resize the MS-DOS window with the mouse and Windows will choose the appropriate font to fit.

If you click on the Font toolbar button – the rightmost one – you will open the Font properties page for the window. This is an alternative way to set the display size.

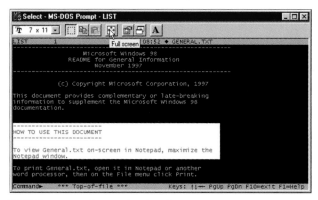

 Next to the text size dropdown is the **Mark** button. Click on this and you can then select blocks of text using the mouse by dragging until the text you want is selected. When you click on the Copy button the selected text is copied to the Clipboard, from where it can be pasted into a different application. Use the Paste button to paste text from the Clipboard to your MS-DOS program. These edit functions are also accessible from a menu if you click on the MS-DOS icon on the title bar.

Moving right on the toolbar, the Full Screen button lets you switch the window to full screen mode. You can also do this from the keyboard by pressing Alt+Enter. The Properties button lets you access the program's property settings. The Background button lets you specify whether the MS-DOS application should run in the background or not: if the button is up the program will only run when its window is in the foreground.

 If an MS-DOS program doesn't run properly when you try to start it under Windows, you may need to set up the program's properties to give Windows more information about the environment that the program needs so that it can run. The alternative is to run the program in MS-DOS itself.

If a program can be made to run under Windows it is better to do so. You'll find it more convenient to be able to launch a program from Windows instead of going into MS-DOS mode to run it. Also, Windows provides some services, such as access to your CD-ROM drive, which are not normally provided in MS-DOS mode.

To access an MS-DOS program's properties, right-click on its icon and select **Properties** from the context menu. If a shortcut to the program already exists, open the shortcut's properties instead.

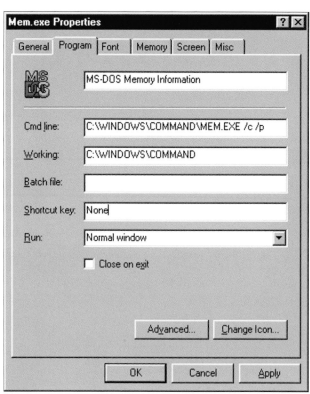

 The **Program page** of an MS-DOS application's properties contains general information about the program. The first field contains a description which appears on the title bar of the MS-DOS window when the program is run. If you don't enter a description the program filename is used.

The Cmd Line field contains the name of the program. If the program accepts command line parameters you can edit this field to add them. The Working field specifies the name of the working folder: the one the program starts up in. This is usually the folder that contains the program.

The Batch File field should normally be blank. In Shortcut Key you can choose a key combination (such as Ctrl or Alt plus another key) which can be used to switch this program's window to the front. Run should be left as Normal Window. The Close on Exit box determines whether the MS-DOS window will close when the program terminates. Uncheck it if you want the window to stay open after the program finishes to give you a chance to read any text it has displayed.

Jargon buster

Conventional memory This is the memory available for MS-DOS applications to run in. The maximum amount of conventional memory is 640KB. Each device driver and memory resident utility uses some conventional memory. MS-DOS applications have to run in what's left over.

Expanded, Extended and Protected Mode (DPMI) memory These terms are used to describe schemes for accessing the remaining memory in your computer. When your PC is running under Windows this is all taken care of for you. But when it is running under MS-DOS you must install a memory manager and set it up to provide the amount and type of memory your programs need.

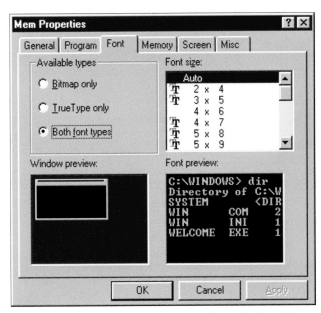

 The **Font property** page lets you choose the size of font that is used to display the text in an MS-DOS window. If you choose a specific size of font, the Window preview panel shows you the resulting window size in relation to your Desktop, while the Font preview panel shows you an example of the font. If you choose Auto for the font size you can resize the MS-DOS window using the mouse.

Font and window size are related because MS-DOS windows are a fixed number of rows high and characters wide. If you switch to the Screen properties page you can choose the initial window size, which by default is 25 rows by 80 characters. Some MS-DOS text-based programs can display 43 or 50 rows in a window. If you choose this option and the program can't display more than 25 rows the bottom half of the window will be left blank.

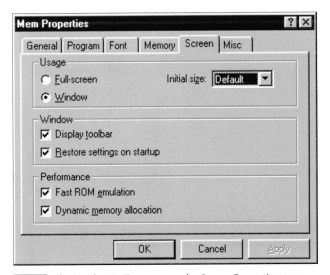

 If you select **Full-screen** on the Screen Properties page, the MS-DOS program will start up full-screen, just as if you are running in MS-DOS mode. You will usually need to select this option for programs that display graphics rather than text, such as games. The Windows check box options let you choose whether the MS-DOS window has a toolbar and whether the font, size and position settings used should be saved and restored when you run the program. The Performance check box options should both be left checked for optimum performance. Uncheck them if the MS-DOS program has problems when running under Windows.

MS-DOS tip

Instead of typing a program name to run it from an MS-DOS prompt, you can drag the program from Explorer and drop it on the MS-DOS window. Type the command line parameters, if required, then press Enter.

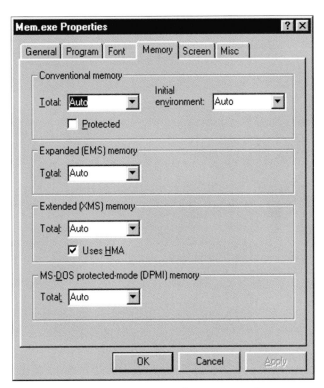

The **Memory property** page lets you set up the memory that the MS-DOS program will see. Unlike Windows programs, MS-DOS programs can't automatically use all the memory in the computer. Windows does its best to work out what memory an MS-DOS program wants, and will provide it if the memory is available, so all the Memory properties are best set to Auto. Change one of these settings only if a program reports that there is insufficient of a certain type of memory.

Conventional memory is the type that usually causes problems when trying to run MS-DOS applications. The maximum amount of conventional memory that you can have is 640KB. However, MS-DOS itself needs some of this memory and every driver loaded in your MS-DOS configuration files uses some more. If an MS-DOS program reports that there is not enough memory without saying what type, it usually means that the amount of free conventional memory is insufficient.

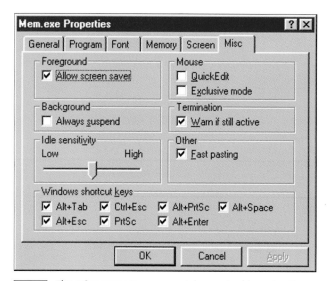

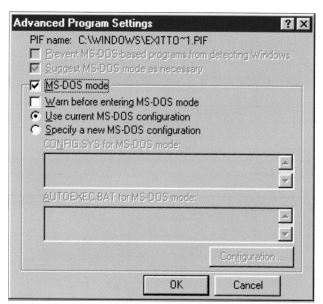

 The **Misc property** page contains a mixed bag of options. MS-DOS programs can waste processor time when they are idle in the background. Windows tries to detect when a program is idle. If performance slows when an MS-DOS program is running, change the Idle Sensitivity slider position. Check Always Suspend to stop the program when it is in the background.

Windows Shortcut Keys controls which keystrokes should be allowed through to the MS-DOS application. Warn if Still Active will display a warning if you try to close the MS-DOS window by clicking on the Close button. Fast Pasting controls how text is sent to the MS-DOS program when you use Edit, Paste.

 If you have an MS-DOS program that won't run after you restart in MS-DOS mode it's no good using the current **configuration**. You need to specify a new configuration by clicking on the radio button on the Advanced Program Settings box and entering Config.sys and Autoexec.bat commands into the edit boxes. An alternative is to modify the MS-DOS configuration used when you restart in MS-DOS mode so your programs will run in that. Edit the properties for the Exit to DOS shortcut in the Windows folder. If the changes you make stop Windows restarting in MS-DOS mode, undo them by selecting Use Current MS-DOS Configuration.

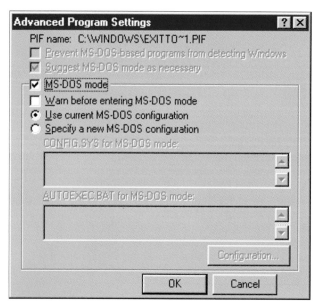

 Some programs will only run if Windows is not running. These programs must be run in **MS-DOS mode**. In MS-DOS mode, Windows and other applications close down and the MS-DOS program is the only program running. When an MS-DOS program runs under Windows full-screen, Windows is still running in the background.

To configure a program so that it runs in MS-DOS mode, select the Program page of the program properties and click the Advanced button. Check the MS-DOS mode box. In MS-DOS mode two files, Config.sys and Autoexec.bat, determine the configuration. If you choose Use Current MS-DOS Configuration, MS-DOS will not use new copies of these files. The settings will be the same as when you shut down Windows and choose Restart in MS-DOS Mode.

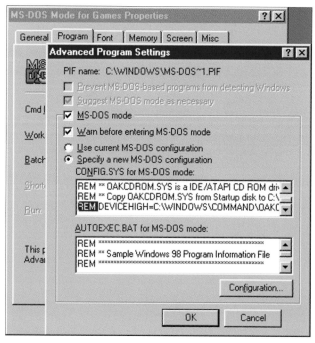

 Windows 98 has some special MS-DOS shortcuts for games players. The **MS-DOS Mode for Games** shortcut is in your Windows folder. Before using them, open their properties and change the Config.sys and Autoexec.bat commands in accordance with comments in the files. These two shortcuts use a generic CD-ROM driver which will work with most PCs. The driver is called Oakcdrom.sys, and you will find it on the Windows emergency startup disk. You must copy this file to the Windows Command folder on your hard disk before you can use it.

Finding lost files

You can turn Windows into a detective when an important file or document goes missing.

There's a lot of information on your hard disk, but can you always find it when you want it? It can be hard to keep track of files unless you organise them properly from the start. Windows 98 makes it easier by encouraging you to use the My Documents folder that was previously only a feature of Microsoft Office. But if you have a large number of files it can still be hard to find the one you want.

Windows provides several ways to get information about files. The Find tool can be used to search for files based on the file name, location,

creation date and the file contents. File Properties pages and the QuickView tool provide other ways to find out what a file is. If it's on your hard disk, Windows has a way for you to find it!

Finding data with Windows

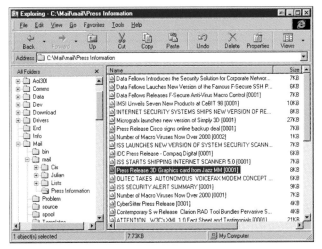

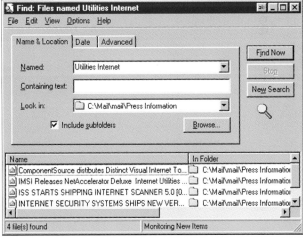

Find — The most important trick for finding information is to make it easy to find in the first place. Store files in folders with descriptive names, just as you would if they were documents in a filing cabinet. Use **long file names** to describe what a file or folder is. That way, you won't have to open the file to see if it is the one you want. File names can have 255 characters, and can contain most of the characters you can type at the keyboard apart from colon, backslash, asterisk, question mark and a few others that have a special meaning. With meaningful names, Explorer becomes a useful tool for locating the files you want, because you can sort the file lists by name, type, size or the date the file was created.

Find — With descriptive names the Find tool also becomes much more useful. It's far faster to search through file names than to search the contents of every file. To locate the files you want, just type a word or words that must appear in the file name for the file to be selected. When you click **Find Now** the Find tool will list all the files that contain one or more of those words. For a group of words to be treated as a phrase rather than as separate keywords, put quotes around them.

To locate files that contain specific strings of text, leave the Named: field blank and enter the search text into the Containing Text: field. The contents search works differently from the file name search. The text you enter is treated as a key phrase, not as individual keywords, so the complete phrase has to appear in the document in order for it to be listed.

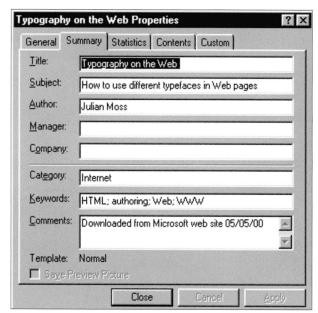

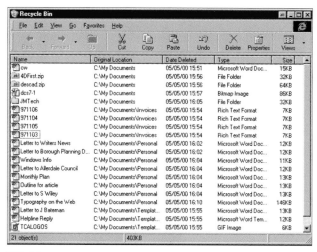

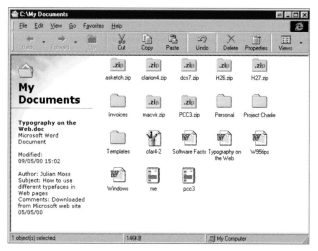

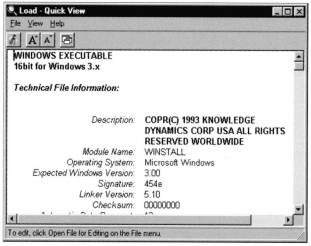

Files are easier to find if you store information about them in their **property pages**. You can't do this with all files. Many file formats — .gif or .jpg files, for example — don't make provision for text-based information to be stored within them. But if you use one of the popular Office application suites, or any Microsoft Office compatible application, you can enter information about a file by selecting Properties from the application's File menu.

To view this data, right-click the file's icon in Explorer or the Find File list and select Properties from the dropdown menu. The data available is dependent upon the application used to create the file and on whether all the available fields were filled in, but the data usually includes who created the file and when, with a description and keywords. The Find tool includes the property data of a file when it performs a text search, so you can use it to locate files such as drawings which might not contain text that it could find.

If you are running Windows 98, it's easy to see the data about a file stored in its properties. If you place the mouse over a file's icon in Explorer, property information such as the file's author, subject and comments are shown in a pop-up box. If you use the **Active Desktop** and choose to view a folder as a Web page, the property information of a file is displayed in the folder itself. To view a folder as a Web page, click on Customize This Folder in the folder's view menu and select Create or Edit an HTML Document. Notepad will open showing the HTML page for the folder. Close it to accept the default page generated by Explorer.

If you can't find the file you are looking for, be sure to check in your **Recycle Bin**. The Windows Find tool doesn't search the Recycle Bin when you use it to look for files, even if you tell it to search My Computer.

To see what files are in the Recycle Bin, right-click on it and choose Open or Explore. You will see a list of files and their names. You can't open files to view them directly from the Recycle Bin, nor inspect their properties. The only property information available when a file is in the Recycle Bin is its size, where it was created and when it was deleted. If you can't tell if a file is the one you want from its file name, you must first restore it to its original folder before opening it.

If you want to discover what a file is, and inspecting its properties doesn't yield any useful information, you can try using the Windows **Quick View** tool to look at it. Quick View can only display information about certain file types, but it is still quite useful for discovering information about application files and other system files. If Quick View isn't one of the options on the menu when you right-click on an Application file, you probably need to install it by going to Control Panel, Add/Remove Programs.

Although Quick View may not know how to display many unusual file types, it can still open them with its default viewer, which should allow you to read any text that is embedded in the file. To do this, simply select the file you want to view with the mouse, press the Shift key and right-click on the file. Select Open With..., then select quickview from the list of programs. Make sure that the Always Open Using this Program box is unchecked unless you want Quick View to become the default choice of program for opening files of that type.

Office detective

Hunt down missing files using the file find feature in Office applications.

Another way that you can track down missing files is by using Office's file finding feature. This handy device can seek out spreadsheet files that have found their way into your Business Graphics folder and love letters that are lurking with long-forgotten DOS games.

File finding is an enhancement to the ordinary File Open dialogue box in Word, Excel and the other Office applications, but it's surprising how few people notice it. Fewer still have ever clicked on the Advanced button.

By finding files systematically you can identify all your documents, wherever they are stored, and move them into grouped folders where they will be easier to access in future.

The file finding capabilities of the Office programs are more flexible than Find on the Start menu. You can search for words in documents, not just in their names, so even if you've forgotten what you called a file, you can still retrieve it.

You will learn

- How to find Office documents by name.
- How to find Office documents by searching for words they contain.
- How to find recent files.
- How to find old files.
- How to make advanced searches.
- How to speed up searches with Find Fast.

Tracking down Office files

1 Documents are loaded into Microsoft Office programs through the Open command on the File Menu. The **Open** dialogue box initially displays files of the type produced by the program you're currently using, so if you're opening a file from within Word, the dialogue box displays Word documents. If you're using Excel, it displays Excel spreadsheets. However, there's nothing to stop you loading Excel files into Word (they appear as tables) once you've found them. By changing the selection in the Files Of Type list box you can choose to view files from any of the Office programs, and many other programs too, regardless of which program you're currently using.

To the left of the Open box in Office 2000 is the **Places Bar** which gives you quick access to your documents. For example, click on the History folder and it will bring up a list of the last 20 to 50 Office files you have worked with.

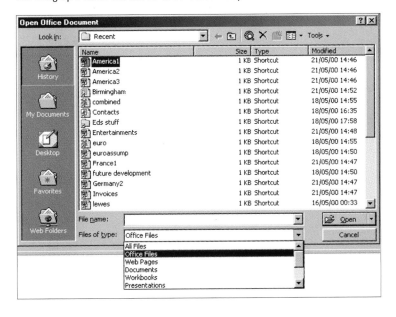

File finding tips

● If you frequently search for text in non-Office documents, it's a good idea to start Find Fast and delete the existing indexes. These are designed solely to keep track of Office documents. Create new indexes, choosing to index files of all types.

● The Find box includes buttons to save and load searches that you run regularly.

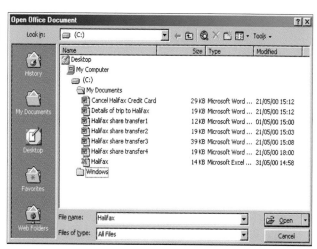

4 The dialogue box now contains seven files, limited to those containing the word Halifax. There's an important point to note here. Seven files were found even though only five begin with Halifax, illustrating that Office programs can find words contained within a longer name. The second point is that the search process is not **case sensitive**, so it doesn't matter if the search is for 'halifax' or 'Halifax'.

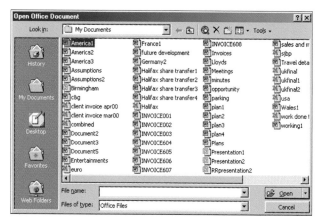

2 The Open dialogue box is being used here from within Microsoft Word to display all the Word files in the folder. To find documents with a specific word in their filename (such as Halifax), you need to first open the Find box. To do this go to the Tools menu on the Open box and select Find.

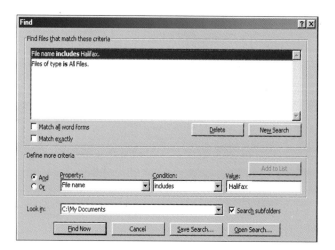

3 In the dialogue box that opens there are various criteria to set for the search. By default the program will search for files of any type. In the section Define more criteria, set out what you want to find using the three boxes labelled Property, Condition and Value. Here the search is for the File name (property) which includes (condition) the word Halifax (value). You could vary any of these criteria so, for example, you could change the condition to search for file names that start or end with the name Halifax. Having decided the search criteria, click on Add to List. In the Look in box the My Documents folder should be selected. This is where the program will search. The tick next to it extends the search to include any subfolders contained within My Documents.

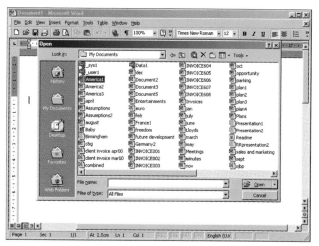

5 Searching for file names, or parts of file names, is most useful when a folder contains more files than can be displayed in the Open dialogue box. This folder contains hundreds of files but only a few of them can be seen at one time. **Scrolling** through this many files looking for a word that isn't at the beginning of the name (like the Halifax documents) is tedious.

File finding tips

● When searching the contents of files you can look for phrases rather than single words by enclosing them in speech marks, for example, "millennium bug".

● You can search for words contained within non-Office documents, but you won't be able to click on them to edit them unless they are in a format which one of the Office programs understands.

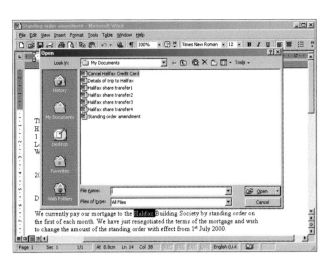

6 Finding comes into its own when you can't remember what a document is called, or even where on the disk you've stored it. As long as you can remember some of the words contained in the document, you can search for these instead. To search for a word contained in a document, go to the Find box and select Text or Property as the property. Write the word you are looking for as the value with 'includes' as the condition. Click on Add to List, select the area to search, as before, and press Find Now. Six documents with Halifax in their names are found, but there's also a seventh. Although this is called Standing order amendment.doc, it contains the word Halifax.

8 If you frequently write documents on similar topics, you'll use the same words in many of them, and your searches will find too many documents, as did the search for the word Millennium in the previous step. By selecting **Last Modified** as the property you can restrict the search to documents that have been recently modified, and thereby exclude out-of-date files that have been gathering dust on the disk for years, reducing the list to more manageable proportions.

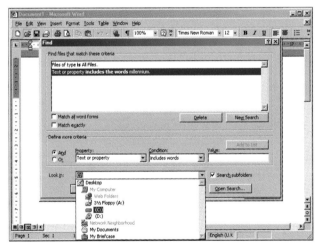

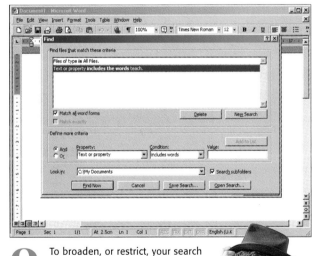

7 To search for a document when you can't remember which folder you stored it in takes a long time, especially if you're looking for the contents of a file and not its name. The technique is to select a disk drive rather than a folder in the **Look In** box. Make sure the search subfolders box next to it is ticked so every folder on the drive is searched. This search of all documents on the drive for the word Millennium took over three minutes and found 36 files. There's a way of speeding up this type of search, and it's demonstrated in steps 11 and 12.

9 To broaden, or restrict, your search there are two further options you can choose – the Match all Word Forms and Match Exactly tick boxes. If you tick Match all Word Forms and then search for a word contained in a file, the search will look not just for the word you type but also for any words derived from it, so a search for Teach will also find Teaching and Taught. A tick in the Match Exactly box forces the search to look for just what you type, including capitals. Needless to say, you can't tick both boxes at the same time.

File finding tips

You can't follow every keystroke in the examples here because the files on your PC aren't the same as those on our test PC, but if you apply the same techniques to your own files, you'll soon have your hard disk under control.

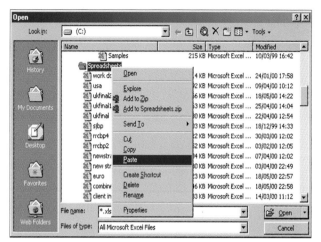

10 Of course, if you organised your documents properly in the first place you wouldn't need to do so much finding. The good news is that if you've got files spread all over your hard disk, you can find them all and move them to the same location. A simple search for Excel files found 68 of them on this drive, only 15 of which were in the Spreadsheets folder. While you can't drag the errant files into the Spreadsheets folder, you can move them one at a time by clicking on a file with the right mouse button and choosing **Cut**. Then highlight the Spreadsheets folder, click on the right mouse button and select **Paste**. This is not as dangerous as it sounds because the file you cut is not deleted until you select Paste.

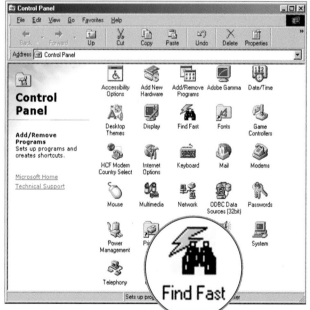

11 If you have tried searching an entire disk for words contained within Office documents you will know that it takes several minutes. This is because every file on the disk has to be opened and searched separately. An Office tool called **Find Fast** can turn these minutes into seconds. Find Fast works by periodically indexing every word in your Office documents and storing them in a database. When you search for a word, Find Fast locates it in the database instead of searching the documents stored on disk. To see whether Find Fast is installed on your computer, click on Start, Settings and Control Panel and look for its icon.

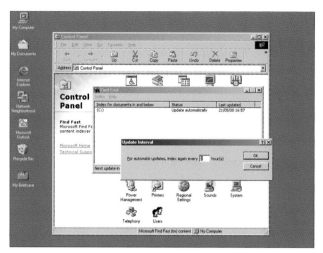

12 If Find Fast isn't on your PC, install it by running **Setup** from the Office 2000 CD. Once Find Fast is installed you can control which drives are indexed and how often the indexes are updated. These options are selected by double-clicking on the Find Fast icon in Control Panel. To take advantage of Find Fast you don't have to do anything special — just use the file-finding features as described in the preceding steps. If there's a Find Fast index, Office uses it to speed up its searching.

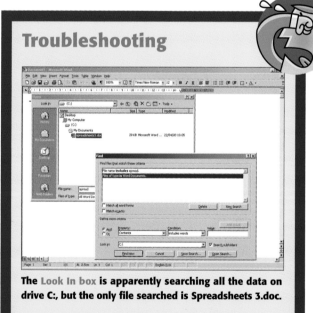

Troubleshooting

The Look In box is apparently searching all the data on drive C:, but the only file searched is Spreadsheets 3.doc.

● There's little to go wrong when finding files but sometimes a search doesn't find as many documents as you expect. This happens when you think you're searching an entire drive and its subfolders but you've already done a search using a file name. The entire drive is still selected in the Look In box at the top of the dialogue box, but when you search for file contents, only the files that have already been found are searched. The solution is to click the New Search button at the bottom right of the dialogue box to clear the results of the previous search.

● Sometimes a search finds more files than you expect. This is because when you elect to search subfolders, the option remains selected and every subsequent search also includes subfolders. Just switch off the option.

Curing viruses

PCs can catch viruses as easily as people, so it pays to have the right medicine for when they fall sick.

PCs are only machines. They can go wrong, but surely they can't catch viruses? Unfortunately, they can. PCs get computer viruses – rogue programs that they can then pass on to other computers, and which may cause them to malfunction.

Computer viruses aren't usually fatal. Many of them are just an inconvenience. They can slow your computer down, and they might make it behave a bit crankily on occasions, but most don't actually do any lasting damage, unless of course files that you haven't backed up are destroyed.

Fatal illnesses

A few viruses are more malicious. They can corrupt or delete files. Some attempt to wipe everything from your hard disk. Others just make it look as if all your data has gone. It is sensible to be aware that your PC could be at risk. Just as you can get inoculated against a human virus, so you can immunise your PC by taking a few simple precautions with the help of anti-virus software.

PC medicine

The following pages describe the problem of computer viruses in some detail, what they are and how they spread, plus where they come from and who invented them.
Symptoms of some of the common viruses are described. Anti-virus tools are summarised on page 72; here you'll find more detailed information on the steps you can take and the software you can buy to protect your PC.

Anti-virus tools are summarised on page 72

Which software?

All anti-virus packages do the same basic job. The differences are in how good they are at detecting and removing viruses. The top products – **Norton's** and **McAfee's** – are the best at detecting viruses, although in practice almost any product you buy will detect all the viruses you are likely to encounter.

When destructive viruses like Melissa and IloveYou strike, it is best to be using a top vendor's product. Within hours of the bug first appearing, the vendor will have an update for their software available to download from their Web site.

When you do install the anti-virus products directly to your PC, the top programs will include highly effective background scanners. They detect all the viruses that standalone scanners can and they let you clean an infected file there and then, instead of making you run another program.

As viruses are often spread via the Internet, it is best to choose a scanning engine that will also check your e-mail attachments and screen any files you download. As files are often compressed to be sent over the Internet, select an anti-virus program that will check these files too.

If you are buying a package because your computer has a virus, choose a program such as Norton AntiVirus which includes a ready-to-use boot disk containing detection and disinfection software. Other anti-virus programs, such as McAfee's, include an Emergency Disk Wizard to guide you through the process of creating your own emergency boot disk on a floppy disk, complete with virus scan information.

You will need

ESSENTIAL

Software An up-to-date anti-virus package, a scheduler for regular sweeps of your hard disk and a write-protected bootable system disk to start the system from if the hard disk becomes infected – many packages include these.
Hardware A modem, as an Internet connection is useful so that you can download updates to the software.

What is a virus?

Jargon buster

Boot sector virus A virus that infects the part of your hard disk that the PC reads when it starts (boots up). This means the virus is activated whenever you turn on your PC. Boot sector viruses are often transmitted in the boot sectors of floppy disks. They copy themselves to the hard disk when you leave a floppy in the drive and accidentally boot from it.

Jargon buster

Macro virus A virus written in the macro language of an application such as Microsoft Word. They are the easiest type of virus to write, and because people often send each other Word files, they can spread rapidly. You have a greater chance of encountering a macro virus in Word than in any other application.

Computer viruses are destructive pieces of software written by pranksters or people with a grudge.

Viruses are software. Your PC runs them just like it runs other programs. The only difference is you don't tell your PC to run a virus. Your PC runs the virus because it has copied itself to a location in a file where it will be run without you realising it.

Double trouble

Once a virus is active it reproduces by copying itself to other locations. This feature distinguishes a virus from other software. Most of the time, if a virus is active on your PC and infecting other disks or files, you won't even know about it. Unless you run a virus checker you'll only find out about it when the virus triggers its payload.

Beware of infection

A virus can't do any harm until it is run. To be successful, a virus must infect things on your PC that have a high probability of being run, like the boot sector of the hard disk. This is a place on the disk that you never even see. It contains a program code that is run every time you start the PC. If a virus gets into the boot sector, it will run when you start the PC, so it will be active all the time.

Leprosy **displays this while reformatting your hard disk.**

Phantom displays this death's head and a message.

Viruses that infect Microsoft Word documents are common. People often send Word files to each other instead of printed pages which makes Word documents ready vehicles for spreading viruses.

Brainy stuff

The first intentional PC virus, called Brain, came to light in 1987 at the University of Delaware. This virus was unusual in that within its code was the address and phone number of its authors – two brothers in Lahore, Pakistan. The brothers claimed the virus had been written to punish people who made illegal copies of their software. It changed the volume label of a floppy disk to the message, '© Brain'. Brain was the name of the brothers' firm.

A month later, students at Lehigh University in the US found floppy disks were being corrupted. This turned out to be the work of a virus. The Lehigh virus, written by a student, counted the number of files it infected. When the count reached four, it overwrote the data on the disk.

Catching on

By 1990 there were only a couple of dozen known viruses. Today, the number is around 50,000. But despite the large number of known viruses, few are a real threat. Most are never found outside the collections of virus writers and anti-virus software companies. Most viruses are not good enough at breeding to become a problem in the wider world.

Jargon buster

Parasitic virus Viruses which infect program files. As the name suggests, they attach themselves like parasites to copies of ordinary programs such as your word processor or your spreadsheet, and are activated whenever these programs are run. Once active, they attach copies of the virus to other programs that you run. They can spread when you give copies of programs to other people.

Virus myths

Viruses harm hardware Software can make your computer behave as if it has a hardware fault, but it cannot actually damage the hardware and cause a real fault. Removing all traces of a virus from your computer's hard disk will always result in a complete cure.

Jargon buster

Trojan Horses A rogue program is not a virus unless it reproduces itself. Some malicious programs are designed to do harm when a particular event occurs, such as 'delete the database if my name is no longer on the payroll'. They are called logic bombs. A destructive program that masquerades as something useful is called a Trojan after the Trojan horse of Greek mythology.

In December 1989 a man calling himself Dr Popp mailed copies of an AIDS Information Disk to 20,000 European PC users. The program assessed your risk of contracting AIDS. Its method of spreading was to ask you to give copies of the program to friends and colleagues. Unbeknown to users, the disk also installed software that counted how many times you started your PC. When the count reached 90, the software scrambled the contents of your hard disk and invited you to send $189 to an address in Panama for an unscrambler program.

Since the AIDS disk didn't replicate itself, it was not strictly speaking a virus. It was a Trojan horse.

PC doctor

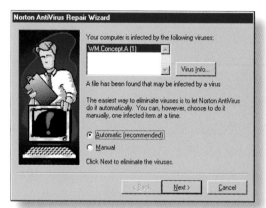

If it detects a virus, Norton AntiVirus launches the
Repair Wizard. **This wizard guides you through the
process of disinfecting the PC making sure you
don't miss any vital steps.**

Regular use of good anti-virus software should ensure that your computer never falls seriously ill.

Viruses make your PC misbehave, destroy your files
and make you unpopular with friends if you pass
them on. You can avoid problems by installing
anti-virus software, and using it regularly.

Most anti-virus packages protect your PC in two
ways. They include a standalone virus scanner that
you run whenever you want to check that your
hard disk, a floppy disk or a file you just received
is virus free. They also include a background
scanner that loads into memory when you start
your PC and checks each file as you access it.

Jargon buster

Scanner This is the name given to
the most popular type of virus detector. It
detects viruses by scanning computer files looking
for the tell-tale signs of known viruses. A scanner
has to know what to look for, and requires
updating in order to detect the most recently
discovered viruses.

Here you select the drives you want to check.

The Options button lets you change the way the
program works.

The Virus List gives information about viruses.

The Log records when the software was run and
what viruses were found.

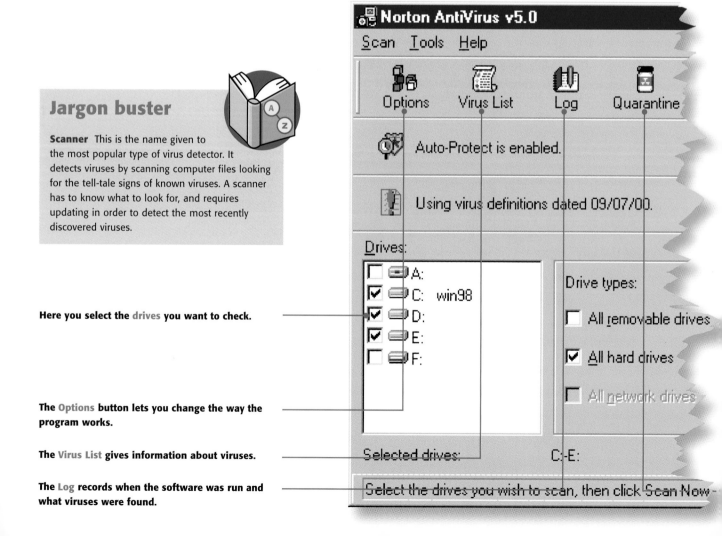

A background scanner removes the risk of running an infected file and activating a virus because you forgot to check it. Some background scanners aren't as thorough as standalone scanners, so it's still worth checking your whole hard disk on a regular basis. Use a scheduler to run a full scan of your hard disk once a week. Many anti-virus packages have a scheduler; with Windows 98 you can use its built-in Task Scheduler instead.

Clean up

If your PC gets a virus, remove it. Some packages make this easier than others. Several include a boot disk or emergency disk that you can use to clean an infected PC. With others, you have to make a rescue disk after installing the software.

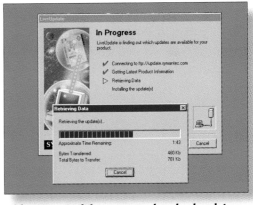

With Norton AntiVirus you can download updates from the Internet to maintain the software's effectiveness at detecting new viruses. Just click the LiveUpdate button.

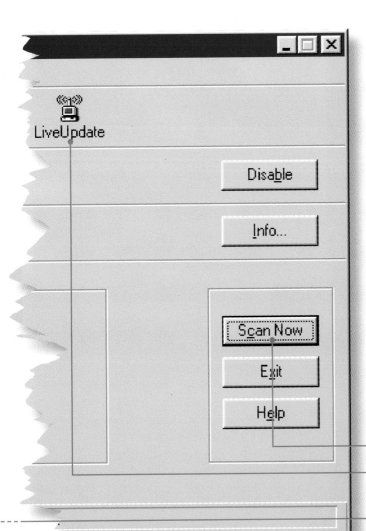

Virus tips

● **Sweeping up** With some products, the background scanner lets you remove a virus automatically as soon as it is detected. Others make you run the standalone scanner to sweep your whole hard disk and clean any infected files it finds. Viruses spread from file to file, so even if your background scanner disinfects the file it found, it's still a good idea to check your hard disk and floppies for any other infections. Some products have a Repair Wizard that guides you through the disinfection process.

● **Updates** Anti-virus software must be updated regularly to maintain its effectiveness at identifying new viruses. If you are on the Internet, you can usually download updates free for a year or for the life of the product.

Click this button to scan your hard drive for viruses.

LiveUpdate lets you download virus updates from the Internet using your modem.

Quarantine sends an infected file to Norton's virus research centre if AntiVirus can't remove it.

Which type of virus?

The three most dangerous strains of virus to watch out for are boot sector, file and macro viruses.

To spread widely a virus has to be active most of the time your PC is running and infect things that are passed around. Brain was a boot-sector virus. It was successful in its time, but it had a flaw. It only infected the now obsolete 5.25in floppy disks. It has become more or less extinct along with them.

Boot-sector viruses common today, like the Form virus, infect hard disks and floppies. They infect the hard disk so they can be active as soon as you turn on your PC, and they infect floppies in order to be passed around. The virus needs just a little help from you to get from floppy to hard disk.

On the floppy

If you have ever switched on your PC with a floppy disk in the drive, you will have seen the message 'Not a system disk. Replace and press any key'. This is displayed by a program in the boot sector of the floppy disk. When you turn on a PC it checks whether there is a disk in drive A:. If there is, it runs the software in the boot sector of the floppy disk instead of that on the hard disk. If the floppy disk isn't a system disk, the message is displayed.

Boot it out

Boot-sector viruses exploit this type of behaviour. When a boot-sector virus succeeds in infecting a floppy disk, it replaces the original contents of the boot sector with a program of its own. Usually it moves the original boot program somewhere else and runs that afterwards, so that when you boot your PC from the disk it will still start up – or display the 'Not a system disk' message – in the normal way. The difference is that the new boot sector program puts a copy of the virus on the hard disk, ensuring that the virus will always be active. Often this type of virus can prevent you from getting your computer to work at all.

Creepy crawlies

File viruses infect ordinary files. When a file virus is active on your PC it adds virus code to other files you access, and modifies them so the virus code is run when the files are accessed in future. The longer the virus is active on your PC the greater the number of files it will infect.

File viruses only infect program files. Data files such as text files, image files or database files are only displayed or updated. They are never run and provide no way for a virus to become active. This means (with one exception) that data files cannot carry viruses. People tend not to pass program files around very often, so file viruses are rare.

Malicious macros

The exception to the rule comes about because some data files contain macros. Macros are a way of building simple programs into a file like a word processor document or spreadsheet. Because macros are so powerful, they are dangerous in the hands of someone with a grudge.

Macro viruses are written in a macro language. The first example was written using the Microsoft Word macro language to show the concept of a macro virus – hence its name, Concept. Concept found its way into a document that was published on CD-ROM, and spread widely. Concept did no more than display a message box.

Dotted about

Word macro viruses spread by adding macros to Normal.dot, the template that determines Word's startup default options. The macros are run when Word starts up. This means that after Normal.dot is infected, the virus will be active whenever you run Word, and any new documents you create will contain the virus. When these documents are opened by someone else they will transmit the virus to their own copy of Word.

Although macro viruses can be written for any application that has a macro facility, Microsoft Word and Excel are currently the only programs affected by viruses that are circulating in the wild. There are over 700 different Word macro viruses, of which about 60 have been discovered in the wild.

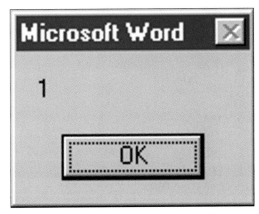

Virus myths

Viruses instantly destroy your data
Some viruses will result in the loss or damage of files, but no virus gives away its presence by doing something as destructive as that immediately after infecting a machine. A virus must remain invisible to you for a while to allow it to spread. If you catch the virus during that time, the likelihood is that no harm will have been done.

Viruses can travel along the mains Viruses are just software. They can only be transferred from PC to PC the same way ordinary programs and data files are transferred: on floppy disks, on CD-ROMs, over a network or from the Internet. Viruses cannot be transmitted down the mains cable, through the air or by mere physical contact with disks that contain viruses.

The **Concept** **macro virus simply displays this annoying little message box.**

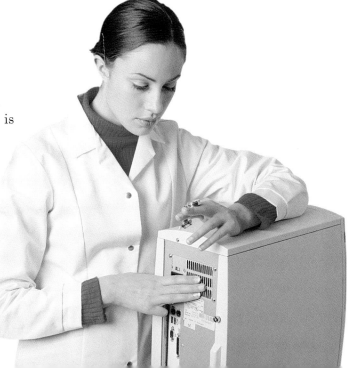

Don't panic

Virus tip

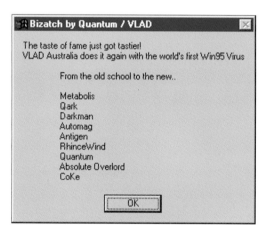

● Viruses have all sorts of effects, from strange messages to lost files and even inability to start your PC. If your PC develops an unexplained problem, a virus check is a quick way to identify or rule out one possible cause.

Bizatch by Quantum / VLAD

The taste of fame just got tastier!
VLAD Australia does it again with the world's first Win95 Virus

From the old school to the new..

Metabolis
Qark
Darkman
Automag
Antigen
RhinceWind
Quantum
Absolute Overlord
CoKe

OK

Boza can breed only in certain conditions.

Computer viruses are not as big a threat as the experts originally thought they would be.

The press and the anti-virus industry have hyped up the effect of viruses. The discovery of Brain in 1987 led to widespread panic and predictions of disaster, which were never fulfilled.

One virus, Michelangelo, first reported in 1991, achieved similar notoriety. Industry figures believed that disaster would occur on 6 March, Michelangelo's birthday and the virus' trigger date, when it would overwrite all the data on the hard disk. Estimates of the cost of the damage were put in billions of dollars. Many people changed the clock on their computers to skip past the critical date and sales of anti-virus products soared. Few people lost any data.

Boza

The discovery of Boza, the first virus to run under Windows 95, was hyped by many anti-virus software developers. The implication was that users of Windows 95 were at risk from this virus unless they bought new Windows 95 anti-virus products. However, Boza didn't spread widely. It seldom spread to program files that were liable to be spread by disk from one PC to another. It isn't found in the wild and is never likely to be.

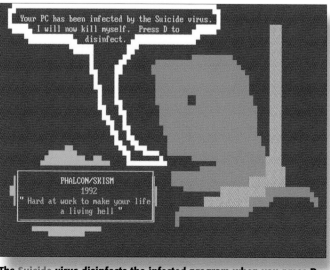

The Suicide virus disinfects the infected program when you press D.

Virus tip

● Active components downloaded from Web sites could contain software that might damage your PC. Use your Web browser's security settings to warn you.

Harmless viruses

Any computer virus is a nuisance, but some have an amusing side. Cascade got its name because its effect is to cause the text on an MS-DOS screen to gradually slide down to make a heap of letters at the bottom. Ambulance causes an animated graphic of an ambulance to whizz along the bottom of the screen, while a siren plays on the speaker.

The Suicide virus displays a crude picture of a head in a noose and the message 'I will now kill myself. Press D to disinfect'. The Casino virus invites you to play a game of Jackpot. The prize? You get to keep the data on your hard disk.

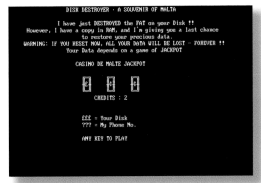

The Casino virus challenges you to a game of Jackpot. If you win, you keep your data.

Virus payloads

How can you tell if you have a virus on your computer? If you don't have any virus-detection software, the first you'll probably know about a virus is when its payload triggers. Every virus has a different payload. Here are the 10 most frequently reported ones:

● **Form** The most common virus of all is quite benign. On the 18th of every month it makes your PC beep each time you press a key. It's a boot-sector virus, spread via floppy disks. It infects your hard disk when you boot from an infected floppy.

● **Concept** Concept is the original Word macro virus. It infects your copy of Word when you load an infected document file. Its sole effect is to display a small message window containing the number 1. There are many modified versions of it.

● **One Half** This virus is transmitted in program files, but it infects the hard disk boot sector so that it is active all the time your PC is on. It scrambles the data on the hard disk, starting from the far end of the disk volume. When half of the disk is scrambled One Half displays the message 'Dis is one half. Press any key to continue…'.

● **AntiEXE** This is a boot-sector virus. It infects your hard disk from an infected floppy. It causes some program files to be modified when they are accessed, which will crash the computer the next time they are run.

● **Empire Monkey** This is a boot-sector virus. It infects your hard disk when you boot from an infected floppy. It makes a change to the system so that the hard disk can only be accessed when the virus is active. This makes removal of the virus difficult.

● **Junkie** This virus infects boot sectors of floppy disks and hard disks, and MS-DOS application files. It disables any anti-virus program that you have running at the time. It has no obvious other effect.

● **Parity Boot** This is a boot-sector virus. It infects your hard disk from an infected floppy. After the PC has been running for an hour or so it displays the message Parity Check, then crashes the PC, simulating a memory error.

● **AntiCMOS** This is a boot-sector virus. When active, there is a random chance that the virus will corrupt your computer's Setup information so that the floppy disk type becomes the wrong type and the hard disk becomes 'Not Installed'. The next time you start the computer, the message 'CMOS checksum failure' is displayed.

● **Ripper** This is a boot-sector virus. It infects your hard disk when you boot from an infected floppy. It gradually corrupts the data on your hard disk. By the time you notice the corruption, much of your data may be damaged.

● **Natas** This is another boot-sector virus which also infects program files. When Natas activates there is a random probability that the virus will reformat your hard disk, destroying all the data on it.

Safety first

Safety tips

● **Know your sources** If you use the Internet, only download software from reputable sources that check files for viruses before making them available. If you receive an e-mail from someone you don't know which contains an attachment, don't open it.

● **.rtf saves the day** When sending Word documents, save them in Rich Text Format (.rtf). Ask people to use the .rtf format when sending documents to you. These files preserve most formatting but won't include any macros.

● **Check it out** If you find a virus on your PC's hard disk, check every floppy disk and CD-ROM you can find, and remember to tell your friends. Anyone you may have given files or disks to should also check for viruses, otherwise you may find the virus returns.

Virus myths

My PC doesn't work, it must be a virus Most PC malfunctions are caused by hardware or software failures, not viruses. Software failures are the most common cause of problems. They are the result of mistakes made by the software's programmers. These mistakes are called bugs. They are more widespread than viruses. If your PC plays up when you run a program, the problem is much more likely to be a bug than a virus.

Only install shrink-wrapped software This is a common myth. In fact, many PC viruses are widespread because they were distributed on mass-produced disks. The Form virus was found on thousands of pre-formatted blank disks. The Concept macro virus was first found in a Word document on a CD-ROM issued by Microsoft. Viruses have even been found on the driver disks of new PCs.

The best way to avoid PC viruses is to keep your PC in good order and avoid taking risks.

Despite the fact that there are viruses around, you shouldn't be too alarmed; there are usually ways to keep your PC alive and kicking. For a virus-free PC, make sure that you take the right precautions for safe computing.

Always back up your system regularly. A back-up is the ultimate protection against data loss, whether through virus action or other disasters.

Keep it clean

Make sure that the people you exchange disks and files with keep their computers virus-free and encourage them to use anti-virus software.

Always remove floppy disks from your disk drive after you've finished with them. And always write-protect the floppy disks supplied with a software package before you install them. This will prevent any virus from infecting the disks so you will know they are clean if you have to reinstall the software.

Archive it

Don't run software that has been copied from someone's hard disk. If it's commercial software, it isn't legal in any case. If it's shareware, you should get hold of the original .zip file. A virus can't infect archived software.

3

Preventing Problems

Housekeeping basics

Dust off your hardware and chuck out all the old and useless software that's clogging up your computer.

At least once a year you should spring clean your computer system, throwing away all the junk you've amassed over the previous year and cleaning what's left. Don't throw away any equipment, but get rid of unneeded files and programs.

What you have to do

Cleaning is a two-level process: one involves removing dirt, dust and fluff from the hardware itself; the second involves scouring the hard disk to make more space and speed up the operation of Windows by relieving it of excess baggage. Your aim is to have a PC that looks good, works faster and is less likely to go wrong in the future.

Preparation

Set aside a whole afternoon for the job. Assemble the various bits and pieces of cleaning equipment you'll need and if you're not absolutely certain which cable goes where in the back of your computer, have some masking tape handy so that when you start dismantling your PC you can label the cables by wrapping masking tape around them.

Before you do anything else, back up your hard disk. This process is described on the next two pages and is essential. If you don't have a back-up drive make copies of your data files on floppy disks. The chances of doing any real harm to your PC are remote but should not be ignored.

You will need

ESSENTIAL
Software All the software you need to keep your PC in peak condition comes with the different versions of Windows 98.
Hardware You may have everything you need to clean the outside of your PC and its accessories already: a lint-free cloth, some non-abrasive, multi-surface cleaner, a kitchen roll, some cotton buds and a small clean paintbrush. The only specialist items you need are proprietary cleaning disks for the floppy and CD-ROM drives, and some disks for backing up.

ALSO RECOMMENDED
Hardware A vacuum cleaner with a tapered nozzle attachment is handy but not essential.

Back it all up

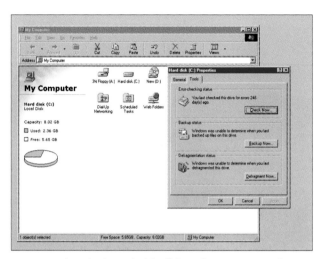

1 To make a back-up, double-click on the My Computer icon on the Windows Desktop. Click with the right mouse button on drive C: and select Properties. Then select the Tools tab and click on the **Backup Now** button.

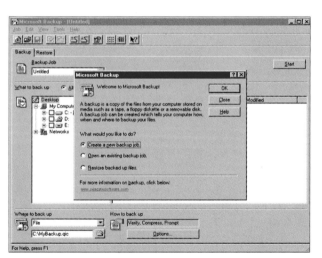

2 This will launch the **Microsoft Backup** wizard. Select the option to Create a New Backup Job and click on OK. On the resulting screen, select Back up My Computer for a full backup of your files and system and click on Next.

Jargon buster

System file Any file on a PC that is essential for it to work properly. In Windows, the majority of system files are in the Windows folder and its subfolders but others are scattered about a hard disk in obscure locations. Some are hidden in an attempt to prevent their accidental deletion.

It's essential to make a full back-up before attempting to tidy up the files on your computer.

Spring cleaning a PC involves removing files from its hard disk and because there's a chance that while doing this you might inadvertently delete crucial system files, you must make a back-up first. That way, if anything goes wrong you can restore the files from your back-up and get your system up and running again. Once you've tidied up your system and it is working at maximum efficiency you should remember to make regular back-ups. (See pages 18–19 and 121–30 for more information on backing up.)

Ways and means
The sort of back-up to make is a full system back-up that includes everything on your hard disk: Windows, programs and data. Use the Backup program that comes with Windows or a more flexible product from a commercial vendor.

The back-up has to be stored somewhere and there are several alternatives. If you have two hard disks you can back up the primary hard disk onto the secondary one. The same applies if you have a single hard disk that has been

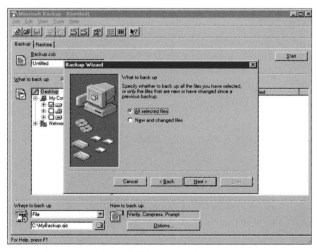

3 As you are doing a full back-up, when the next screen appears, choose to back up **All Selected Files** rather than just those that have changed. Click on the Next button and select where you want to store the back-up.

partitioned into two or more logical drives.

Of course, if you're lucky enough to have a back-up tape drive you can use that, but any form of removable storage will do. Zip disks that store 100MB or 250MB and LS-120 disks (SuperDisks) that store 120MB are fine, although none of these are likely to be big enough for a complete back-up, so make sure you've got plenty of blank disks. High-capacity removable hard disks such as the Iomega Jaz drive which can store up to 2GB are a better bet.

More cash, more dash

If you're in the market for a back-up program Drive Image from PowerQuest offers a unique solution. Instead of backing up each file on a disk, it makes an image of the entire disk and stores it on virtually any type of media – tape, removable disks or another hard disk. It's much faster than conventional back-ups – as little as five minutes per gigabyte – and the clever part is that you can restore a damaged system from the DOS prompt by booting from a floppy disk. The drawback is that you can back up and restore complete disks only, not individual files.

Zip it up

If you haven't got a drive suitable for storing back-ups, buy one as part of your housekeeping regime. Remember that Zip drives are best for partial back-ups or saving selected files – a full back-up would mean buying a lot of disks, which would be expensive.

Microsoft Backup tip

Backup is not installed during a typical Windows installation. If it's not on your PC, add it by double-clicking on Add/Remove Programs in Windows Control Panel. This displays a properties box. Select Windows Setup and tick next to Backup in the System Tools category. Click on OK.

Jargon buster

Partitioning A way of dividing the space on a hard disk so that its host computer sees it as two or more disks. Partitions may be further subdivided into logical disks, each of which can be formatted without affecting the others.

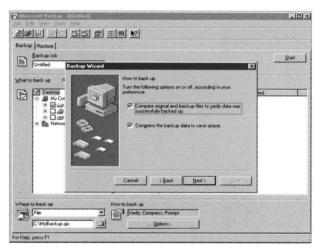

4 Before the back-up starts, two further options appear. Compare Original and Backup Files to Verify Data was Successfully Backed Up will check the copied files against the originals to make sure they are correct. This will double the time the back-up takes. The second option lets you compress the data – useful if you have limited space on your back-up device.

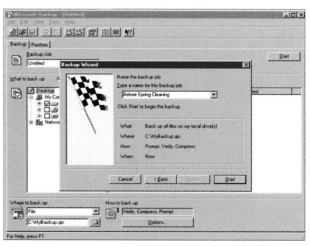

5 Give the job a descriptive name and click on the Start button. The program calculates the number of files it needs to copy and the space they take before it starts the back-up.

Hardware care

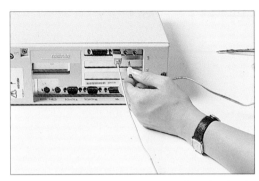

When reassembling your computer after cleaning it, insert and remove the audio cables **several times to clean their contacts.**

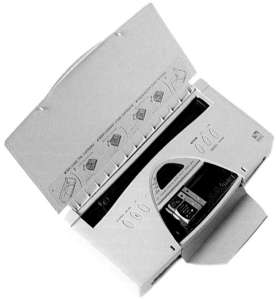

Remove dust and paper particles from the inside of an inkjet printer **but don't remove an ink cartridge to clean its nozzles. There will be a button on the outside of the printer or a utility in its Windows controller for this purpose.**

Keep your computer and peripherals as clean as you can to extend their lives and stop them breaking down.

Keeping the outside of your PC and its accessories clean isn't just a matter of pride, although it's undeniably satisfying to see a PC looking as clean as the day you first took it out of its box. The main reason for keeping kit clean is to prevent dust and dirt finding its way into floppy and CD-ROM drives, ventilation slots and even into the PC itself, where it can clog up cooling fans and cause overheating.

Cleaning your PC

Disconnect the cables from the back of your PC and move the system unit somewhere you can turn it around and get at it easily. Remove all the thick dust using a damp cloth or a piece of kitchen roll. Use a vacuum cleaner fitted with a tapered nozzle to suck dirt out of the ventilation slots, the fan grille on the back and the gaps around disk drives.

You can buy tiny PC vacuum cleaners for this purpose but a domestic machine works just as well provided you're careful with it. Use a clean, dry paintbrush if you have nothing else. Ingrained marks can be removed with an all-surface cleaner, but make sure it's non-abrasive and choose one that doesn't have to be cleaned off with water.

Internal checks

Remove the case from the system unit and earth yourself by touching the metal frame of the PC and briefly holding a nearby radiator or pipe. Examine the inside of the PC for dust and carefully remove

Push in the flap of the floppy disk drive **and remove any obvious dirt and fluff with a brush or cotton bud. To clean the heads inside you need a special cleaning disk.**

Blow away any dust and wipe the tray of a CD-ROM drive **with a damp cloth. Clean the inside using the same sort of cleaning disc that's available for audio CD players.**

Remove dust and fluff from ventilation slots **using a soft brush or a vacuum cleaner.**

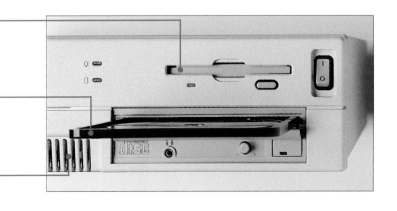

any build-up around fans and ventilation slots using a dry paintbrush or cotton buds. Most of the chips in a PC are soldered to the circuit board, but some are mounted in chip carriers. Over time, expansion and contraction caused by heating and cooling causes these to rise out of their sockets. Push each one into place without using undue force and without flexing the main circuit board.

Check that all cables, connectors and expansion cards are firmly in their sockets and tighten the screws retaining any cards that have worked loose.

Accessories

Mice, keyboards, printers, monitors and scanners all attract dirt, yet they're easy to clean and work much better when they are. Clean the outside of your mouse with a damp cloth and remove its ball. Wash the ball in soapy water or washing-up liquid, rinse it and leave it to dry. Clean the exposed rollers (there are usually three of them) with a tissue. Stubborn contamination can be loosened with a cotton bud soaked in isopropyl alcohol, which is what's in the cleaning fluids sold for cassette and video tape heads.

Keyboard clean

Clean your keyboard by turning it upside down and shaking it gently. You'll be surprised at what comes out, especially if you smoke or eat at your PC. Clean the keys with a small brush. Stubborn dirt can be blown out using a can of compressed air or sucked out with a vacuum cleaner.

When you're putting everything back together it's a good idea to insert and remove the audio cables several times to clean their contacts. Once you've powered up the PC you're ready for the final stage, which is to clean the floppy and CD-ROM drives.

Final touches

Eject the CD-ROM tray, blow away any dust and wipe it clean. The working parts of CD-ROM and floppy drives can only be cleaned using special cleaning disks. If your floppy drive isn't giving you problems you can probably ignore it, but CD-ROM drives need regular attention. Don't waste money buying a CD cleaner if you already have one for your audio CD player. They work in the same way.

Cleaning tips

Treat the cases of your monitor, printer and scanner in the same way as the PC's system unit. The monitor's screen and the glass plate of a flatbed scanner should be cleaned with a proprietary non-abrasive glass cleaner. Don't open your scanner to clean inside unless its performance has deteriorated, in which case follow the manufacturer's recommendations.

Inkjet printers don't need much attention. The main cause for concern is tiny particles of paper dust that can cause the paper to slip as it feeds through. Prevention is better than cure, so open the cover of the printer and brush away any dust and paper particles. Treat laser printers in the same way and carefully remove any particles of stray toner with a damp cloth. Wear gloves and avoid breathing in the carcinogenic toner.

The mouse ball picks up dirt and this sticks to the rollers. Clean the rollers with a cotton bud soaked in an alcohol-based cleaning fluid.

Hard disk health

1 To check for hard disk faults run **ScanDisk** from the Start button by selecting Programs, Accessories, System Tools, ScanDisk; or right-click on drive C: in My Computer, select Properties, click on the Tools tab and the Check Now button.

Watch out!

One reason that a hard disk might be performing badly isn't picked up by ScanDisk. It's caused by changes made to the startup files when installing a new piece of hardware. The worst offenders are the older types of removable disk drive designed to work in MS-DOS as well as Windows.

Check for these and similar problems by right-clicking the My Computer icon on the Windows Desktop and choosing the Performance tab. You should get a message saying your system is configured for optimal performance. If there is a problem, a brief description appears in the message box instead. Click on an item and then click on the Details button that appears, for help with tracking down the cause of the problem.

A fit and healthy hard disk means healthy files and programs as well as an efficient computer.

You can't physically service your hard disk because it's a sealed unit which should never be opened except in laboratory conditions. But you can maintain it at peak efficiency using utility software to check its physical state, repair minor damage and reorganise its contents.

To clean or redecorate?

Before spring cleaning your hard disk you must decide whether to reinstall Windows and your software or simply spruce them up. If programs have been crashing for no apparent reason, a full reinstallation is in order. But if Windows and your other programs are stable, all you need is a tune-up. This will make your PC run faster and free up some space on the disk.

Double glazing

There are two ways of reinstalling Windows: on top of the existing version or by formatting the hard disk and starting again from scratch. If you install over the current version you won't

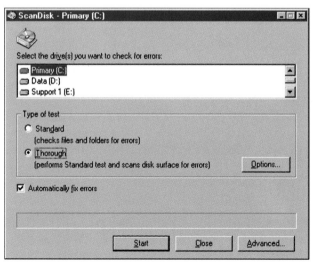

2 In ScanDisk's Options box ensure that the type of test is set to **Thorough**. The Standard test, which doesn't check the disk surface for errors, is for quick daily or weekly checks. Put a tick in the box labelled Automatically Fix Errors and click on the Advanced button.

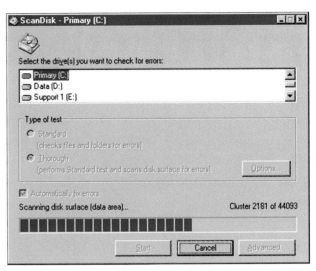

have to reinstall your other software, but you may have to reconfigure any dial-up software that connects you to the Internet and tidy up menus, shortcuts and preferences. Freshening Windows in this way is relatively painless. It restores elements of Windows that may have been deleted and can revitalise a flagging PC.

To reinstall Windows from scratch takes at least a day and isn't something a novice should attempt without expert help, but it's a viable option if you have a recovery CD. Before you start, make a note of any Internet access numbers and passwords you've been using and, of course, back up your data files.

Checking your hard disk

Windows' ScanDisk utility detects and repairs faults on the surface of a disk and in the way files are organised. Minor faults are nothing to worry about because it's normal over time for small sections of a hard disk to go bad. When this happens, Windows marks them and avoids them in future. ScanDisk identifies areas already marked as bad and checks for others not yet discovered by Windows. It repairs them if it can or marks them as bad and avoids them.

4 Ensure the Automatically Fix Errors box is checked. The first part of the test takes a minute or so, but when the main action begins, which is a thorough check of the **surface of the disk**, you could be in for a long wait. The bar along the bottom indicates progress but, because of your selections under advanced options, you don't need to sit at your computer.

5 This disk is perfect and has no bad sectors. If errors had been found, the top line of the **Results box** would have stated ScanDisk found errors on this drive and fixed them all. The only time you should worry about bad sectors is when they multiply every time you run a check.

3 Set the **advanced options** as follows: Display summary, Always; Log file, Replace log; Cross-linked files, Make copies; Lost file fragments, Convert to files. Then put ticks next to Invalid file names and Check host drive first. Click on OK.

Recovery tip

PC suppliers often provide a recovery CD-ROM to reinstall Windows and the software supplied with the PC. The process is usually fully automated and you just have to swap disks when requested. Recovering a system is a great way of revitalising a PC, but your data files will be wiped out and should be copied onto floppy disks before you start. You'll also lose programs installed after taking delivery of the PC.

Hard disk tuning

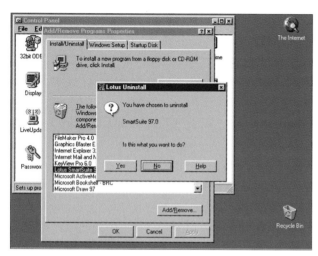

Clearing out and rearranging your hard disk frees up space and can speed up your computer.

Nearly all Windows programs have an uninstall facility to remove them. If there are programs on your PC that you never use, remove them through Add/Remove Programs. Some removals leave files behind, so when you delete any programs use Windows Explorer to scan the Program Files folder on drive C: for strays.

1 To **uninstall** a program, open the Control Panel and double-click on Add/Remove Programs. Highlight the chosen program in the scrolling list box and click on the Add/Remove button. Usually a confirmation box like the one above appears. Use it to check that you've picked the right program.

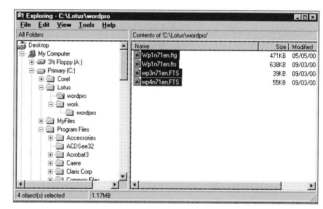

2 After uninstalling Lotus SmartSuite several folders remain on the hard disk and waste over 1MB of space. These can be removed using Windows Explorer to highlight each file before right-clicking and **deleting**

Disk cleaning tip

Several Uninstall programs are available at reasonable prices. Norton CleanSweep is one of the better ones. It logs programs as they're installed enabling it to remove them without trace if you no longer need them. Also, it has a Wizard to find all the redundant files on a disk in one go. It even clears out Internet cache files, which you'd normally have to do yourself from within a Web browsing program or by using the Disk Cleanup accessory.

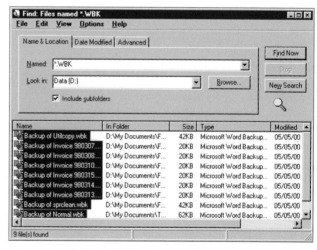

3 When finding files for deletion make sure you search the correct hard disk and that the **Include Subfolders** box contains a tick. If not, you'll miss some files. The search in this screenshot is for back-up files generated by Microsoft Word.

Seek and destroy

Next seek out temporary and back-up files that can be deleted. Select Find, Files and Folders from the Start menu. Instruct Find to look for files named *.bak, which brings up a list of back-up files. Highlight those you don't need and press Delete. Repeat the process with system back-up files (*.syd), temporary files (*.tmp) and ScanDisk repair files (*.chk).

When files are deleted they're sent to the Recycle Bin. To get rid of them, right-click on the bin and choose Empty Recycle Bin. You might choose to reduce the amount of space Windows reserves for recycled files, increasing the space available for other programs. As long as you empty the Recycle Bin regularly, you can reduce it to one per cent of the drive's capacity.

Pack up your troubles

Defragmentation takes fragments of files all over a disk and packs them together so there are no gaps. Running the defragmenter before clearing out files is pointless because new gaps are created every time you delete something. Defragmenting is therefore the last stage of hard-disk maintenance and is described here.

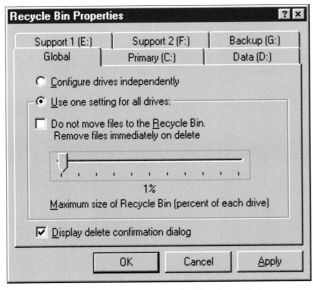

4 Reducing the size of the **Recycle Bin** gives Windows more space. To open Recycle Bin Properties, right-click on the bin. A setting of one per cent means you can store 10MB of files for each 1GB of hard-disk space. Keep the percentage low.

5 Start Windows Disk Defragmenter by opening My Computer, right-clicking on drive C: and selecting Properties. You can alter the settings by opening Programs, Accessories and then System Tools.

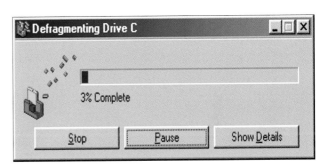

6 Click on the Tools tab and the **Defragment Now** button to begin. Defragmentation can take anything from several minutes to a few hours depending on factors such as the amount of defragmentation and the size of the disk.

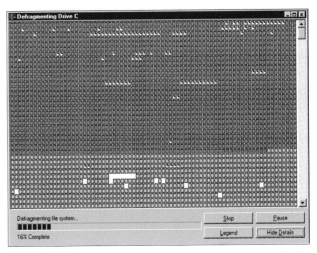

7 If you want something to watch while you're waiting, click on the **Show Details** button.

Keep it in shape

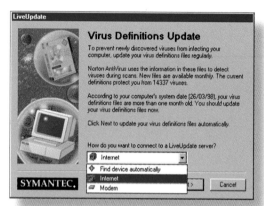

An integral part of keeping your PC in shape, of course, is to run anti-virus software. **Norton Anti-Virus** can be kept up to date by downloading new virus definitions direct from Symantec or over the Internet.

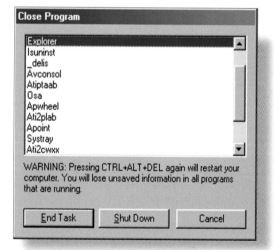

Ctrl-Alt-Del will soon show you whether you have any programs open but remember to press this once only otherwise your PC will restart.

There are some things you can do to avoid interference before you begin running disk cleaning programs.

Before running utilities such as ScanDisk and Disk Defragmenter on your hard drive – or restoring backed up data – it is advisable to disable other programs running under Windows 98 that may interfere with them. Although you might think you've got nothing open, press Ctrl-Alt-Del and the dialogue box will prove you wrong. It shows a list of all the programs currently running. Programs to look out for include:

● Microsoft Office Find Fast which regularly indexes your folders to speed up searches for Office documents. This can be disabled through the Control Panel.

● Uninstaller programs which sit in the system tray ready to monitor the installation of any new programs. These can usually be disabled by right-clicking and selecting the appropriate option.

Similarly with anti-virus software which will stay 'on' monitoring your system and be confused by the changes made by the disk utilities into thinking your PC is under attack.

● Any scheduled program, such as one set up under Task Scheduler, suddenly bursting into action could upset the disk maintenance program. These can be disabled through the Scheduled Tasks folder.

● Any communication software – such as answering machines or fax receiving software which are set to open automatically. Again these can usually be disabled by right-clicking on the icon in the system tray and selecting the appropriate option.

Backing up

Microsoft Backup should be run before any major changes to your system.

Once you have decided what type of back-up you want to run, the Microsoft Backup program gets to work calculating how many files you will have to copy and the space they will take up. The program also makes sure there is enough room available on the back-up disk or tape that you've chosen.

When everything is correct, copying commences. To speed things up, you can opt for Microsoft Backup to compress the files it is transferring to

the back-up device. Not only does this make backing up quicker, it also means the files take up less space.

However, you must be careful. If the files you are copying are already compressed – or the drive you are copying them to is compressed – trying to compress them down further may lead to them taking up more rather than less space.

Using Microsoft Backup

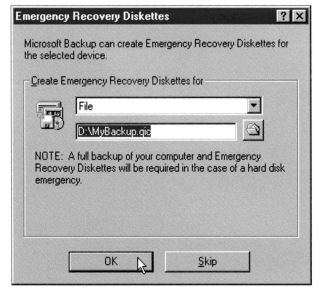

1 You'll probably have to install Backup from Control Panel, Add/Remove Programs: it's under System Tools. You run it from Programs, Accessories, System Tools, Backup. When you start **Microsoft Backup** for the first time, the software should detect your tape drive. If it can't find one, Backup will ask you whether you want to run the Add New Hardware Wizard to load the tape drive's drivers. If you don't have a tape drive and will be backing up to a removable disk cartridge or floppy disk, then click on No.

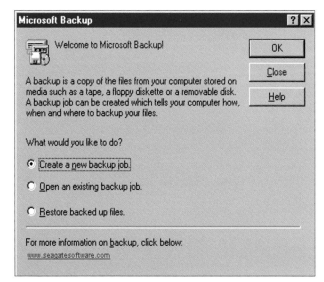

2 Windows 98's first screen asks if you want to create a new **back-up job**, open an existing back-up job or restore backed up files. Back-up jobs are instructions that tell Backup which files to back up. If you have a removable disk drive, create a back-up job to back up your whole system. You should also create jobs to back up your work files, which you should run every day.

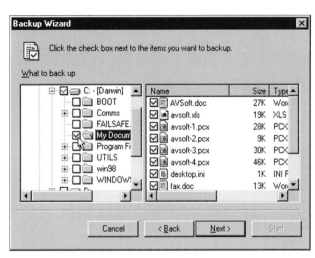

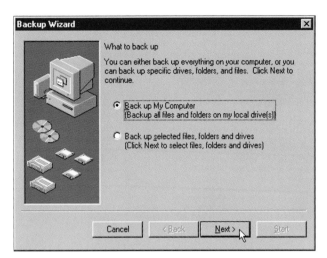

3 To create a whole system back-up job, choose the option **Back up My Computer**. When you click on Next, accept the default option to back up all selected files. Click on Next again, and you will be asked where the back-up should be made. The choices will be your tape drive or a file on your hard drive.

Select whether Backup should verify that the copy of your files is correct by comparing each file with the original. If you are using a tape drive you should select this option, although it will double the time the back-up takes. If you are using a removable cartridge you can omit it. Choose to compress the data unless you are backing up to a drive that already uses data compression such as DriveSpace.

5 When creating back-up jobs to run every day, it's best to make the number of files to be backed up as small as possible so that the back-up runs quickly. That way, not having enough time won't be an excuse for not backing up your data properly. This is especially important if you will be backing up on floppy disks. If you organise your work into folders, you can create back-up jobs for individual folders or groups of folders, such as your My Documents folder.

When the Backup Wizard runs, choose **Back up selected files** The wizard will take you to a selection screen, where you can choose which folders or files to back up by checking or unchecking the boxes beside them. The other options in the wizard are the same as for a full back-up.

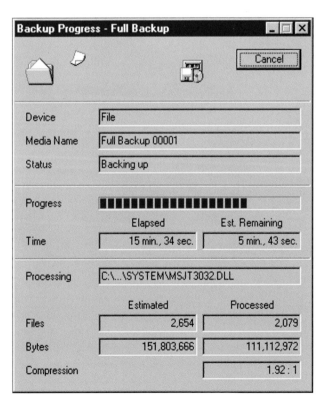

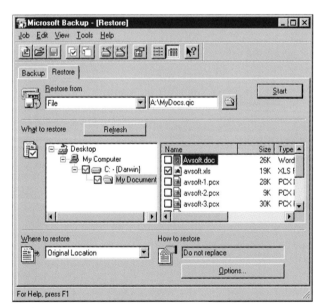

4 The final step is to choose a descriptive name for the back-up (such as Full Back-up) and click on Start. Microsoft Backup will begin backing up your data. While the back-up is running, Microsoft Backup will display a **progress window** showing how far it has got, which files are being backed up and how long the back-up will take. If you are using compression, it will also show what compression ratio is being achieved. Usually, files compress to almost half their normal size, so you can expect to get nearly 200MB of data onto a 100MB Iomega Zip cartridge.

6 When you get into the swing of using Microsoft Backup you can close the Backup Wizard that appears when it starts, and choose your back-up job from the **main interface**. This gives you the opportunity to change some of the options. For example, you can choose to back up only new and changed files, which will save a lot of time. If you do that, you must make sure you do not overwrite your earlier back-up files containing those files which have not changed.

To restore a file from a back-up, load the back-up disk or tape and then locate it in Microsoft Backup. The program will display the drives and folders contained on the back-up. Choose which folders or files to restore by checking the box alongside them, then begin restoring by clicking on Start.

Storage facilities

Increase your system's storage capacity and keep your valuable computer data safe.

There's a difference between storage drives and back-up drives. Whereas a storage drive can be pressed into service to make back-ups, the reverse is seldom true because back-up drives use tapes instead of disks. (See pages 18-19.)

The tape is not dissimilar to an audio cassette, but the tape itself is wider and the cartridges are more sophisticated. Data is recorded magnetically and arranged sequentially on the tape, with one file following another, just as one track follows another on a pre-recorded audio cassette. To further complicate matters, the data is usually compressed to squeeze twice as much onto a tape. This means that restoring a single file from a back-up involves waiting while the tape spools to the correct location and the file is decompressed.

Disks or tapes?

Removable disk drives are much faster in operation and easier to use than tape back-up drives. As with the hard disks built into computers, files can be randomly accessed at high speed because the read head inside a drive can jump straight to any file on a disk regardless of its position.

Fact file

AIT Advanced intelligent tape drives and DLT (digital linear tape) drives push tape back-up capacities to over 70GB, but are prohibitively expensive for ordinary users.

Gigabyte (GB) A measure of how much data a disk can store. A gigabyte is 1,000MB.

IDE Refers to the disk controller fitted to most PCs. The most common type is EIDE (enhanced IDE) which permits the attachment of a hard disk, CD-ROM drive and two other storage devices.

SCSI An interface that is seldom fitted to a PC as standard equipment but may be added by slotting a controller card into an internal expansion slot. SCSI may be used for hard disks, tape drives and diskless devices such as scanners.

Streamer Another name for a tape back-up drive, so called because it stores data as a continuous stream of information and not as separately accessible files.

Travan There are five variants of this tape back-up system (with compressed storage capacities from 800MB to 8GB) plus a special high-capacity, high-speed version for network servers.

Buying tips

● Hard disks are very rarely fully packed with data, and program files don't need backing up if you've got them on CD-ROM, which makes it possible to back up a 3GB or 4GB hard disk onto a much smaller removable disk of 1GB.

● As well as storing 120MB on its own disks, a SuperDisk (LS-120) drive is able to read and write ordinary floppies. This makes it a good choice for a PC that has no spare drive bays because it can be installed as a replacement floppy drive.

● Choosing between SCSI, IDE or parallel port drives is not difficult. Buy internal IDE drives for ease of installation or SCSI for slightly faster access. External drives don't have IDE interfaces so choose SCSI for top performance or a parallel port drive if you want to share it between several computers.

Watch out!

The capacity of a tape drive is often quoted as the amount it can store after compression. The true capacity is half the compressed figure. This is misleading because some files compress very well and others, such as program files and compacted JPG graphics, barely compress at all. There is no guarantee that compression will always double the actual storage capacity.

Top five brands

● **Hewlett Packard** 0990 474747
● **Iomega** 0800 973194
● **Seagate** 01628 890366
● **Sony** 0990 424424
● **Imation** 01344 402000

The main advantage of tapes over disks is that they store more data. The most popular tape format, simply because it has been around the longest, is Travan. This can store up to 8GB of compressed data on a single cartridge whereas the most capacious removable disks store only 2GB (4GB using compression). A newer tape format called DAT (digital audio tape) can store 24GB on a tape that costs no more than a single 1GB removable disk, but the drives are expensive.

Iomega, has tried to add some of the advantages of removable disks to its Ditto Max tape drives. These use a tape format called DM-Extra, which provides a maximum of 10GB of compressed storage plus a special 125MB area of the tape that can be accessed in as little as five seconds.

Use the same make

If you choose a removable hard-disk system rather than a tape drive, you should be aware that not all disk systems are compatible. For instance, while you can use 1GB Jaz disks in a 2GB Jaz drive, you can't use 2GB disks in a 1GB drive. So if you want to be able to share disks with others, make sure you all have compatible drives.

When the function of a drive is to store large data files or back up portions of a hard disk instead of its full contents, a Zip or SuperDisk drive should be considered. These store up to 250MB and 120MB respectively, but the disks, based on floppy disk technology, are quite expensive if you need to buy a large quantity.

You should also consider how you want to connect the new drive to your PC. Most tape drives require a SCSI interface, which means buying an adapter card for your PC, whereas removable disk drives can be wired up to USB, SCSI, IDE or parallel port connectors. Drives are made for a single interface so you need to decide which one is best for you before you buy.

Emergency startup

Create a startup floppy disk as a back-up in case you ever have trouble booting your PC.

When you switch on your PC it will boot – load the operating system software from your hard disk. But PCs can also boot from floppy disks. This dates from the days when PCs didn't have hard disks and it was the norm to have to boot from a floppy disk.

Booting from floppy disks is still a useful facility. It allows you to get at your files to correct problems that may prevent Windows from loading. It can also be a convenient way to get to a DOS prompt so that you can run games that don't run under Windows (see pages 89–92).

Windows provides a way to create a boot floppy for use in emergencies. The steps here look at how to make a startup disk and how to use it to boot your PC to a command prompt.

Creating a boot floppy disk

1 To make a startup disk, open Control Panel, run Add/Remove Programs and click on the **Startup Disk** tab. Click on the Create Disk button. Windows will prompt you to insert the Windows CD-ROM. Afterwards, click on OK and Windows will prepare the files to go on the startup disk. Next, Windows will ask you to insert a disk called Windows 98 Startup Disk in drive A:. Make sure the disk is not write-protected – there should be a plastic tab covering the hole at the top right corner – and that it doesn't contain any files you may want later. Click on OK after inserting the disk. Windows will copy to the disk all the files you need to make a startup disk. After the disk has been created, write-protect it to prevent it from being infected by a virus.

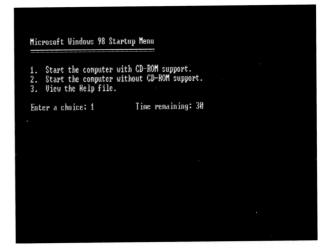

2 How you use your startup disk depends on whether you have **Windows 95** or **98**. The startup disk created by Windows 98 is more useful and easier to use. Whichever version you have, the procedure for starting your PC using the disk is the same. Shut down the PC and turn it off, then put the boot disk in the A: drive and turn it on again. If you have Windows 98 the startup disk will display a menu like the one above. To start the PC and have access to the CD-ROM drive, choose option 1. To start the PC without access to the CD-ROM drive choose option 2. To display a help text file describing the contents of the startup disk and what you can use it for, choose option 3.

Jargon buster

RAM drive An area of memory made to look and act like a disk drive. It has its own drive letter, and you can create and store files on it.

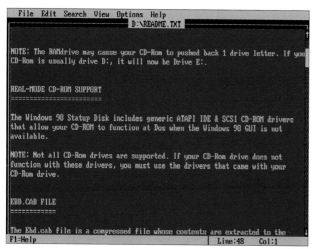

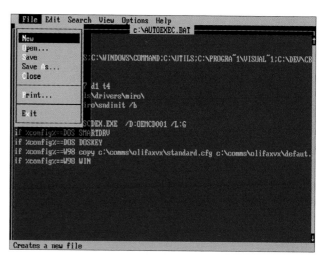

3 The startup disk **Help** is just a text file that is viewed in the MS-DOS Editor. Use the cursor keys to scroll through the text. To close the editor type Alt+F, X. The startup disk uses generic drivers to provide access to your CD-ROM drive. This will work for the great majority of drives, but not all of them. If you cannot access your CD-ROM drive after choosing option 1 from the startup menu, you will need to modify the startup disk so that the drivers specific to your CD-ROM drive are loaded.

The startup disk creates a RAM drive and copies troubleshooting utilities to it. The drive letter for the RAM drive follows on from your hard disks, so if you normally have just a C: drive, the RAM drive will be D:. This means that the letter used for your CD-ROM drive may be different from what it normally is.

5 The tools copied into the RAM drive by the startup disk should be sufficient to enable you or an expert to repair any problems that prevent Windows from loading. One tool included is **ScanDisk**, which you can use to check your hard disk for errors. To run it, type scandisk /all. If you suspect that your hard disk has suffered physical damage you should get ScanDisk to perform a surface test by typing scandisk /all /surface instead.

You can use the MS-DOS Editor to edit configuration files. Just type edit followed by the name of the file, or use the File menu to open the file you want. Edit is similar to Windows Notepad, but there is no mouse support when using the startup disk so you must do everything using the keyboard. Use Alt plus the initial letter of a menu option to pull down a menu, then the highlighted letter to choose an action.

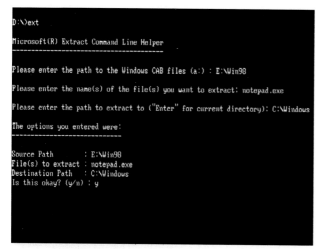

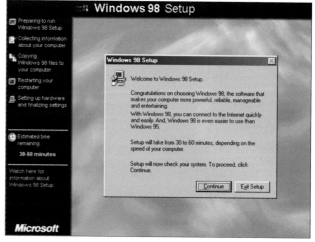

4 The startup disk is useful if you need to restore Windows files that have been damaged or overwritten. To do this, start your PC using the startup disk and choose menu option 1 for CD-ROM support. Place the Windows 98 CD-ROM in your CD-ROM drive. At the command prompt type **ext** and hit Enter. Ext extracts named files from the compressed container files, called cabinet or .cab files, on the Windows CD-ROM.

Enter the location of the .cab files. This will probably be E:\Win98. If your CD-ROM drive, when using the startup disk, has a different drive letter from E, use that letter instead. Next enter the name or names of the files you want to extract. Finally enter the destination location for the files. It is important to get this right. The usual locations are either the main Windows folder, C:\Windows, or the system files folder C:\Windows\System. Ext gives you a chance to check what you have entered is correct. If you answer Y to Is This Okay? the tool will extract the files you requested to your hard disk.

6 If replacing missing or damaged files, or editing configuration files doesn't solve your startup problem, more drastic measures are called for, using some of the other tools on your startup disk. If, during a normal startup, you see an error message about a missing or incorrect operating system, you can replace the operating system from the startup disk by typing sys C:. It is important that you use a startup disk created using the computer that has the problem.

If you want to try reinstalling Windows 98, type **setup**. This will install the operating system over the existing copy. It will preserve most of your existing settings, and will not affect your other applications or data files, but it might preserve the cause of your problem, too. To wipe the hard disk clean and prepare for a fresh installation type format C: /s first. Back up all your important files before you do this, because everything on the hard disk will be lost.

Register it

Protect your computer by making a back-up of its configuration files.

PCs are controlled by an operating system, usually Windows, which must be set up for the hardware that is installed. The hardware can be customised to suit your preferences. These settings are stored in a repository called the Registry or in other data files. Collectively these files are called configuration files.

If your configuration files are lost or damaged your PC may not work correctly. Windows may fail to start, or some of your hardware may not work. The configuration files are therefore important to the health of your PC, and it is a good idea to take steps to protect them. Windows provides tools to help you back up, restore and maintain your configuration files.

Backing up your configuration

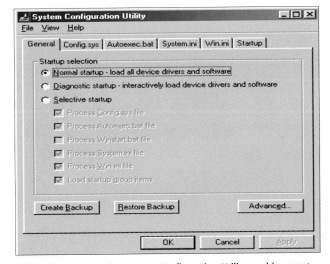

Under Windows 98, the System Configuration Utility enables you to make vital back-up copies of your system files. In addition, it is a useful troubleshooter if things go wrong at startup. The program has a number of check boxes which enable you to pick and choose which parts of the startup procedure are run.

To start the back-up, open the System Information Utility in Programs/System Tools. From the Tools menu select System Configuration Utility. On the General tab select Create Backup to back up your system files or Restore Backup to go back to the previous working settings.

An alternative way to open the program is to go to the Run box on the Start menu. Type msconfig.exe in the dialogue box and click on OK.

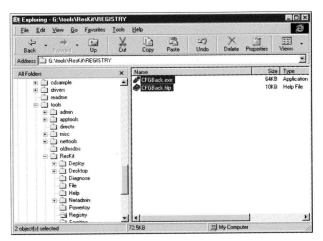

1 One configuration back-up tool you can use yourself is the Microsoft **Configuration Backup Utility** (CFGBACK). This utility, which originally came with Windows 95, is not one of the standard ones accessible from the System Tools section of your Start Menu. It may be available from your Windows CD-ROM. Use Explorer to navigate to the \Tools\ResKit\Registry folder. This folder should contain two files, Cfgback.exe and Cfgback.hlp. Copy these to the Windows folder on your hard disk. Create a shortcut to the Configuration Backup Utility by dragging it to the Desktop. Alternatively, the program can be downloaded from Microsoft's Web site – see tip on page 130.

Back-up tip

Back up your configuration data regularly and often. If you don't, and you need to restore from a back-up which is out of date, important configuration changes made since the back-up was taken will be lost.

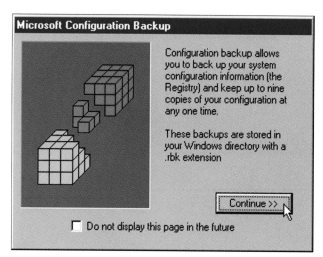

2 The Configuration Backup Utility creates back-up copies of your system **Registry** on your hard disk. The Registry is the most important configuration file. Information in it controls how Windows runs, the look of your Desktop, the preferences used by your applications and many other things. If this information becomes damaged for any reason, Windows or an application may not work. If you have a back-up then you can restore a previous working configuration to solve the problem.

The Configuration Backup Utility lets you keep up to nine copies of your Registry, each with a descriptive name so you know what it is. You can restore any named configuration using the same tool.

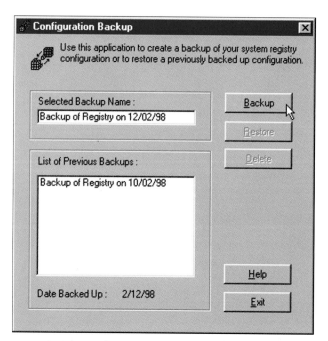

3 Run the Configuration Backup Utility from the Desktop shortcut you created, or by clicking on Start, Run and typing **CFGBACK**. When you start it up, CFGBACK displays some pages that tell you how to back up and restore your configuration. If you do not want to see these pages in the future, check the Do Not Display This Page in Future box. The tool will then start straightaway in its main screen.

Taking a configuration back-up is very simple. Just type a descriptive title for the back-up and click on the Backup button. The utility will ask you to confirm that you want to back up your configuration. If you click on Yes it will then display a progress bar while your configuration is backed up. This usually takes just a couple of minutes.

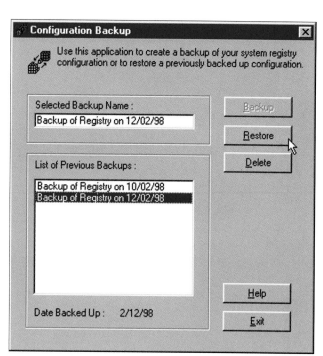

4 To **restore a configuration** from a back-up, run the Configuration Backup Utility as before. This time, select a back-up from the list of previous back-ups, then click Restore. The saved configuration will be copied over the current configuration files, which will take a couple of minutes. When this has finished you will be prompted to shut down and restart the PC.

To delete a saved configuration, select a back-up from the list of previous back-ups and click on Delete. There is no point in keeping very old back-ups because if you restored them, many wanted configuration changes would be lost.

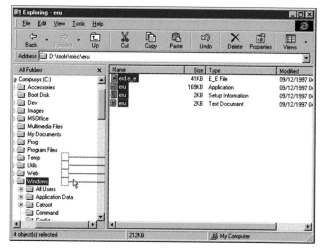

1 Another tool you could use to create back-ups of your configuration files is the **Emergency Recovery Utility** (ERU.) Like the Configuration Backup Utility this is not a standard Windows system tool. You must copy the program from the Windows CD-ROM or the Microsoft Web site.

Load the Windows CD-ROM into your CD-ROM drive. Then use Explorer to navigate to the \Tools\misc\eru folder. This folder should contain four files. Copy these files to the Windows folder on your hard disk. If you want, you can now create a desktop shortcut for the Emergency Recovery Utility by dragging from the application file to the Desktop. Or you can add it to your Start Menu System Tools folder using Start, Settings, Taskbar & Start Menu.

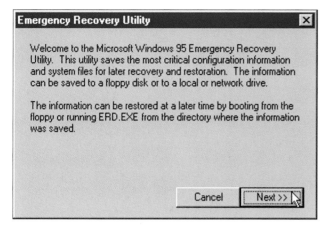

2 The advantage of the Emergency Recovery Utility over the Configuration Backup Utility is that it creates a back-up copy of all your **main configuration files**, not just the Registry. ERU also includes a tool for restoring the backed-up configuration from a command prompt. This is very useful if your current configuration is so damaged that you can't even start Windows in Safe Mode. However, you can't restore a configuration backed up using ERU from within Windows at all, which makes it less convenient as a way of reversing configuration changes that don't actually affect the ability of Windows to start.

Another difference of Emergency Recovery Utility is that it can create a configuration back-up on a floppy disk. However, if it does, the Registry is not backed up because the files are too big to fit on a floppy disk. ERU cannot create a back-up that requires more than one floppy disk to hold all the data.

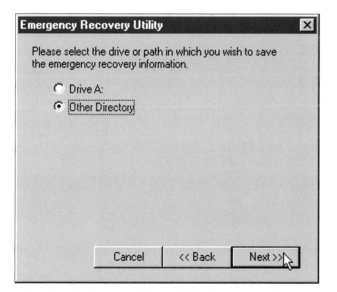

3 Run the Emergency Recovery Utility from your newly created shortcut, or by clicking on Start, Run and typing ERU in the box. The utility is designed like a wizard, so all you have to do is make a choice on each page and then click on Next. The first choice is whether to save the emergency recovery information to floppy disks or a folder on your hard disk. Click on Drive A: to use floppy disks, otherwise click on **Other Directory**.

You cannot back up the Registry files to floppy disk so it is better to save the information to your hard disk. If the folder on your hard disk where the files were saved is inaccessible you probably need more than the Emergency Recovery Utility to get your system running again in any case. You will probably need to restore from a full back-up, which is why these tools should not be viewed as alternatives to backing up your system.

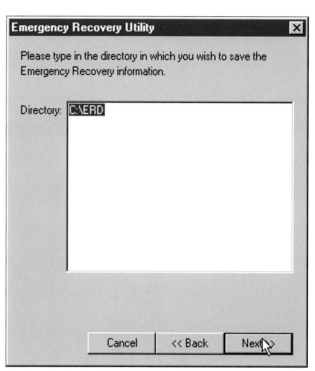

4 The next option you will be asked to specify is the name of the folder in which the emergency recovery information is stored. By default, ERU will use the location **C:\ERD**.

Unlike the Configuration Backup Utility the Emergency Recovery Utility isn't really designed to let you keep multiple configuration file back-ups. You could get round this by specifying different folder names, such as C:\ERD\Config1, C:\ERD\Config2 and so on. However, for most people, storing a single configuration back-up should be sufficient. You can use the Configuration Backup Utility to make regular configuration file back-ups, and update the Emergency Recovery Utility back-up only after you have made major changes to the configuration, such as by installing new hardware.

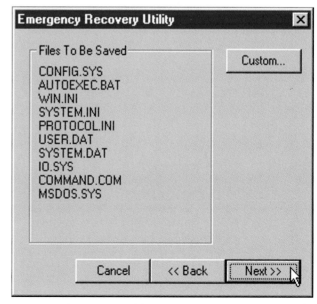

5 On the next page of the Emergency Recovery Utility wizard you will see a list of the **files to be saved** in the back-up. If you are creating the back-up in a folder on your hard disk there is little point in not backing up all of the files listed. The files that take up the most space are the Registry files, but it is still important that these files are backed up.

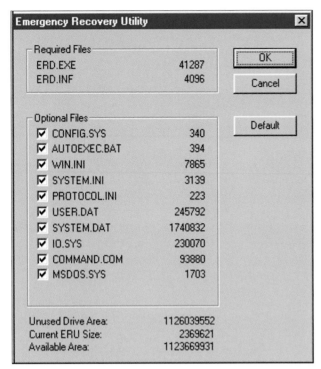

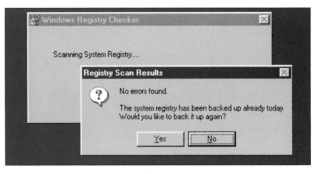

6 If you click on the **Custom button**, the Emergency Recovery Utility will show you a list of all the files that will be included in the configuration back-up, this time with the current size of each file, the total size of the back-up and the space available on the selected drive. If you want to make a floppy disk back-up, you can deselect certain files by clearing the tick in the check box alongside them, until you have a back-up set that will fit onto the floppy disk.

1 The Registry is so important that Windows 98 has yet another tool for looking after it. The **Windows Registry Checker** scans your system Registry for errors, and allows you to make a back-up of it. The Registry Checker should already be on your hard disk in the Windows folder, but it doesn't appear on any menu. To run it click on Start, Run and type Scanregw in the Open box. If you like, make a shortcut to Scanregw.exe in your Accessories, System Tools menu.

The Registry Checker checks to see whether the Registry is damaged at all. It cannot tell if the data is intact but invalid, so it cannot cure all problems related to the Registry. If no errors are found, the Registry Checker displays a message box asking whether you want to back up the Registry or not. The registry is automatically backed up when Windows starts.

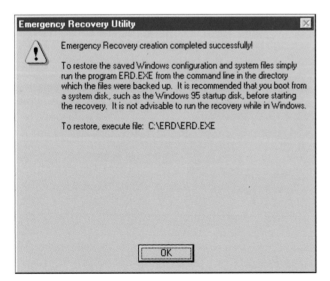

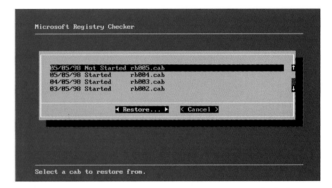

7 Click on Next again and Emergency Recovery Utility will begin copying your configuration files to the back-up directory. It will also create the ERD program needed to restore them. When it has finished it will display a message box containing instructions on how to restore your configuration from this back-up should you need to.

To **restore a configuration**, use the Windows boot menu or your startup disk to boot to a command prompt. Then type the command shown in the message, for example C:\ERD\ERD.EXE. The program will ask you to confirm whether you want to restore the configuration files. If you type Y and press Enter the configuration will be restored.

2 The Registry Checker has a complementary tool which you can run from a command prompt if you have Registry problems that prevent Windows from starting. If this happens, boot to a command prompt, type Scanreg and hit Enter. The text-based interface lets you check the Registry, make a back-up or view and restore from previous back-ups. Registry back-ups are stored as .cab files (a compressed format) and Registry Checker shows you the date the back-ups were made so you can pick one that pre-dates the problem. For an even easier way to solve Registry problems from the command prompt, type **Scanreg/restore**, which will restore from the previous day's back-up, or **Scanreg/fix**, which will attempt to fix any problems in the current Registry.

Back-up tip

If you are unable to locate the Configuration Backup Utility or the Emergency Recovery Utility, you can obtain them from Microsoft's Web site. The Configuration Backup Utility is at http://support.microsoft.com/support/downloads/dp1702.asp and the Emergency Recovery Utility is at http://support.microsoft.com/support/downloads/dp1704.asp

Data protection basics

Protecting your PC from physical damage or theft is important, but protecting data is absolutely vital.

Your PC is valuable but the data and programs it contains are worth even more. If your computer is stolen or irreparably damaged in an accident you might be insured for its full replacement value, but however generous the compensation, it won't begin to cover the real cost of your lost data.

Time machine

What can never be replaced is the time you put into getting your PC to work properly and into creating, collating and entering data. Even on a domestic computer system there'll be letters, household accounts, homework projects and all manner of documents that could take ages to retype – and then only if you're lucky enough to have printed copies to work from.

Reconstituting the data on a business system for which there's no back-up might be impossible, unless scrupulous paper records have been kept. At best it's an expensive and time-consuming process.

Configure it out

Entering data is a tedious enough affair, but you might also have to spend days or weeks reinstalling programs, customising them and creating templates and report layouts for your word processor, spreadsheet and other software. So while protecting your PC against total loss or theft is important, preserving your system configuration and data is vital.

Plan ahead

Fortunately, there are many precautions that you can take without spending anything at all, and some of them are described on the following pages. If you're also prepared to make a few relatively minor investments in security hardware and software, you should be able to sleep peacefully.

You will need

ESSENTIAL
Software Security software like anti-virus, encryption and recovery programs can be bought separately or in suites such as McAfee's Nuts & Bolts and Symantec's Norton Utilities.
Hardware A PC system running Windows can be made reasonably secure but additional hardware such as a removable tape or disk back-up drive is highly recommended.

Physical security

Supplied by Boss at www.boss-int.co.uk

Lockable cables are a cheap form of security that's not too expensive for home use. Several pieces of equipment can be protected by a single cable, yet still be easily moved when required.

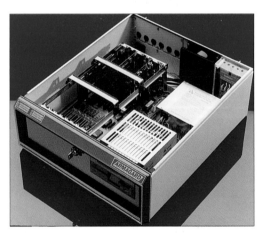

Disk drive locking devices prevent the use of unauthorised software and protect against intrusive fingers and objects.

Motion-sensitive alarms are great if somebody hears them, but there's always the danger thieves will trash equipment to silence the alarm.

There is plenty of equipment you can buy to protect your hardware and software from damage or theft.

If your home is broken into and you lose your TV, hi-fi or camera, the cost of replacement should be covered by the sort of all-risks policy provided by reputable insurance companies.

There are also insurance policies which will cover against the cost of restoring stolen or fire-damaged computers, programs and data. But it's small compensation for the immense effort needed to get the new systems up and running smoothly.

There are firms that offer back-ups or storage of critical data over the Web, so it can easily be retrieved in an emergency. Some also provide a disaster recovery service where replacement computers can be delivered within hours.

Anti-theft devices

The main risks to PCs are theft, fire and accidental damage. In business, you take the same measures to protect against opportunistic theft by employees as you would to safeguard other items of business equipment. These include asset tagging and security marking, securing rooms and kit when not in use, and implementing access control to keep staff or visitors straying from public areas into offices.

Insurance tip

In the UK, the Association of British Insurers advises those who think that their computer equipment is covered by a household policy to check the terms of the policy regarding high-value items. Typically, cover is limited to around £1,500 per item, but many insurers regard a computer system as a single item and the value of a PC, printer, scanner and other peripherals taken together is almost certain to exceed the single item limit on many insurance policies.

Disclosing your possession of a high-value computer system to your insurance company does not necessarily result in increased premiums unless you specifically want to cover the uninsured risk, which costs much the same as additional cover for jewellery, pictures and other high-value items.

Though not the prettiest of security devices, an equipment cage **is highly effective and it's the form of security preferred by insurance companies.**

Professional theft is the most difficult to prevent. Keeping thieves out of your premises is the highest priority but, assuming that a determined thief will gain entry, individual items of equipment can be protected. Most systems involve fixing the computer to something that's immovable or difficult to move, such as a desk or workstation. This can be done using a cabling system that connects several pieces of equipment to a single locking point.

Cage it

Another approach is to lock equipment directly to work surfaces using bolts or industrial adhesives. This is an effective but drastic step that makes PCs hard to service and may invalidate manufacturers' warranties. It's more common to bolt steel security cages around equipment. Cages are available that allow PCs to be used even with the cage in place. Motion-sensitive alarms can be attached internally or externally to key items of kit, but these are of little benefit if there's nobody around to hear them.

In the home, cable systems or alarms are the practical choices. When fitting a cable security device, it's important that it should also prevent the removal of the case because thieves are just as likely to take valuable processors, memory and hard disks as they are to remove a complete system.

Fire precautions

There are no specific fire risks attached to PC equipment, which is protected by whatever standard fire prevention measures apply to the rest of a building. What is important is to protect the data that's stored on PCs. The key concern in the event of a fire is to protect back-up tapes or disks so they are not destroyed along with the PC itself.

In business, this means a fireproof safe, which also protects against the loss of back-ups through theft. A specialist fireproof safe need not be too expensive because tapes and disks are not bulky. Fireproof safes do not cost a huge amount of money and can be accommodated almost anywhere.

In the home, where a fireproof safe may not be necessary, store back-up media in a room as far away as possible from the PC itself. The total destruction of buildings through fire is not common so this may be enough to preserve your back-ups.

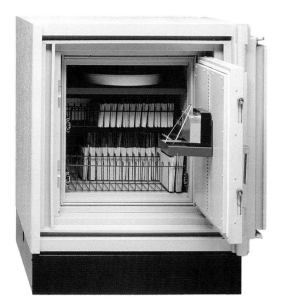

A fire safe **makes sure that your back-ups don't get fried along with your computer.**

Virus tip

Accidents can happen in the home where dogs chew cables and small children poke unsuitable objects into disk drives. But the worst type of accident, because it's the hardest to correct, is introducing a computer virus by installing software from dubious sources. Fitting locks to the floppy and CD-ROM drives of a PC is one solution, but it should be augmented with anti-virus software, which will also guard against viruses downloaded from the Internet.

Keep it private

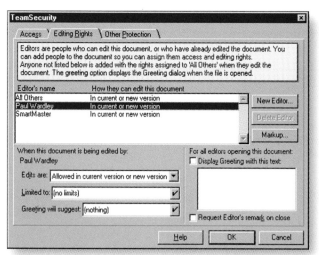

Password options in Lotus Word Pro, the word processing module of SmartSuite, are very sophisticated. Access them through File, Save (or Save As) and click the Protect File button.

In Helix's Nuts & Bolts, Stronghold is an encryption program for any type of file. The DES algorithm is a standard encryption method developed by IBM and the US government. Stronghold can be set to shred a file after encoding it. Helix is now owned by McAfee.

Jargon buster

Executable This is just a fancy synonym for program, although it has a rather specialised meaning in terms of file encryption. An executable is a program you can run on any computer, regardless of what other programs are installed. The significance is that if you encode a file as an executable, the recipient doesn't need a copy of the encryption program to read it.

Keep your data safe from prying eyes using password protection and encryption technology.

Preventing others from seeing what's on your PC isn't paranoia and doesn't mean you've got something to hide. If you use your PC to write personal letters, for instance, you may not want other people who use the same PC to read them.

On a home PC there might be information you'd rather your children didn't read. They've probably got secrets they don't want you to see either. In business there could be commercially sensitive data that not everybody in the company needs to know. Businesses also have a legal obligation to maintain the confidentiality of personnel information and client records governed by the Data Protection Act.

Passwords

On a network, security is the responsibility of an administrator who will implement a system of passwords so that users see just what they're supposed to see. There's nothing to stop users protecting their PCs with passwords too, and the same techniques can be used on single PCs.

The easiest way to stop unauthorised users from reading your files is to use a password-protected screensaver. This won't stop dedicated snoopers from starting your PC with a floppy disk but it deters the merely curious.

The next level of protection is to password protect your files. Because passwords are not a feature of Windows, you set them in programs' Save dialogue boxes. Password facilities vary, but there is always an option to stop people loading a file without the password. It may also be possible to set levels of restricted access, such as being able to read but not change a file.

Secret messages

To stop someone bypassing your passwords by opening protected files with a different program, when you set a password it also scrambles the structure of a file so that even if an expert opens it with another editor, the contents are junk.

If you need to encrypt a file from a program without its own password facility, you'll have to use an encryption utility (see pages 144–6). These are available separately or as part of utility suites such as McAfee's Nuts and Bolts. Coded files can be turned into executables and sent safely by e-mail. The recipient runs the program and enters a password you've provided to decode the documents within.

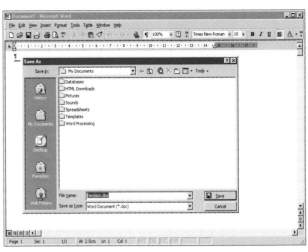

3 To assign a password to a file in **Microsoft Word** choose Save or Save As from the File menu. Type in a file name and then select Tools/General Options.

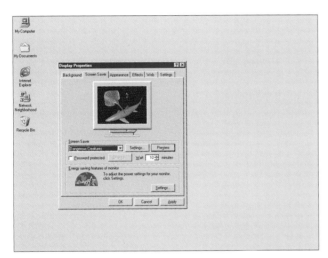

1 To install a **password-protected screensaver** right-click on the Desktop to bring up the Display Properties box. Click on the Screen Saver tab and choose a saver from the list. If there are no screensavers listed, install them using Add New Programs in the Windows Control Panel. They're in Accessories.

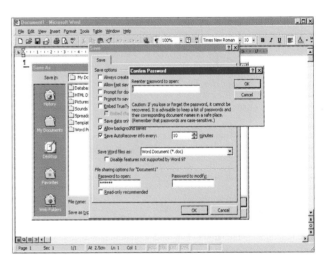

4 Type a password in the **Password to Open** box if you want to restrict access to those who know the password. Type one in the Password to Modify box if you want to let people open but not edit the file. When you click on OK you're asked to confirm the password.

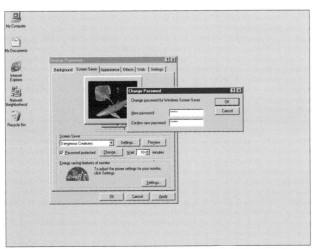

2 Tick the box next to the words Password protected and then click on the Change button. Enter your password in the **New Password box**. Confirm it in the box below (this is just to make sure you haven't misspelled it) and click on OK.

Watch out!

For the ultimate in confidentiality, store work on removable disks and keep them locked away. But if you work from a hard disk and simply copy the finished file onto a removable disk and then delete the original from the hard disk, you leave behind an invisible image of your work that a data thief can use to reconstruct the file.

When you delete a file you are simply removing its name from the hard disk's index. The pattern of letters and words it contained is still on the disk and can be recovered. Symantec's Norton Utilities includes a utility to unerase files in this way, and you don't need to be an expert to use it.

The solution is to not just delete your files but shred them too. For this you'll need a file shredding program to overwrite its image on disk. But don't shred a file unless you're sure you'll never need it again.

When to back up

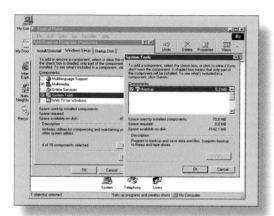

Microsoft Backup is part of Windows 98. If it's not on your system you can install it through Windows Control panel. Select Add/Remove programs then Windows Setup. You'll find it under System Tools.

Iomega Jaz disks can be used to run programs and store data as well as to make back-ups.

Back-up tips

● **Back-up sets** A common mistake is to have only one set of back-up tapes. If your system develops a problem and you don't notice it, there's a possibility when using a single back-up set that you'll copy a damaged system over a good back-up. Keep at least two sets of tapes or disks and use them in rotation.

● **Disk organisation** To make backing up easier, keep your data separate from your programs. Keep all your data in a single folder such as My Documents, or, better still, when you're setting up a PC, split the hard disk into two partitions and keep programs on one and data on the other. You can then back up complete partitions or folders without having to select individual files.

● **Incremental back-ups** Save time by using incremental back-ups. The first back-up you make should be a full one that includes everything on a disk. For subsequent back-ups, copy just the files that have changed or been added to.

Make backing up a regular task and you could be up and running again sooner than you think.

Back-ups are the first line of defence against the total loss of your programs and data. Should there be a disaster – your computer is destroyed or stolen, for instance – you can duplicate your previous system within a few hours of getting a new machine. This involves having a regular back-up schedule. The professionals recommend a weekly back-up cycle of the material you want to have safe. During the rest of the week you should do incremental back-ups – that is, save the files which have changed.

These incremental back-up files are appended to the full back-up. The following week follow the same procedure but use a different set of back-up tapes. The system can be damaged without you noticing and you could end up copying bad files over good.

Extra precautions

It's also important to decide what to back up. Many people back up their data, but not their programs on the basis that if anything happens these can be reinstalled from the original program disks or CD-ROMs. But these can be destroyed or stolen too. Even if they aren't it is an undertaking to install a

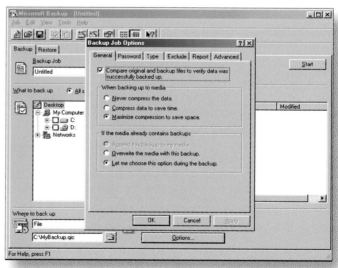

It is a good idea to include the Windows registry with the full back-up, although it can be done separately. In Backup Job Options, click on the Advanced tab and check Back up Windows registry.

full set of programs. Setting up Internet accounts, installing upgrades and utilities and re-establishing program settings and preferences can take days. It is worth doing a program back-up once a month.

Although you can back up the Windows registry separately, it is as well to include it in any back-up. To do so, click on the options button or go to Job on the menu and select Options. Select the Advanced tab and tick the Backup Windows Registry (see pages 127–30).

A tape drive is an inexpensive, reliable back-up medium but high-capacity, removable drives such as the Iomega Jaz or Syquest Syjet are more versatile (see pages 18–19 and 112–13).

Syquest Syjet disks cost more than tapes, but they are more versatile and can store up to 2GB.

If you are worried that others could access files if the back-up tape falls into the wrong hands, you can password-protect access. In Backup Job Options, click the Password tab, select Protect this back-up with a password and enter the appropriate details.

In the hurry of the working day it can be difficult to remember to run a back-up, but Windows can help. Regular tasks can be scheduled so that the program will run automatically at a set time.

To schedule a task go to Start, Programs, Accessories, System Tools and Scheduled Tasks. Click on Add Scheduled Task and it launches a wizard which takes you step-by-step through the process of setting up a new task.

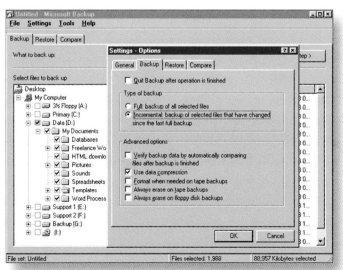

Microsoft Backup makes full back-ups by default. Once you've made one of these, switch to incremental back-ups to speed things up. From the Settings menu select Options and then the Backup tab. Change Type of Backup from Full to Incremental. Click on OK.

Multiple users

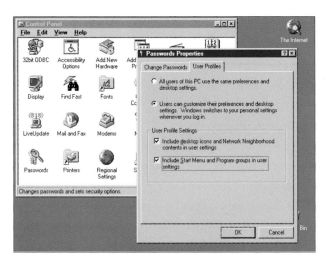

1 To make it safer to let your kids loose on your PC set up a **password control system**. Double-click on the Passwords icon in Windows Control Panel. When the Passwords Properties box appears, click on the User profiles tab. Click on the radio button that permits users to customise their preferences and then tick the two boxes underneath. Click on OK.

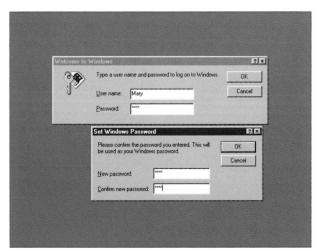

2 Windows has to be restarted before passwords can be used. When it restarts enter the name of a child and a password in the **Welcome to Windows** dialogue box. Click on OK and then confirm the password in a second dialogue box. If the password is not identical it won't be accepted.

Password tip

Desktop icons that are not shortcuts can't be deleted in the usual way. But a utility called TweakUI, which for Windows 98 is found in the Tools menu, Reskit and then Powertoy, can prevent them appearing on the Desktop.

Set up your system so children or colleagues can only see files or programs you want them to see.

Connecting PCs on a network is a great way of sharing resources. Networking systems have access controls built in, and there's usually an expert around to set things up properly. But it's crucial for users to know how to restrict access to personal folders they don't want to share.

Personal files

To restrict access to folders on a network use My Computer to select the folder to protect. In the File menu, click on Properties (or right-click on a disk or folder) and select Sharing. Type a password that people must have in order to be able to read or write to the folder.

There are no similar mechanisms to restrict people who share a single PC. Adults sharing a PC are unlikely to tamper with another person's work, although they might browse around the system to see what others are doing. Setting passwords on files when they're saved is the best way of protecting against such intrusions. (See page 135 for help with setting passwords.)

No children

It's much harder to protect a system that's used by children who might inadvertently start programs and accidentally delete important files. There are plenty of programs you can use to set up password-protected, simplified Windows systems that children may safely use. Kid Desk is one of the better ones.

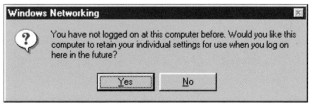

3 A message box appears asking if the new user wants to retain **personalised settings** to be used at every log on. Click on Yes. Windows will finish loading and any changes you make to the icons on the Desktop and the programs on the Start menu will now be preserved for this child only.

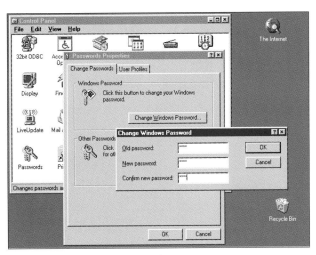

You can achieve a degree of protection by defining personal Windows settings for children. The process is shown here, but it's not perfect. It lets you remove software from the Desktop and Start menus, but doesn't stop talented kids from browsing My Computer or starting programs from the Start menu's Run prompt.

6 Repeat steps 2 to 5 for each child or individual who will use the PC and don't forget to make a careful note of the passwords. Every time Windows starts, it displays the name of the most recent user and prompts for a password. Other users can overtype the displayed name with their own and passwords can be changed at any time by clicking on **Passwords** in the Windows Control Panel.

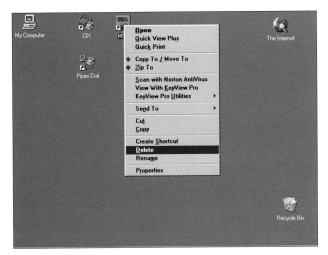

4 Start by **removing** the Desktop icons you don't want your child to use. Obvious candidates are shortcuts to Internet access, spreadsheets and databases. To remove an icon right-click on it and select Delete from the context menu.

Jargon buster

● **Peer-to-peer network** A simple network in which no single computer is in control. PCs connected in this way can share their resources (disks and printers) through a Network Neighbourhood icon on the desktop.

● **Read and write access** If you share a folder with users on a network and allow read access to your files they may be viewed but not modified. If you allow write access, other users can change the contents of your files.

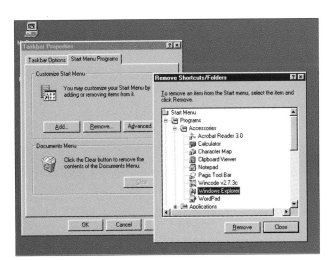

5 To remove programs from the Start menu, right-click on the taskbar at the bottom of the screen and select Properties. Click on the tab marked **Start Menu Programs** and then the Remove button. In the Remove Shortcuts/Folders box highlight the Start menu groups and individual programs you don't want the child to use and click on Remove after each one. It's a good idea to deny access to Windows Explorer.

Copyright

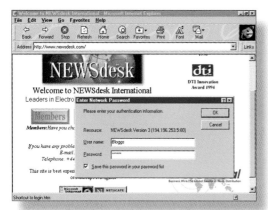

Passwords are fairly common on commercial Web sites, especially ones where you have to sign up and pay a fee, but you can use them to preserve the confidentiality of your site.

Prevention can be better than cure when it comes to enforcing copyright. Who'd want two sample tracks of a CD in low-fidelity mono when for a small amount you can have the entire CD in stereo?

Protect the information on your Web site by claiming copyright or issuing passwords to people you trust.

If you want to protect information on a Web site from indiscriminate use by others, you should claim copyright. Under the Universal Copyright and Berne Conventions this is straightforward. All you do is display, in a prominent position, the word copyright and a © symbol, along with the name of the copyright owner and the year of publication. The first page of a Web site is prominent enough for a copyright notice, but if you'd rather put it on its own page you can link to it from other pages.

Keep out

Copyright applies to pictures, sounds and music as well as the written word, but you can't copyright your thoughts. So if someone expresses ideas from your Web page in different words you can't do anything about it.

In practice, it's so easy to cut and copy data from a Web page that whatever rights you claim, it's very difficult to assert them. If you really want to prevent people from using your material, as you would on a Web site intended for a closed group of users, the safest way is to require visitors to enter a password on the first page of a site and issue passwords only to those you can trust. A site password is a specialised type of input form which can be created with Web design programs like Microsoft Front Page or Claris Home Page.

Jargon buster

● **Hierarchical passwords** A system of multiple passwords in which the PC system is regarded as a layered structure. Each layer has a password so you can control how deeply staff can delve by restricting their passwords to specific layers.

● **QIC/Travan** These are the two most common types of back-up tape drive. There are several variants of each type and their tapes are not compatible. When comparing the stated capacities of drive/tape combinations, check that the figures are for uncompressed data. Compression squeezes up to twice as much onto a tape but at the expense of speed.

Power problems

Protect your PC and computer equipment from unexpected surges or cuts in the electricity supply.

If you're lucky, you've probably never known the sense of despair that comes from spending hours working on your computer, only to have it crash just when you go to hit the Save button. While there are lots of things that can cause a crash, one of the most annoying is a power problem.

Lightning strikes

A nearby lightning strike, a momentary flicker of the lights or a complete power cut can affect your computer. The result could be a simple crash or everything switching off at a crucial moment. Either way, you stand to lose whatever you're working on, and potentially much more. Not shutting your system down properly can damage your hard disk resulting in the loss of other data you have saved. There are other risks. Your modem can be damaged by lightning striking the phone line, which could potentially damage other parts of your computer too, if it's not properly protected.

Are you at the mercy of the phone and electricity companies? Fortunately not. There are a lot of things you can use to protect your PC and other equipment, in the shape of surge suppressors and uninterruptible power supplies (UPSs).

Spiky stuff

Surge suppressors do more or less what you'd expect them to. They contain special components that prevent serious spikes in the electrical supply from reaching your PC. They're also available in versions designed to plug into your phone line, protecting modems and fax machines.

The smallest suppressors are slightly larger than an ordinary plug. You fit them on the cable of your computer instead of a plug, and it's instantly protected. There are larger suppressors that the existing cable can plug into, and even multi-way connectors with up to six sockets, so you can connect all your computer equipment, such as printers, scanners and monitors.

Top five brands

● **APC Smart-UPS XL** These are some of the most popular line-interactive UPS systems around, available in a wide range of sizes to suit anything from a small desktop PC to a server. www.apcc.com

● **APC PowerChute Plus** If you want to make the most of a UPS, this software lets it do more than just take over when the mains supply fails. It can test the batteries so you know when they need replacing, calculate how much time you have left, and even be programmed to let your computer stay on until there's a predetermined amount of battery power left. www.apcc.com

● **Belkin SurgeMaster** This is a low cost six-way connector block that will protect all your computer equipment from surges. It also has a socket for protecting your phone line, so you can make sure the modem is safe. www.action.com

● **OPTI-UPS** These offer uninterruptible power for PCs, covering blackouts, surges, and other power blips. They also have power management software, OPTI-SAFE+, which saves data in the event of power failure. www.opti-ups.com

● **Liebert PowerSure** This is a compact offline UPS designed for single computers, in a range of sizes, with upgrade options and replaceable batteries. www.liebert.com

Buying tips

● Check the ratings of your equipment and of the UPS. UPS ratings are usually quoted in VA, which is roughly the same as the rating in W on the back of your PC.

● Find out how long the UPS will run. Is it long enough to shut down your PC easily and safely?

● Is software supplied to run on your computer that will let the UPS tell it to shut down when the power fails, so everything is safe, even if you're away from your desk?

● How long do the batteries in the UPS last, and can you replace them easily, or will you have to buy a whole new unit?

● Does the UPS or surge protector have a connector for protecting a phone line, to look after your modem or fax machine?

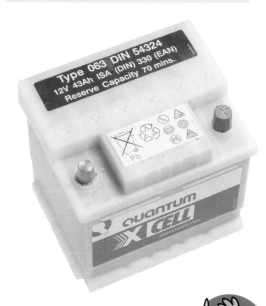

Fact file

● **Line interactive** A type of UPS that continuously monitors the power supply to even out surges and dips.

● **Online** A type of UPS that creates clean power continuously.

● **Run time** The number of minutes for which a UPS will supply power at a stated number of VA.

● **Standby** A type of UPS that switches to battery power when the mains supply fails.

● **VA (Volt Amps)** A rating of how much power a UPS can supply. Similar to Watts (W).

● **W (Watts)** The amount of power consumed by a piece of computer equipment. You'll usually find this on a label near the power connector.

Constant power

UPSs are much more complicated. As the name implies, they promise to provide constant power to your computer. They have a battery inside them which takes over in the event of the mains power supply failing. They contain circuitry to boost the battery power to the required level, and to monitor how much battery life is left.

There's more than one type of UPS. Your choice depends on what you want to use them for. Offline or standby UPSs simply pass mains power to your computer, switching to battery when the mains fails. These are the simplest and cheapest sort, but they don't usually incorporate surge suppression.

If you use an online UPS, the power that your computer receives is created by the UPS all the time, either from the mains supply, or from the battery. This means you always have a perfectly clean power supply, with no surges, no dips and no interruptions. Online UPSs are more expensive.

The most common UPSs in use are inline or line-interactive. These are a cross between standby and online UPSs, which constantly monitor the power supply to your PC, evening out surges and dips. Most of the power comes directly from the mains, unless there's a power cut.

Shut down safely

How you choose to protect your computer depends on what you are doing with it. If you simply play games, you will probably feel that all you need is a surge suppressor to protect your system from damage. If you work at home, a cheap offline UPS that can run your system for long enough for you to shut it down safely when the power fails should do the trick. But if you want to protect a server that's providing files to other computers, then it's worth looking for a unit that's better protected, like a line-interactive UPS.

Check to see what sort of battery life is being offered. You need to match the size of the UPS you choose to the equipment you're hoping to protect. Just as there's little point putting the battery from a Ford Fiesta into a large truck, so there is little point having a small UPS to protect two computers, a printer, a scanner and a modem. The battery will go flat in no time.

Before choosing a power supply, check the power ratings on the back of your equipment to see how much electricity they consume and bear in mind that this is usually a worst-case figure. If you have a computer you simply have to have on all the time, buy the biggest UPS you can afford, to try to outlast all but the longest power cuts.

Restricted access

Restrict what different family members can see and do on your PC.

Windows is designed to be used not just by private individuals on their personal computers but by people in offices and large corporations too. In a business environment, computers are usually managed by specialist staff, who set up the hardware and software for the users. In that kind of environment, the people who manage the computers don't want the users to tinker with the settings. Windows includes a tool called the System Policy Editor that allows them to remove various features from the view of the user.

If your PC is used by all the family, with the System Policy Editor you can restrict the options available under each user profile in a more comprehensive way than by using just password protection (see pages 138–9).

Using System Policy Editor

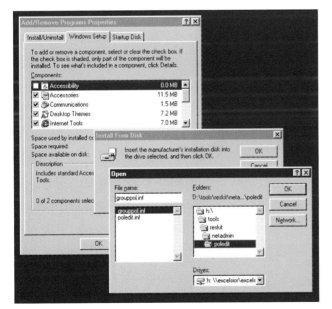

The System Policy Editor is not installed as standard by Windows, so before you can use it you must install it from the Windows CD. Open Control Panel, double-click on the **Add/Remove Programs** icon, click on the Windows Setup tab and then Have Disk. In the Install From Disk dialogue box click on Browse, then navigate to D:\Tools\Reskit\Netadmin\Poledit (if D: is your CD-ROM drive). Select Poledit.inf, then click on OK twice to close the dialogue boxes. The Have Disk dialogue box will appear. Select System Policy Editor and click on Install. The System Policy Editor will be installed on the Start menu under Programs, Accessories, System Tools. Launch the System Policy Editor by running it from this menu.

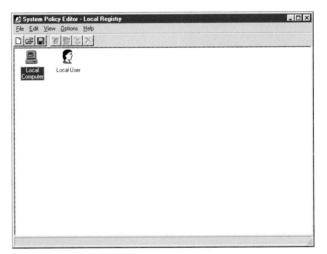

The System Policy Editor is designed to allow system administrators to create sets of restrictions called **policies** that can then be applied to various groups of users on a network. This method of applying restrictions is inappropriate for use on a home computer system, so some of the options of the program will not be needed.

On a single computer you can use Windows' System Policy Editor to make alterations that immediately affect that computer. You do that by editing the Registry. From the File menu, select Open Registry. As the name suggests, the changes that the System Policy Editor makes are recorded in the Registry.

The System Policy Editor provides an easier and safer way to make these changes than the Registry Editor does. But it is still a good idea to back up your configuration before making any changes, in case you want to change things back to how they were and can't remember how to do it (see pages 127–30). Take note that the changes you make will affect only the particular user profile you are currently logged in on.

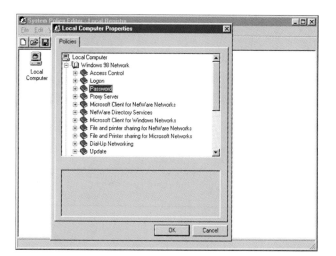

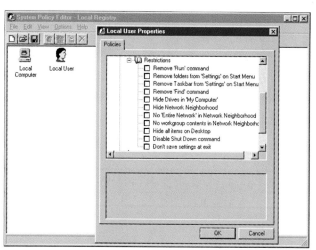

 When you open the Registry in the System Policy Editor you will see two icons: **Local Computer** and **Local User**. Local Computer lets you make changes that affect the PC and all users. To see what properties you can change, double-click on the icon. The Local Computer Properties dialogue box displays the properties which you can change as a collapsible tree. There are two main branches: Network and System.

Most of the options that it may be useful to change using the System Policy Editor are under Local User. Double-click on the icon to see the options available. The only settings available under Network determine whether the user can share their files and printer with others. Under **System**, the options are Shell, Control Panel, Desktop Display and Restrictions. Under Shell, Restrictions are settings that let you remove certain Windows options from view. For example, you can remove the Run command from the Start Menu, which would help prevent someone running programs other than those that are actually on the Start Menu. To stop your carefully arranged Desktop layout from being messed up you could check the box against Don't Save Settings At Exit.

The Control Panel settings let you deny a user access to Control Panel icons. You can specify which tabs of that control panel the user is allowed to see. The Desktop Display settings can be used to enforce a particular Desktop wallpaper and colour scheme.

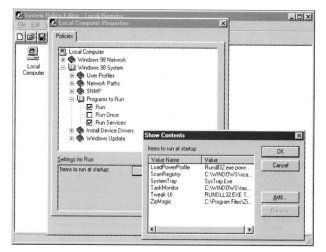

 You will not want to change many of the options under System. You can disable User Profiles, which is useful if having tried them you want to revert to having a single default login. The Network Paths and SNMP options are only for networked PCs, and the Install Device Drivers and Windows Update options are useful only to system administrators.

If you expand the **Programs To Run** item, select one of the Run options and click on the Show button that appears in the panel below, you'll see the Show Contents dialogue box listing programs Windows runs at startup. You can remove a program from the list by selecting it and clicking on Remove. Don't do this unless you are sure a program is not required, or is causing a problem. Most of the programs in this list are run for a good purpose.

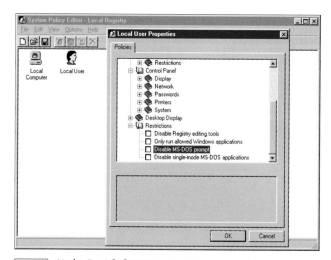

 Under **Restrictions** you can prevent a user from using Registry editing tools. Once you've done this, you won't be able to edit the Registry to change the setting back again. You can also remove access to the MS-DOS prompt — a back door way for the more knowledgeable user to run forbidden programs.

The most powerful restriction is Only Run Allowed Windows Applications. After enabling this option, click on Show and create a list of programs that the user is allowed to run. The list must consist of program names like winword.exe and excel.exe. Once you have used this option, any attempt to run a program that isn't listed will result in the message This Operation Has Been Cancelled Due To Restrictions In Effect On This Computer being displayed. Unless you allow poledit.exe you won't be able to change any of the settings for this profile ever again, so if you try this do be very careful.

PolEdit tip

To have a program run at startup using a method that other users of your PC can't easily tamper with, use PolEdit to add the program name to the Run list under Local Computer, System, Programs to Run.

Encrypt it

You can keep all your private files safe from prying eyes with encryption software.

'Innocent people have nothing to hide' is a popular saying, but anyone who's ever kept a diary, or thought about looking for a new job before leaving the one they are in knows that's not strictly true. There are lots of times when you might not want other people to know all about what you're doing.

Keep it private

Now that so many people use computers for just about everything, it's not always simple to keep things as private as you might like. While you can lock a diary in your desk drawer or tuck it under the mattress, or keep a love letter with you all the time, what do you do with the job application you're writing on the PC, or the invitations to the surprise party for your partner's birthday? Or maybe you want to send information over the Internet, and don't want to risk it being read by prying eyes along the way.

Whatever your reasons, there is a way to keep information private when it's stored on a computer. It's called encryption, and it can be a very useful tool, whatever the reason you have for wanting to keep your information private – although see the box called *Encryption Issues* on page 146 to check the legal situation.

Cracking the code

Encryption is the use of cryptography, the science of making and breaking codes. When you encrypt something, what you're doing is turning it from one format into another. For example, the simplest form might be just moving every letter one space to the left in the alphabet, turning 'apple' into 'zookd'.

Of course, that sort of encryption would be very easy to turn back into the original text, so there are much more sophisticated techniques available. Most of these work using a system called Public Key Cryptography. That's where you have two keys which can be used on

The **RSA system** is used by Web browsers, office e-mail systems and many other programs.

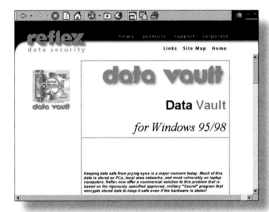

Data Vault can divide your hard drive into a number of 'safes', all of which can be encrypted and password protected. If you need to leave your PC for a while, any open 'safes' can be locked to keep your information secure until you return.

Encryption issues

Encryption can certainly be useful, but there are times when people would rather that the information they want to see was freely available. Law enforcement agencies, for example, may want to check the e-mail messages being sent between different people as part of an investigation into something illegal.

Obviously, if a message is encrypted, that's much more difficult, and in some cases, either impossible or so time-consuming as to mean that there's no point trying.

Working on the principle that innocent people have nothing to hide, some countries have strict laws that regulate the use of encryption. In some cases, that means that you can access only what are called weak systems, which the authorities will be able to crack easily.

Other countries rely on a system called key escrow, which means they can use encryption, but you have to give a trusted agency, possibly part of the government, the key that can be used to decode your messages if a court orders it. Some countries outlaw encryption completely, so if you decide to download and use an encryption program, you could run the risk of prosecution.

In the UK there are no restrictions on using encryption programs at the time of writing, but the issue is under review and may change.

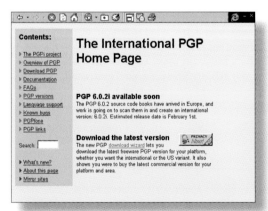

Pretty Good Privacy offers a simple encryption system that is suitable for e-mail.

Where to go

- ● **RSA** www.rsa.com
- ● **Data Vault** www.reflex-magnetics.co.uk
- ● **PGP** www.pgpi.com

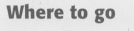

your messages, a public one, and a private one. If you want to send information to someone, you look up their public key, and use that to turn the information into a code. It can only be decoded by using the private key. You can also use your private key to sign a message; by checking it against your public key, people will know that something is really from you.

The key is the key

If that sounds complicated, imagine it like this: you have a message in English, and want it to be hard for people to read. Your public key is an English to German dictionary, so anyone can turn a message into German and send it to you. If you're the only person with a German to English dictionary, it'll be very hard, but not impossible, for anyone who sees the encoded message to work out what it means.

Encryption can be broken. For example, the encryption used by the majority of Web browsers outside the US can be broken in just 22 hours using powerful computers. The strength of encryption is measured in bits. The more bits the encryption software uses, the harder it is to break the code, so when you're looking at software to keep things private, check how many bits it uses. Web browsers typically use 56 bits, but 128 is much more secure.

Web encryption

One of the most well-known encryption companies is called RSA, which licenses its encryption to many firms. It's the RSA system that's used in Web browser, office e-mail systems and lots of other programs. The company also provides a good Web site where you can find out more about encryption.

What other software is available for encryption? One of the most popular programs is called Pretty Good Privacy, and you can find information about it at www.pgpi.com. It's a simple program that can be used to turn a file into an encrypted form which you can then send via e-mail. There are other similar programs, some free, some commercial, that do a similar job.

That's not the only type of encryption available for a PC, however. There are programs available that will encrypt your whole disk automatically. For example, Data Vault is a program that runs on your computer and makes it look like you have an extra disk drive. Each of the extra drives can have a password of its own, and anything you save to that drive is automatically encrypted, so you don't need to remember to run a separate program like PGP – you'll know instead that everything you save is safe from prying eyes.

Filter adult sites

With a little knowhow you can avoid sites containing sex and violence.

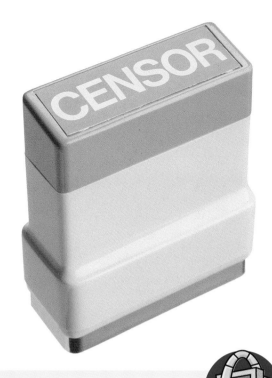

Adult sites containing bad language, violent imagery or pornography teem on the Internet. If you occasionally stumble across these sites, it follows that children can quite easily find them as well, accidentally or not.

If you don't want your children to have access to such material, there is action you can take. The first line of defence is to configure your browser to filter out offensive content. Internet Explorer has a Content Advisor which uses a ratings system to classify sites. You enter acceptable levels of violence or sexual content and access is denied if someone tries to enter a site exceeding these levels.

There are dozens of programs that act as filters, and work with Internet Explorer and Netscape Navigator. These either respond to keywords (sexual terms and offensive language), or by comparing a site address to a list of disallowed sites stored online.

You will need

● **Software** Microsoft Internet Explorer 4 or later.
● **Hardware** A modem or other means of connecting to the Internet and an account with an Internet service provider.

How to censor the Internet

1 Start up Internet Explorer, go to the Tools menu and select **Internet Options**. This will pop up the options configuration window, complete with a series of index tabs across the top. Select the Content tab to move to the relevant section where you will find the Content Advisor options.

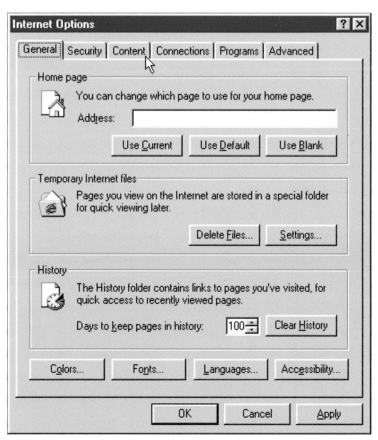

You will learn

● How to use the filtering software built into Internet Explorer.
● How to block out bad language and violence as well as nudity and sex online.
● How to configure Internet Explorer correctly so that educational sites that may contain nudity or sexual reference are still available.
● How to secure your filtering configuration to ensure that your kids can't sneak in and change things without you knowing.

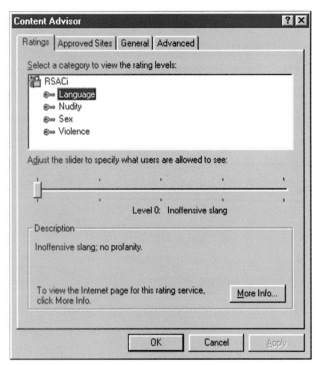

2 At the top of the Content section is the **Content Advisor**.
Click on the button marked Enable. This opens a window
with more index tabs across the top and a slider bar in the
centre. Selecting any of the categories in the RSACi window and
dragging the slider bar alters the level of censorship. You can filter
out language varying from inoffensive slang (level 1) up to explicit
or crude (level 4) with others in between. The same applies to sex
(from none to explicit sexual activity), violence (none to wanton
and gratuitous) and nudity (none to provocative frontal nudity).

3 Click on **More Info** to connect to the RSACi Web page
which explains what the ratings options mean, and how
they work. Once you have done this you should feel
confident about configuring the ratings levels. So go back to the
configuration window and make your choices for each category.
Remember, if you find your choices too restrictive or not restrictive
enough, you can always come back and balance them.

4 The second tab at the top of the Content Advisor window
is **Approved Sites**. Click on this and you can add Web
sites that you want your children to be able to access
even though they break the rating settings. Examples could be
educational sites that look at human reproduction or health sites
covering AIDS or breast cancer. You can also enter sites you want to
permanently ban, whether they pass the ratings filter or not.

5 Next move on to the **General** tab, which opens a window
containing several options. The first lets you decide if users
can see sites that have no ratings. If you disallow this, you
will impose a lot of control over the sites your kids can visit. But
you will also limit the usefulness of the Web, since many innocent
sites are not rated. The supervisor password option allows you to
type a password which will enable access to a banned site. This
feature is useful because it means you can have an adult option for
yourself while maintaining filtering for your children. To use it you
need to set a password. Click on Change Password.

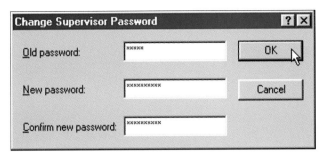

6 If you have not yet entered a **password**, don't be put off by the box that asks you to enter your old password before changing it. Simply leave the top box, marked Old Password, blank and enter a password in the lower two boxes (marked New Password and Confirm New Password), then press OK to confirm the password setting.

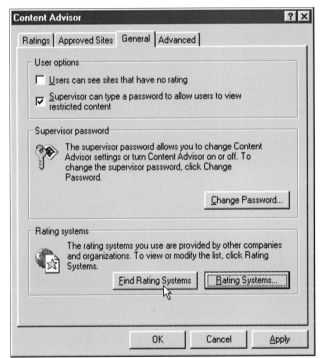

7 At the bottom of this general options window is a section dealing with ratings schemes. By default Content Advisor knows all about the RSACi scheme, but you can add other ratings schemes to make the filtering process even more effective. You may purchase a third party software product which lets you integrate a ratings scheme into Internet Explorer, or you may use a freely available scheme such as SafeSurf. In order to use SafeSurf you first click on the **Find Rating Systems** button which will take you to a page on Microsoft's World Wide Web site. From here, you follow the link to SafeSurf.

Jargon buster

● **RSACi** The Recreational Software Advisory Council's Internet ratings scheme helps your software to determine a site's content before allowing access.

● **PICS** The Platform for Internet Content Selection is a technical specification used to help label content of sites for ratings purposes.

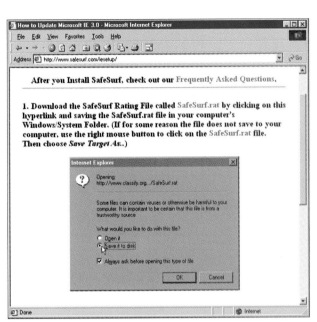

8 At the SafeSurf Web page follow the link marked **Update Explorer** where you will see the step-by-step instructions for downloading a small file called safesurf.rat, and details of how to save this in your Windows/System folder. Follow these instructions and then return to the Content Advisor window.

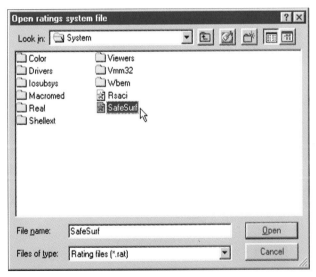

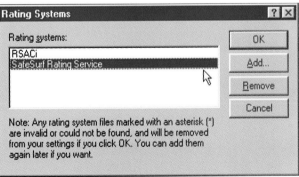

9 Now click on the Rating Systems button and a window will appear which lets you add further schemes to Content Advisor. Click on the option marked Add and select the safesurf.rat file from the directory list displayed. Select Open and you should now have both the RSACi and SafeSurf rating schemes displayed in the rating systems window.

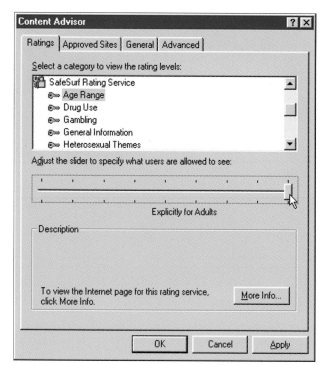

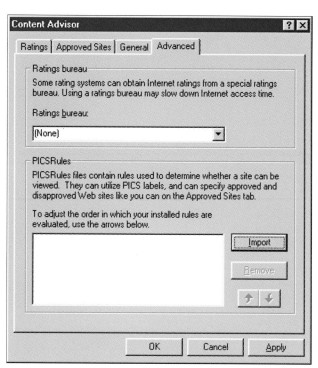

10 Go back to the Ratings window, and you will see that the original four categories have been joined by 12 **SafeSurf** categories that cover areas such as drug use, intolerance, profanity, homosexuality and gambling. Selecting any of these will enable you to use the slider bar to set appropriate rating guidelines for each. One useful addition is the Age Range category that lets you set levels for sites that have SafeSurf age ratings applied, from all ages through many steps right up to adults.

11 The final index tab is marked **Advanced** and contains options which apply to those users who have purchased third party software filters that use either a ratings bureau or special sets of filter rules. If either of these apply you will find details in the manual of your filtering software product. If you are using Internet Explorer Content Advisor without such third party products, you can safely ignore this advanced section and just click on the Apply button to bring the Content Advisor configuration into play. You will then be asked to enter a password to ensure only you can disable and configure the Content Advisor.

Troubleshooting

Although enabling Internet Explorer's Content Advisor filter, and possibly using one of the many third party Internet censoring packages available will make using the Net a considerably more wholesome activity for your kids, there is no guarantee of 100 per cent success.

Content Advisor relies on a rating system akin to that used to rate movies, but not all sex sites are rated. Most filtering packages rely on lists that contain the Web addresses of offensive or adult sites, checking against the list before allowing access. For this to be effective you need to update the filter list regularly, and even then, given the rate at which new Web sites appear, there will always be sites that manage to slip through the gaps.

You should look upon software filtering as an important part of your overall approach to supervising your children's Internet access. You should also let your children know that you will be monitoring their online access and checking to ensure they haven't been visiting adult sites. You can do this by making use of the Web browser history and data cache resources. Software such as CyberSitter at www.cybersitter.com can keep track of every attempt to connect to an inappropriate site or search for a sexually explicit word on a search engine. The knowledge that this software is in operation will often deter a child from trying to access these sites in the first place.

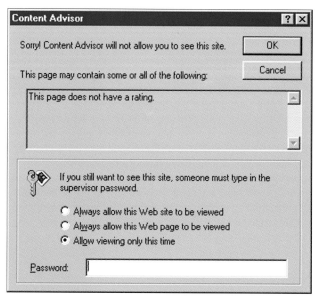

12 When you try to access a site that is outside the rating guidelines, a **warning window** should appear before you are connected. This will explain which ratings category is being breached, or if you have set the Only Allow Access To Rated Pages option, that this is a non-rated page. To access the site the supervisor password must be entered and you can choose to allow access just once, always to a specific page or always allow access to the whole site. Without the password your kids cannot get any further and cannot access the site or page.

4

Improving Performance

Speeding up

You can get your old PC working like new without spending a fortune on new hardware or software.

The PC you bought 18 months ago probably felt like the leading edge of technology. Yet today you're bombarded by ads ramming home the point that you can now buy more computing power, more extras and more memory for less than you paid.

Better and cheaper

That's the way with computer technology. It changes quickly, with components getting better and cheaper all the time. Economy of scale, intense competition, and economic factors in the producing countries also force prices down.

Here's the good news: you don't need the latest go-faster PC. What you've got will almost certainly do what you want. And even if you could use some more oomph, it is possible to give your system a boost on a modest budget. The following pages look at the options. Some are free, none are too pricey. So what can you do to keep your PC in trim?

● Regularly delete the temporary files that clutter up your disk. Remove the fonts you don't use — they have to be loaded every time Windows starts up. Check the disk's health occasionally, and use a disk defragmenter every week. Your copy of Windows should have everything you need.

● Check out the latest versions of every bit of software you use. As well as bug fixes, the later versions usually offer performance improvements.

● Invest in a disk maintenance utility that extends and automates the housekeeping process with more and better tools.

● Open the hood and get out the screwdriver. Add more memory, a second hard drive, a go-faster graphics card, even a new processor. The performance gains will vary from one setup to another.

You will need

ESSENTIAL
Software Most of the software you need to fine tune your computer system is supplied as standard with Windows 95 and 98, but it is also worth investing in a maintenance utility such as Norton SystemWorks.
Hardware A Pentium PC which has at least 16MB of RAM.

Upgrade tip

Don't spend any money unless you absolutely have to. Stripping out unnecessary or unwanted programs, files and other extras will improve your PC's performance. It's simply a matter of getting into good habits. Windows already has a basic set of housekeeping tools to get you started.

Tune it up

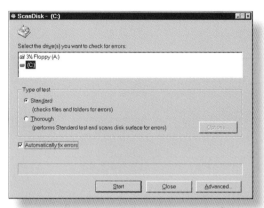

Windows' ScanDisk utility is easy to use. Make sure the Automatically fix errors box is ticked to automate the process.

Performance tip

If you use Microsoft Office with Windows 98, you can get a slight increase in performance by removing Find Fast from your Startup folder. Find Fast is a utility that from time to time goes through the files on your hard drive and creates an index of keywords that can subsequently be used to speed things up when an Office application goes looking for something. To reclaim the space used by the Find Fast index, go to Control Panel and click on the Find Fast entry. Select your drive and from the Index menu, choose Delete Index.

Windows 98 comes with a number of maintenance tools – all you need for a fine tune-up.

As well as old favourites like ScanDisk and Disk Defragmenter, Windows 98 includes utilities to clean up unwanted files and Maintenance Wizard to schedule automatically when programs are run.

Clean sweep

All the tools can be found by going to the Programs menu, Accessories and then System Tools. Select Disk Cleanup and it will search through your hard drive to find all the unnecessary files that are clogging up your valuable hard-drive space. These include Web pages you've viewed recently which are cached away in a temporary folder for quick access if you want to see them again. The size of this cache and how often it is emptied are set through the properties box in Internet Explorer, but Web pages can take up a lot of space.

Other prime targets for deletion by Disk Cleanup are temporary files set up by some programs when they run or are first installed. It is also easy to forget to empty the Recycling Bin! You can view any files before they are deleted. Under the Settings tab you can also select Disk Cleanup to run automatically when disk space is low.

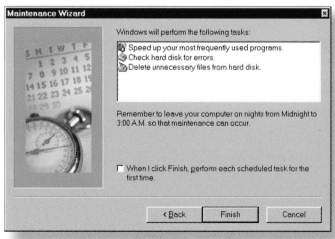

Windows 98 includes the helpful Maintenance Wizard, used to schedule a regular spruce-up of your hard disk.

Regular runners

ScanDisk checks the health of your hard drive and locks out any impaired areas so they can't be used. It should be run once or twice a month.

Disk Defragmenter is more useful as a tuning aid. Windows saves programs and data on a disk by filling up one block of space and then looking for the next free block to continue. This might not be next to it, so the file ends up being scattered all over the disk. Although Windows will still know which bits are linked to each other, it can slow things down. Disk Defragmenter reorganises the drive so all the bits of a file are, where possible, together. It also improves performance by keeping track of the programs and files you use most often. It moves these files to the fastest area of the disk so they start quicker. Use Disk Defragmenter once a week to keep things running sweetly.

The Maintenance Wizard can automate all this housekeeping. When selected it runs ScanDisk, Disk Defragmenter and Disk Cleanup automatically. It can be set to run at whatever time you want. Alternatively, it will do an immediate tune-up if you open the program and select Perform maintenance now.

Similarly, Task Scheduler enables you to set up programs or tasks to be run automatically at set times – usually periods when you're least likely to be needing your PC for other work. You can access Task Scheduler by selecting the Scheduled Tasks folder in System Tools or by double-clicking on its icon in the Taskbar.

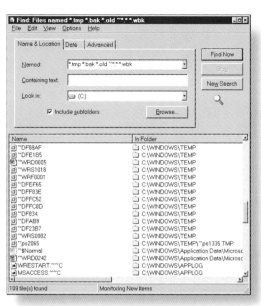

Use the Windows Find tool to locate unwanted files on your hard disk and then delete them.

Cache tip

If your PC has over 16MB of RAM, change its Typical Role to Network Server to make Windows increase the size of the caches it uses to read from the disk, for faster access.

Go to the Control Panel, click on System, select Performance, and click on the File System button. Select Network Server in the dropdown box alongside Typical Role of this Computer.

While you're in the System properties box, click on Performance and select Graphics. Move the Hardware Acceleration slider over to the right.

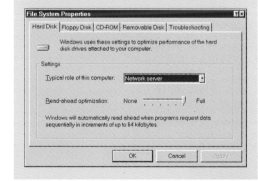

Check the Web

Several Web sites include tips and tweaks for Windows and the more you can use the faster your computing will be. Try these:

● **Computertips**
www.computertips.com/contents.htm
● **PCWin Resource Center**
www.pcwin.com/

● **Pure Performance**
www.pureperformance.com/
● **System Optimization**
www.sysopt.com/
● **TipCity**
www.swschool.com/tipcity.htm
● **TipWorld**
www.tipworld.com/tiphome.html

● **Windows magazine**
www.winmag.com/Win95/
● **WinFiles**
www.winfiles.com/tips/
● **WinfoHQ**
www.winfohq.com/tips/index.html
● **Your!PC**
www.yourpc.net/Home.html

Disk utilities

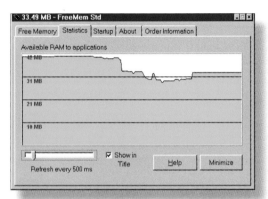

Run FreeMem and it will free up as much RAM as possible for your applications. The result is faster operation all round.

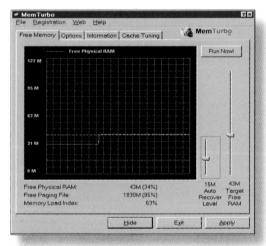

MemTurbo is designed to increase the available RAM on your system by flushing out unused sections of programs and fixing memory leaks – memory that was allocated and forgotten by Windows or other applications.

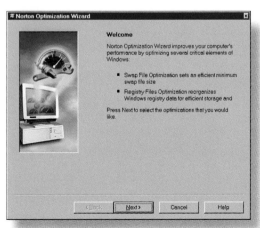

Use SystemWork's Optimization Wizard to get Windows' Registry working efficiently.

There are loads of software tweaks that you can make to get Windows running as quickly as possible.

With Windows, many variables and parameters can be set to make things run smoothly on your PC. Windows also alters its environment from one minute to the next. Inevitably this results in some inefficiencies, and regular housekeeping is essential. There are several utilities available that claim to keep your PC in tip-top condition. (See pages 163–70 for more information on utilities.) This collection will keep it in line:

FreeMem Standard

Windows 95 and 98 have a memory management system that enables programs to use more RAM than is installed in the PC. Unused sections of an application are temporarily moved out to a cache area on the hard disk. At the same time, Windows can use part of its RAM as a cache for files stored on hard disk. It tries to anticipate what the user will need next and loads that data into the cache so that it doesn't take as long to get it into play.

This doesn't always work as it should. Windows may allocate too much memory, and sometimes unused chunks of programs take up precious RAM. FreeMem (which is free) is an elegant solution. It is available from shareware libraries.

FreeMem Professional (which has more functions than the Standard version) reduces the amount of RAM programs need by switching off unnecessary background programs. For example, Microsoft Office Fast Start is a program that just loads a lot of libraries. This is meant to make the applications from Office load faster because the libraries are already in RAM, but the effect is nullified the moment the libraries are swapped out to disk.

MemTurbo

MemTurbo is similar, but more comprehensive. The commercial version can defragment your physical RAM, reorganising it to make your system more efficient. You can run MemTurbo as and when required. The program can also be set to kick in when RAM levels reach a critical low.

O'Reilly Utilities gives you Solutions for Windows 98 Annoyances with point-and-click options, and thus helps maximise your PC's performance.

Waste Whacker

There are several tools to automate the removal of rubbish from your hard drives. Waste Whacker lets you prioritise the disposal of files; they can be sent to the Recycle Bin, completely removed from the system or archived for later retrieval. Waste Whacker is available at several shareware libraries.

Norton SystemWorks

The Norton Utilities bundle has been around almost as long as PCs. The current version of this superb collection of essential housekeeping utilities includes some useful performance enhancers, like the Speed Disk defragmenter – an advanced version of the defragmenter supplied with Windows.

Also included are Space Wizard and Optimization Wizard. Space Wizard identifies files that may be cluttering up your hard disk – temporary files and anything in the Recycle Bin. It will also hunt for duplicates, infrequently used and very large files, and anything else discardable. The Optimization Wizard tweaks several critical elements of Windows. In particular, it can clear out the Registry – the database used by Windows and other applications to store key configuration data.

WinTune

WinTune System Analyzer summarises data about a PC's components and advises you if your setup can be improved. It comes with a database of systems that have been tested, which allows you to see how your PC compares. If your system is properly configured and running at or near the norm for its class, you won't get any tips. WinTune is available as shareware at www.winmag.com/.

O'Reilly Utilities

This collection of utilities for Windows 98 includes dozens of point-and-click features which fine tune performance and give users more control over their desktop, browsers, files and folders. It's possible to achieve the same results by tampering with the Windows Registry, but that's not something the average user should attempt. This 30 day demo version, available from download libraries, is a safe and effective alternative.

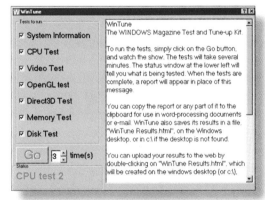

WinTune is one of the few utilities that claim to identify ways of optimising the performance of Windows. When you run WinTune on your system, it goes through an exhaustive series of tests and comes up with a list of tips and problem areas. It's then up to you to do something about them.

Rev it up

The quickest, simplest, cheapest and most effective boost you can give your PC is to add more RAM.

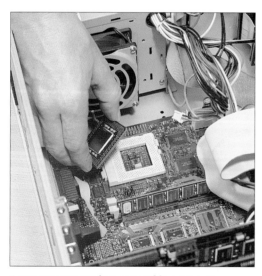

A processor upgrade means taking out your existing processor chip and replacing it with one that allows you to run applications faster.

Memory tip

Be careful about paying too much for branded memory that appears to be made specifically for your PC. There aren't many different types of memory for PCs. Branded memory is made in exactly the same way and probably even on the same production lines as RAM that would be labelled industry standard.

If you're brave enough to open up your computer, you can replace or add to the key components.

Increase your RAM

Your PC uses RAM to store the data it's currently working on. It also needs RAM for the application you're running and the sections of Windows being used. If it runs out of RAM, it has to access some of the data it needs from the hard drive. The more RAM you've got, the faster your PC can perform.

You'll see a dramatic improvement moving from 16MB to 32MB, a noticeable gain going from 32MB to 64MB, and for particular types of work a definite result from increasing to 128MB.

Installing the memory should be simple enough, and there are several useful guides on the Web. Try www.micron.com/crucial/html/installationguides.html.

The only real concern in upgrading is to match the capacity and speed of the new memory strips with whatever is already inside your PC. You may be able to figure that out from your computer's handbook. If not, ask your supplier for advice.

Upgrade your processor

The type and speed of the processor is one of the main differentiators between one PC and another. You can't usually find a replacement for the newer Intel processors, and some processor types are not upgradable at all. The fastest and most expensive upgrades available are rated at 333MHz, so if you are running anything faster than that, don't bother. But if you are running a 486 or an older Pentium (rated at 75MHz and up), you should consider it. You'll get a worthwhile speed increase. Tests suggest that moving from a 75MHz processor to a 333MHz Pentium will boost performance fivefold. Programs which use a lot of graphics, such as games or image editors, or which do a lot of number crunching, like spreadsheets and databases, will benefit greatly.

Go for graphics

A go-faster graphics card won't do much for word processing, Web browsing or other applications that don't make a lot of use of multimedia effects. But if you want zippy games, smooth video and superfast

Regular use

Collecting useful performance-enhancing utilities may be good fun, but it's a waste of time if you don't use them regularly to keep your PC in good shape. Set up the automated-function options wherever possible so that the utility gets used regularly; or use the Task Scheduler (Windows 98) or System Agent (Windows 95 Plus! Pack) to schedule operations.

Watch out!

If you have a 386 or 486-based PC, there is no point in trying to upgrade it as you won't be able to find enough replacement components.

If you're nervous, the inside of a computer can be a scary place to start teaching yourself practical electronics. And if your PC is still covered by a guarantee, even opening the hood will probably invalidate the warranty. Finally, it is wise to check out how much your bill is likely to be. If it is going to be half the price of a new computer, it's worth considering paying the extra to get a new system and a warranty on the whole thing.

screen redrawing, there's never been a better time to upgrade to one of the new accelerated 3D graphics cards. This is an easy upgrade. Just slot in the new adapter card, plug in your monitor and run the software supplied.

Space solver

Disk drives now come with huge capacities and quite low costs – which is just as well, because modern software takes up a lot of space. Most PC cases already have a spare compartment into which the new drive slots, and there should also be spare cables already in there. The extra disk space will give Windows more room for its temporary caches, which translates into faster operation – smoother running for applications, easier switching between applications and speedier Web browsing.

Installing a second hard drive or replacing your existing drive should be easy and inexpensive.

Cash in on cache

This is one for the more experienced PC owner. Increasing the size of the processor cache is one of the best upgrades you can make. The cache is used as a temporary store to relieve the processor's workload, and it comes as one or two strips of dedicated, very fast memory chips. If you can up the cache size, your processor will be able to work faster, more smoothly and more efficiently.

The current cache size should be listed somewhere in your handbook, or may be found in the power-on setup screen. If it's 128KB or less, check whether your computer's main circuit board has plug-in cache chips. Again, the handbook should tell you, or you may be able to work out where to find the cache memory on the board and check it visually.

Then contact a specialist memory supplier — many advertise on the Internet or in the back pages of computer magazines — and find out what it can do for you. You might need to note the serial numbers on your existing cache chips, because that will help the supplier identify exactly what you need.

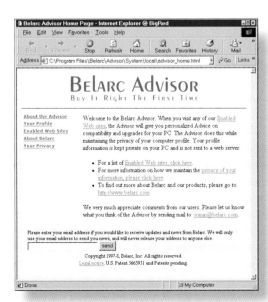

The Belarc Advisor is a small free utility that runs a check on your PC setup and tells you where things could be improved. Get it from www.belarc.com.

Slicker software

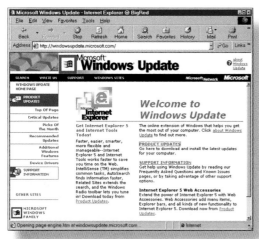

Updates **for Windows can be found at Microsoft's purpose-designed Web site.**

The **Driver Detective** utility gives you the low-down on the drivers you have installed.

Jargon buster

Device driver A program that controls a device on the PC. Every device – like a modem, printer, keyboard, mouse, disk drives and so on – must have a driver associated with it. Some drivers come with Windows and others are on the Windows CD. But most new devices come with drivers supplied by the manufacturer, and when you connect the device to your PC you'll have to load the new driver before it will work. Drivers are regularly updated by manufacturers as bugs appear and new functions become possible.

It's not always worth the effort to update your software every time a minor change is made to it.

It's always tempting to have the latest version of any software. But before you upgrade make sure it has some real benefit. What the maker may regard as a major improvement might come down to some improved Help files, support for recently launched and esoteric devices, and extra components that may be irrelevant to you.

Do you need a fix?

For instance, Microsoft regularly rushes out patches for Internet Explorer whenever any potential, if obscure, security breaches are discovered. The danger is very real and the update is worthwhile, except that the situation is unlikely to arise for most users. It's a fix that you might need, but more likely you can forget it.

If the upgrade fixes major problems or adds features that will be of value to you, go for it. Make sure you know exactly what you're getting and why the software maker has deemed it necessary to produce an update. To find out exactly what the upgrade offers, look at the Read Me file which is usually linked to it.

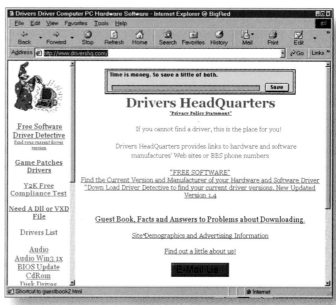

Specialised sites cover areas like virus and device driver DLL files.

Be wary of the hardware and operating system requirements. The newest version of any application may demand the latest version of Windows, and the software suppliers could easily be assuming that you're running the same modern PC with a lot of spare RAM and disk space.

Bugs out

If you do have the latest versions of the software you use, you can be sure bugs will have been corrected, perhaps with new features added and some extras included. Updates for Windows can be found on Microsoft's Web site at http://windowsupdate.microsoft.com/. This is an online service that can check what you already have and then recommend what you need.

Major Microsoft updates are also available from the principal shareware libraries, such as WinFiles at www.winfiles.com and Filez at www.filez.com. These libraries also hold updates for other software, utilities and system components like device drivers.

Specialised sites cover virus and device driver DLL files. The DLL libraries include Drivers HeadQuarters at www.drivershq.com, from where you can download Driver Detective, a useful utility that can give you the version numbers of the drivers you have installed.

The latest drivers

It pays to download the latest drivers from the original manufacturer, although it can be tricky to identify who that is. Your printer and modem makers should be obvious. Other manufacturers may be identifiable from the Device Manager list in the System properties panel in the Control Panel. The Microsoft Web site also holds updates for all MS applications.

Jargon buster

DLL Stands for Dynamic Link Library. A collection of functions that can be used by a particular Windows program. Some DLLs are provided with Windows and can be used by any Windows application. Others are written for a particular application. A missing DLL can slow a program or stop it running.

Which number?

The version numbering used by software manufacturers will often give you a clue to the significance of a new release.

Moving a whole integer, say from version 3 to 4, denotes an important revision of the product. It will incorporate any minor changes and bug fixes that have already been announced, but it will also have significant new capabilities. You may not want to install this update; it may have hardware requirements that fit only the most up-to-date PC.

A point release, with a change to the digit following the decimal point, should be of interest. For instance, the move from 3.0 to 3.1 is likely to mean major changes to the efficiency of the program and fixes for problems without significant changes to how the product works. Minor changes are indicated by the second and subsequent digits following the decimal point. So 4.011 is likely to have no performance advantage over version 4.01, although minor problems might have been fixed.

Web updates tip

You will find a number of free services that will notify you about updates on the Web. Typically you sign up and the service scans your PC, figuring out exactly what software you have on board. It can then tell you if there's a more up-to-date version available, and offers you the chance to download it there and then. Subsequently you might be e-mailed when the manufacturer issues an update.

The two best examples are the explicitly named Versions at www.versions.com and Updates at www.updates.com. Norton SystemWorks includes LiveUpdate Pro, another such facility that can identify and automatically download latest versions of your installed software. This one, however, is a subscription service.

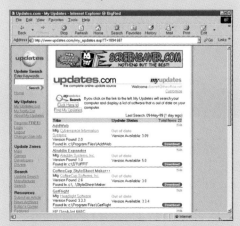

Updates is a free Web-based service that identifies and lets you download any newer versions of your software.

Problem solving

Troubles tip

On Microsoft's Web site you will find a useful collection of troubleshooters for most Microsoft products. They aren't quite Wizards, but on the basis of a few key questions they can direct you to information elsewhere on the site that might help. And quite often it does. The troubleshooters are at http://support.microsoft.com/support/tshoot/.

If your computer suddenly starts to slow, don't panic. The problem could be simple and easy to fix.

Few things are more frustrating than a computer that starts to misbehave. It's bad enough if the thing suddenly locks up, makes grinding noises or won't start up. It's worse if the occasional hiccup starts becoming a regular occurrence.

Genius not required

Don't despair – not until you've tried some basic remedial measures. And you don't need to be a PC genius to apply a few troubleshooting principles.

First, identify the problem. If your PC appears to be wading through treacle, it's likely to be a software issue, and it's almost certainly related to Windows. If it wasn't always that sluggish, you can probably speed things up using standard Windows housekeeping tools. Strip out unneeded files, delete unnecessary fonts, defragment the hard disk and don't have more than two or three programs running at once.

A simple fix?

If the problem started suddenly, you might have installed some software that Windows doesn't like. Use the Add/Remove Programs tool in the Windows Control Panel to kill anything you have recently installed and see if that makes a difference. If not, a minor hardware upgrade could improve performance. The easiest and usually the most effective investment is more RAM. Put in as much as you can afford to take the PC to at least 64MB.

You could upgrade your hard disk, either by replacing the existing drive or adding a second. The latter is the easier and safer option, but you should then transfer Windows and your principal programs to the larger, faster and more modern drive.

The final step to consider is a processor upgrade. Surprisingly, this isn't the obvious way to speed up your computer. The processor isn't the only or even the most significant bottleneck in the average PC system. CPU upgrades start at little more than a chunk of additional RAM, but to get major increases in speed you'll have to spend a lot more.

Using utilities

Utilities extend the power of Windows and can make your applications even more versatile.

As good as Windows is, it can't do everything. Just as you have to buy applications before you can use your PC for word processing, accounting or playing games, you need extra programs to help keep your PC in good working order and make it easy to use.

What are utilities?

From their name it's obvious that utilities are useful, but not in the same way that programs like Lotus 1-2-3 and Microsoft Word are useful. While spreadsheets and word processors can be used for an almost infinite variety of tasks involving words and numbers, they're not clever enough to do really useful things like compressing their own files to save disk space. Even Windows can't do this. But there is no shortage of utilities that can.

What do utilities do?

Utilities are designed to perform tasks that are beyond the normal scope of Windows. Some of them work in the background performing essential operations such as checking for viruses or clearing out redundant files that are cluttering up a hard disk. Others are used in the foreground in the same way as applications programs. This category includes file managers, encryption systems and utilities to catalogue graphics files and convert them from one format to another.

A graphics utility like Hijaak differs from an application like Corel Draw in that it can't be used to create original pictures. But it can transform an existing Corel drawing into a format that is useable by a wide range of programs and computers.

You will need

ESSENTIAL

Software Most of the programs featured here are available on magazine CD-ROMs or from the Internet.

Hardware Any type of PC running any version of Windows. Most of the utilities featured on the following pages are for Windows 95 and 98, but a vast selection for DOS and other versions of Windows is available. A CD-ROM drive and a modem are very useful because the two most abundant sources of shareware utilities are magazine CD-ROMs and the Internet.

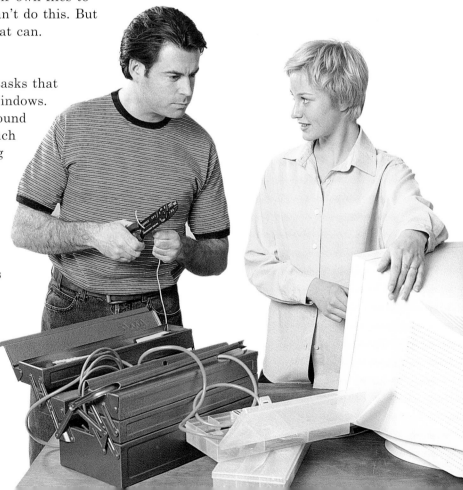

Choosing utilities

Kid Desk protects your PC from your kids. The screen shot shows a safe Desktop for a child called Eileen from which she can run just three programs: Word, Bookshelf and Paint Shop Pro.

Shareware applications abound on the World Wide Web and the CD-ROMs on the front of magazines.

Utilities can be packaged complete with warranties and manuals or distributed as shareware. Buying a commercial utility is more convenient than having to register a shareware version, which may involve sending money abroad. But shareware gives you the chance to try out a program to see if it's any good before parting with your cash.

Can you trust shareware?

Shareware titles can be very good. Many commercial utilities started life as shareware before being snapped up by big publishers. Some of the best utilities, like PowerDesk and Paint Shop Pro, are available as both shareware and retail products.

Most people get their shareware from CD-ROMs on the covers of PC magazines. The other main source is the Net. Magazine CD-ROMs are carefully checked for viruses and are as safe as buying from a shop. But files you download from the Net should be checked for viruses before you install them.

The large shareware download sites on the Web can be regarded as virus-free zones, but smaller sites run by individuals cannot. The best place to

Utility suppliers

Here are the best shareware sites on the Web together with contact information for the publishers. They were chosen because they specialise in utilities or are responsible for market-leading products. Some of their programs are available in computer stores, but for the widest choice and best prices you should check out the lists of mail-order software suppliers.

SHAREWARE WEB SITES

● **www.winfiles.com**
Provides extensive information about programs before you download them.
● **www.tucows.com**
The best place for Internet-related utilities.
● **www.download.com**
Well organised and with a good search system to find exactly what you need.
● **www.jumbo.com**
The best place for screensavers and sound files as well as a selection of useful utilities.

COMMERCIAL PUBLISHERS

● **Symantec**
www.symantec.com
● **McAfee**
www.mcafee.com

KeyView Pro is an alternative file viewer to the Quick View system built into Windows. Not only can it view and convert word processor, spreadsheet and graphics files, it also handles video and sound.

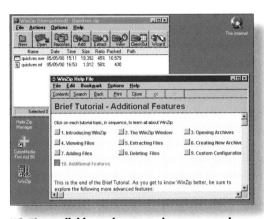

download a utility is from a manufacturer's Web site. You can be sure that it's the latest version and virus-free. You'll also know in advance how and where to register it, should you choose. The worst source of shareware is floppy disks passed on by friends. Always check these rigorously.

Something for everybody

Norton's Utilities have been evolving since the early days of PCs and are still the standard by which other utilities are judged. PK-Zip introduced a way of compressing files and is now universally recognised. Inso's file-viewing utilities were an even bigger success. These were so popular that Microsoft built them into Windows.

The following pages take a closer look at utilities in three categories: system helpers, graphics tools and Internet enhancers. But there are thousands of others less easy to categorise. Pagis Pro, for example, is a document management system that lets you scan, fax and e-mail from a single toolbar. It includes an OCR (optical character recognition) program and a search tool that can find any word in any file on your hard disk.

Kid Desk is a way of setting up your PC so your children can use it without being able to see your files, use your programs or log onto the Net when you're not there, all without you having to know anything about how your computer works.

WinZip, **available as shareware, is a very popular file compression program. In common with other shareware programs, it includes comprehensive instructions and a tutorial.**

The WinFiles.com Web site offers more than just shareware. It's a source of features, tips, program updates and product information.

System utilities

Norton CrashGuard, **available in Norton Utilities and also as a separate product, watches for errors and interrupts them before they cause a crash, giving you various recovery options.**

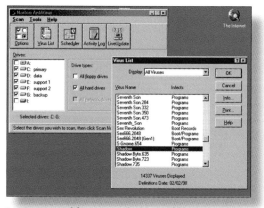

In common with most anti-virus utilities, Norton AntiVirus **includes an encyclopaedia of viruses and live updates via a modem connection.**

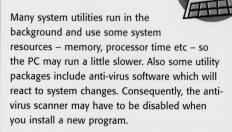

Watch out!

Many system utilities run in the background and use some system resources – memory, processor time etc – so the PC may run a little slower. Also some utility packages include anti-virus software which will react to system changes. Consequently, the anti-virus scanner may have to be disabled when you install a new program.

System utilities can knock your computer into shape and keep it working at the peak of fitness.

As computers become ever more complicated, system utilities have been developed to help keep PCs working smoothly and efficiently. Some of these utilities come packaged with Windows itself, but a much broader range is provided in commercial packages.

Guardian angels

System utility packages, such as Norton Utilities or McAfee's Utilities, include a variety of tools. Some utilities will find and fix problems, while others are aimed at preventing trouble developing, troubleshooting or tuning up the PC's performance.

Windows itself has utilities, such as ScanDisk and Defragmenter, to find and fix troublesome parts of the hard drive and tune it up. But most system utility packages will go further. They will enable you to transfer data out of the bad files, or to salvage files that have been mistakenly deleted.

More importantly, they run imaging routines which provide a record of all the files on your hard drive and the way they are organised. This snapshot of your system is useful if you have to run a recovery program after a hard-drive failure.

Crash protection

Windows is prone to crash. Most crashes are caused by memory problems, usually bugs written in the programs where one program 'bumps' into the memory space being used by another. One has to give way and be shut down in order for you to continue. Windows lets you know through a dialogue box announcing an 'invalid page fault'. If it's a bad invasion of memory space it could lead to a fatal exception error – or blue screen of death – where you would need to restart the machine.

While Windows is clever enough to see what's happening and pass on the message, there are products such as Norton CrashGuard that go one step further and try to prevent the crash or at least alert you to the problem before it's fatal so you can save any data you may be working on.

These system crash prevention tools work by hooking into Windows and running in the background. Once set up they need little intervention. Instead they watch what's happening with Windows. Other monitoring tools will warn you when the amount of free disk space is low.

Uninstallers

One of the reasons why a PC that once ran Windows perfectly becomes unstable is that every time you add a program invisible changes are made to crucial system files.

Although Windows 95 and 98 has the Add/Remove Programs Control Panel, removing a program this way doesn't always reverse all the changes made deep within the system. While some programs do come with their own uninstaller, an uninstall utility can be useful.

Uninstallers, such as McAfee's Uninstaller or Norton CleanSweep, monitor what a program does when it's installed, so they are better able to restore the PC to its original state when it is removed.

Anti-virus checker

Whatever other utilities you have on your PC, you must have an anti-virus program. See pages 99–108 for detailed information.

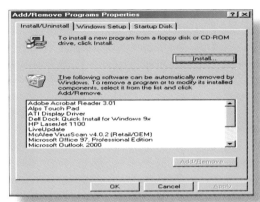

Add/Remove Programs is the basic uninstaller that comes with Windows.

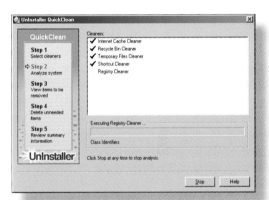

McAfee's Uninstaller removes programs and redundant files from hard disks, restoring the PC to its original state.

The graphical approach of First Aid 2000 is ideal for beginners. All they have to do is click on an item on the desktop to find out if it's working properly. If there is a problem, First Aid tries to fix it.

Watch out!

System utility suites come with recovery systems for use when Windows is so badly damaged that it won't start. Most of them rely on taking a snapshot of your PC's settings and system files. This snapshot is saved on the hard disk or on the recovery disk. In the event of problems, you start your PC with a recovery disk and this reinstates the last working version of Windows from the snapshot.

It's important to know that a recovery system is not the same as a back-up. Neither your work nor your programs are protected, so if your PC fails because its hard disk is physically damaged a recovery system won't help. You should make copies of your programs and data. See pages 112–13, 121–4 and 136–7 for information on backing up.

Internet utilities

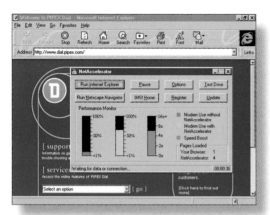

NetAccelerator works in the background to speed up Internet browsing. To find out how well it's working there's a performance monitor, but this tends to exaggerate the actual benefits.

Jargon buster

Cookie A short text file downloaded to your PC when you visit a Web site. It identifies you and stores information about your preferences. Cookies are meant to be used when you revisit a site, but other sites can gather information about you by analysing them.

Browser tip

By installing an anti-virus utility and correctly setting up your World Wide Web browser you can duplicate many of the features of Internet security utilities. In the Options dialogue box of Internet Explorer click on the Security tab and you can choose whether you want to download and run ActiveX controls and Java applets. If you decide to do so, then you should set the safety level to medium so you'll be warned before they're used.

On the Advanced tab choose whether or not you want to accept cookies on your computer. The Settings button on the same screen allows you to save disk space by reducing the percentage of your disk used to store temporary Internet files.

Speed up World Wide Web browsing and protect your computer from unwanted files and viruses.

Connecting to the Net via a modem can be slow; there's the danger of virus infection; thousands of space-hungry files are downloaded to your hard disk; and it's easy to get lost on the Web trying to find what you want. It's therefore not surprising that utility writers have jumped onto the Internet bandwagon and brought out a slew of programs designed to tackle these and other problems.

Speed enhancers

You can often spend longer waiting for a Web page to load than you do reading it. Speed enhancement programs can't make your modem faster, but they make browsing smoother by looking ahead. While you read a page, utilities like NetAccelerator and Speed Surfer pre-load pages linked to it. If you're lucky, when you click on a link the new page will already have been loaded.

Another irritation when Web browsing is waiting to connect to busy sites. Jackhammer is a utility that keeps hammering away at busy sites while you browse elsewhere. When a connection is made, Jackhammer displays it in a separate window.

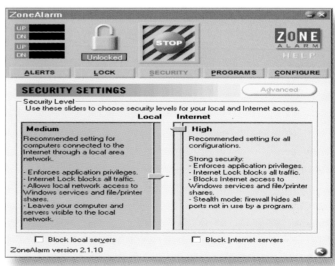

ZoneAlarm is a program that can detect and stop hackers accessing your information. It is available from www.zonelabs.com.

Finding your way

WebSleuth and WebCompass are alternatives to the search engines on the Web. With both programs you enter words and phrases of interest and then leave them to connect to the most-used search engines on the Internet. Where these programs differ from similar multiple-search facilities on the Web is that once you've got a site list you can sort, index and analyse it, and save it for future use.

Similar programs, such as Anaware's Gravity, are available for searching and sorting newsgroups. Messages can be downloaded for off-line reading, replies can be typed while you're off line and Gravity will post them to the appropriate newsgroup the next time you connect.

Safety and security

A good anti-virus program will protect your PC from viruses while you're on the Web but there are other Internet files that also pose threats. The concern about cookies is that left by one site they could be read by another site, but in practice cookies seldom store any personal information of significance. More problematic are ActiveX controls and Java applets. These are mini programs that a hacker can use to read data on your hard disk or cause other damage. Check whether your anti-virus program scans for these hostilities.

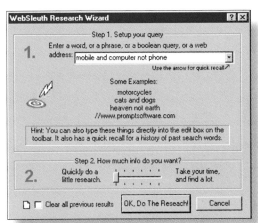

Configuring WebSleuth **to search the Internet is a simple matter of choosing which Web search engines to use and how many references to find. The multi-window approach is at first confusing but a wizard guides you through the initial stages.**

Jargon buster

Java applets Small programmes that can be downloaded from a Web site and run on your PC by a Java-compatible browser, which Netscape Navigator and Microsoft Internet Explorer both are. Java is a programming language used on the Web.

ActiveX controls A way of sharing information between applications. ActiveX controls can be embedded in Web pages, in the same way as Java applets.

Watch out!

● Some Internet utilities (NetAccelerator for example) only work properly if they're started before your browser, while others can be started afterwards. If you're using several Internet utilities you may have to load them in a certain order.

● Remember too that World Wide Web accelerators speed things up only if you spend long enough reading a page for the accelerator to pre-load any linked sites. If other utilities are running searches or hammering sites at the same time, the accelerator's share of the modem won't be enough for it to do its job.

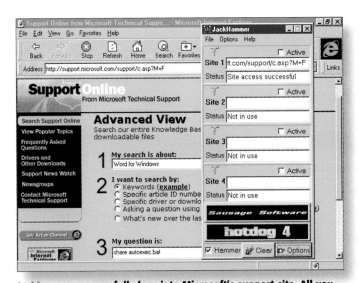

Jackhammer successfully logs into Microsoft's support site. All you have to do is copy a URL into one of its site panels and leave it to keep trying a connection while you move on to something else.

Fun stuff

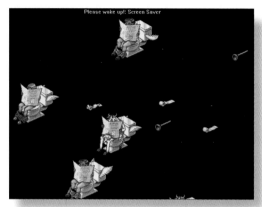

One of the screensavers from the selection in After Dark Totally Twisted. **This variation on the flying toaster theme is one of the more restrained in this particular collection.**

Screensaver tip

All you have to do to install extra screensavers is copy them into the Windows\System folder. They then appear in the Display Properties dialogue box. Start this by right-clicking on the Desktop, then click on the Screen Saver tab and choose the one you want from the list box.

Screensavers do a useful job at the same time as providing plenty of fun and entertainment.

The screensavers supplied with Windows aren't very exciting but hundreds more can be downloaded from the Web. After Dark screensavers are the most sophisticated. Modern monitors don't suffer from the screen-burn that savers were designed to prevent, but they're useful as a form of password protection and as a way of protecting your work from prying eyes. After Dark can also control the power-saving features of EnergyStar monitors.

Themes and variations

Microsoft's Themes are a source of screensavers. These are sold as separate products and as part of the Microsoft Plus! 98 pack. Each theme includes a background wallpaper, sound effects, animated cursors and a distinctive combination of colours.

You can make your own wallpaper using utilities such as ACDSee. Scan a photo or create a picture, view it in ACDSee, right-click and select Wallpaper from the Context menu. Alternatively, copy a picture with the PrintScreen key and paste it into Windows Paint. Save it as a .bmp in the Windows folder. You can then select it as your wallpaper from Display Properties by clicking on Background.

Desktop themes – such as The Golden Era shown here – may not make Windows easier to use but do give a very striking effect.

Enabling technology

The technology is available to help everyone get the most out of computing, whatever their ability.

If you're disabled, most of the computer operations that the rest of the computer-using world takes for granted may not be all that easy. But while some aspects of the technology may be hard to access, other aspects could cancel them out and make your life a bit easier.

A powerful tool

Computers can be powerful tools, helping people with disabilities to deal with many parts of their day-to-day lives in ways that simply wouldn't have been possible ten or 20 years ago. Voice-controlled computers, for example, can be used to write letters or to control devices around the home. The hard of hearing or those with speech problems can use e-mail and other services to communicate, and blind or partially sighted people can have a computer read out their messages to them.

Those are just the straightforward, obvious applications. Computers can do much more when you start to add specialised equipment, allowing people with little control over their bodies to perform complex tasks.

PCs for all

A few years ago you would have needed a very big budget for specialist equipment; now it's much easier to find products that will help overcome disabilities. Tools like speech recognition programs are more advanced, more widely available and cheaper than ever before. They can control all the functions of your PC. Devices to let your PC control the home are fairly easy to come by too, and even the basic software that comes with every computer now includes features to make it easier for everyone to use. Of course, some people will still need specialised equipment, but taking the first steps towards improving your life with a computer is now easier than ever.

You will need

ESSENTIAL
Software The exact needs of every person will differ, but you'll need either Windows 95 or 98. For controlling a computer by speech, you need speech recognition software.
Hardware A soundcard and a microphone, either for speech control or to have the computer read messages back to you.

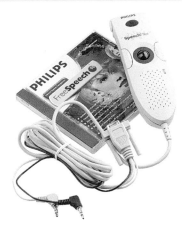

New technologies such as voice recognition are making it easier than ever to control a PC.

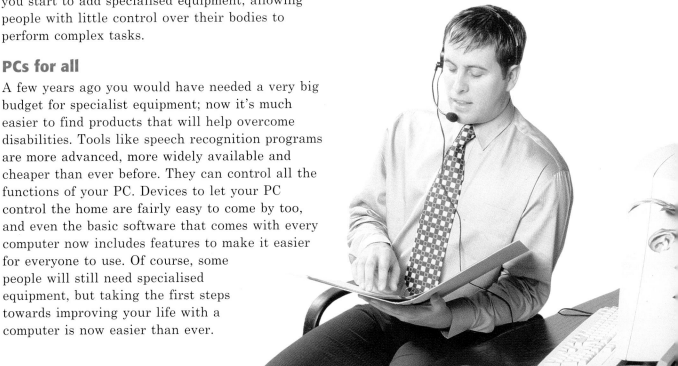

Helpful hardware

There is plenty of equipment to help people with computing, although some of it is very expensive.

For many people with disabilities, using a computer requires a lot of thought and effort. Fortunately, there is plenty of equipment that can make it much easier to control things, and whatever the disability, there's certain to be a product that will help overcome it.

Mouse alternatives

One of the simplest pieces of equipment to use is a trackball. For many people, using a mouse can be complicated, but a trackball stays in one place, and models are available with larger balls, which can be even easier to use.

Another alternative is a touch-screen display, which can be bought either as a dedicated replacement for a standard computer monitor, or as an add-on. Either way, all the user will have to do is touch part of the screen to select options.

People without the use of their arms have the possibility of using devices such as a head-operated mouse. Several companies make them, and there is also the head wand, which allows you to press keys on a keyboard or touch a screen.

There are also specialised keyboards, ranging from those designed for children, with large, easy-to-press keys, to specialised models designed to be controlled with a mouse stick, or to allow typing using just one hand.

Switch on

To control things around the home, the X10 system at www.x10.com lets a PC switch on lights and other equipment with signals sent over the mains

Equipment tip

While some people will require very specialised equipment, don't overlook some of the more common devices such as trackballs and children's keyboards, which will solve some accessibility problems more easily and cheaply than a specialist solution.

Breaking barriers

Professor Stephen Hawking has famously overcome some of the difficulties of his motor neurone disease using a speech synthesiser. But in fact the voice that you hear isn't typical of a modern speech system. The latest speech synthesisers produce a much more natural sound; the main reason that users of older models haven't changed over is that their voice is recognised by the people who know them.

The book, *The Diving Bell and the Butterfly*, by Jean-Dominique Bauby, was dictated using the blinking of his eyelid. Although he didn't use a computer to help – visitors read the alphabet to him – technology is making it easier for people who can't move at all, and similar techniques can easily be computerised.

Compatibility tip

Before buying equipment, remember to check that it's compatible with the software you're using and any other hardware you have. For devices such as special keyboards you may need drivers, so you'll have to ensure that they're compatible with the version of Windows that you have installed on your computer.

wiring. The system has been popular in the US for years, and is now available in the UK. Combining a system like this with special keyboards or speech recognition means you can have more control over your environment as well as your computer.

Magnify the screen

It's not just getting information into a computer that can be a problem. For many people, reading a computer screen isn't possible. Apart from obvious solutions like a larger monitor, there are graphics cards that can magnify one part of the screen, making it easier to read, and screen readers that will read out the words on the screen for you.

While printers are essential for many people, for those who are blind or visually impaired, they are less useful. But being unable to see doesn't mean that you have to have the computer speak to you, or miss out on hard copies of information.

Using a device called a Braille Terminal from HumanWare at www.humanware.com, your PC can translate the words on the screen into a form that you can feel, just like printed braille, by raising and lowering pins beneath a smooth surface. They can even be used to edit text on the screen, but the downside is that they are also one of the most expensive add-ons for a computer, largely because mechanically they are very complicated.

Touch-screen displays can be bought to replace a standard computer monitor, or as an add-on.

Devices are available from companies such as HumanWare that can translate the words on screen into a form that you can feel.

Special deals

The bad news is that you are unlikely to be able to buy special equipment at a discount, simply because the companies supplying it are always selling to people with disabilities.

However, if you contact charities or support groups for your particular disability, some of them may be able to recommend suppliers who offer equipment at a special price.

It's unlikely that any single company will have expertise in putting together a complete solution, so the convenience of buying everything from one supplier is not available. Once again contacting a charity or support group is the best way to find someone who understands your needs and can deliver a computer that does everything you need it to.

It's worth remembering, when you're budgeting, that if equipment is a medical necessity, you may be able to claim back the VAT on some of it — your local Customs and Excise office will be able to help you with more information.

Some people find trackballs or similar devices much easier to use than conventional mice.

Helpful software

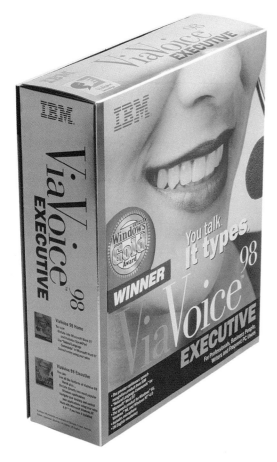

Much of the software included as standard with PCs is designed to help people with various abilities.

There's a wealth of software that can help people with disabilities and some of it is included with a standard computer. There are also lots of ways that the programs on your computer can help to make it easier to use.

Talk is cheap

One of the most common is speech recognition, which makes the computer respond to spoken messages. A few years ago, good quality speech software was expensive. But now it's used by many people, and can be bought very cheaply. Some software packages, such as Lotus SmartSuite, come with speech recognition as an option.

Some of the cheaper speech recognition programs give control over only a limited range of functions on the computer, and they may include their own word processor. Others allow you to do almost anything, and to use the programs of your own choice. So if, for example, you really have to use Microsoft Word, make sure you buy a program that will allow you to type into it with voice recognition, such as Dragon Systems Naturally Speaking (www.dragonsystems.com) or Philips

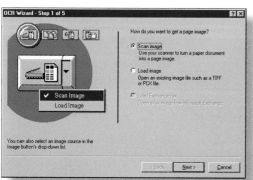

Text recognition programs like OmniPage make it easier to understand complicated printed pages.

Jargon buster

Text to speech Text to speech is the opposite of recognition. It allows the computer to read the words that are on the screen, making it much easier for visually impaired people to use the computer.

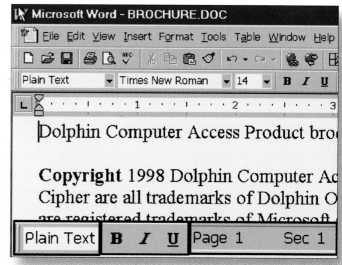

SuperNova can make sure key parts of the display are enhanced, so you can easily see them, whatever you're doing in a document.

FreeSpeech 2000 (www.speech.be.philips.com). Some of these systems, including Philips FreeSpeech, also provide text to speech facilities. Couple that with a scanner and text recognition programs like TextBridge (www.textbridge.com) or Caere's OmniPage (www.caere.com) and you can use the computer to read out letters and other documents.

All in one key

If you can type, but have difficulty, there are other programs you can consider, like macro systems that let you assign a whole sequence of commands or typing to a single key. You could press a function key, for example, and have the PC start the word processor, and automatically insert your name and address at the beginning of a letter. One of the most popular programs for doing this sort of task is QuicKeys (www.quickeys.com).

Another useful tool, whatever sort of system you use to type, is word prediction software. Programs like HandiWord (www.microsys.com) guess what word you're typing from the first few letters, and offer a selection of choices, which can mean you achieve the same results with fewer keystrokes.

Braille processing

For more specialised needs there are other programs, like the Monty Braille word processor (www.humanware.com) or the Duxbury Braille Translator, which will let you take an ordinary document and convert it to Braille for printing out, or vice versa. The visually impaired can also benefit from screen readers – programs designed to read from the computer screen. Screen magnifiers are designed to enlarge the text on the screen. Some products, like Dolphin SuperNova (www.dolphinuk.co.uk) combine all these features in one package but, again, expect to pay more for specialised programs like this than for more general ones like the Philips or QuicKey products.

There's software available from the BBC called Betsie (www.bbc.co.uk/education/betsie) that can be added to a Web site so that a version of the site that is easier for screen-reading programs to use will automatically be generated.

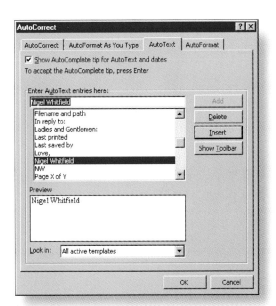

Word processors like Microsoft Word can speed up typing by predicting some phrases using the AutoText feature, from the Tools, AutoCorrect menu.

Windows tips

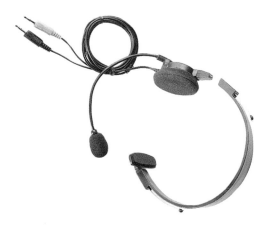

Many aspects of Windows can be configured so that they are easier to use for everyone.

From larger text to greater colour contrast, there are many ways to adjust both Windows 95 and Windows 98 to make them easier for anyone to use.

Sticky business

Using StickyKeys makes it easier to select the key combinations Windows uses for special functions. Instead of having to press a key like Ctrl and hold it down while you press another, with StickyKeys you can press one after the other. Other features allow you to have the PC make a sound when a key like Caps Lock is pressed, so you know which state it's in, even if you can't see the lights. The SerialKeys option allows you to control the computer using devices other than the keyboard.

Click on the Users Control Panel to enable profiles, with different settings for each person who uses your computer.

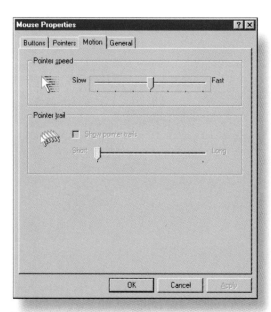

The Mouse Control Panel allows you to use mouse trails and change the size and shape of the pointer to make it clearer to see.

The Appearance tab of the Display Control Panel allows you to choose a high-contrast colour scheme with larger fonts.

Larger text

For people with visual difficulties, the Display Control Panel can be used to make text larger, and you can also select a colour scheme that gives much greater contrast. There are other features too – mouse trails, where the mouse pointer will leave a trail on screen, and sonar, which will display a series of circles around the mouse pointer when you press a key. Both will help people who have difficulty following movement.

Add a spot of colour

Windows has colour schemes to cope with a wide variety of visual conditions, and also pointers, so you can select a larger arrow, or one that changes colour automatically depending on what background it's moving over. The idea is to help you see it wherever it is on the screen.

There's a magnifier program, so that you can have the area of the screen around the mouse pointer magnified in a separate window.

There's also a new Accessibility Wizard, designed to help you change the settings on your PC that make it easier to use (full details are on page 181). The Wizard will guide you through creating a disk with those settings so that you can easily move them to another computer. Windows also has a version of Internet Explorer with extra options that make it easier to work with screen readers.

However, as Microsoft points out, specialist products have more features than this and may therefore be better for some people.

Customise for users

Both versions of Windows 98 can be configured with User Profiles. These allow you to have different settings for different users by typing your name when you start the PC. It makes it much easier for people with different levels of ability to use the same computer without having to change the settings each time.

Watch out!

If you buy a computer from an ordinary vendor without telling them that you have a disability, the Accessibility Options in Windows may not have been installed for you.

Fortunately, it's very easy to add them. Click on the Start button, choose Settings and then Control Panel. When the Control Panel window appears, double-click on the icon labelled Add/Remove Programs. Click on the tab marked Windows Setup and you'll see a list of options. In Windows 95, you need to make sure there's a tick in the box labelled Accessibility Options. For Windows 98, there's also a box called Accessibility Tools which you need to check.

When you've checked the boxes, click on the OK button, and you'll be asked to insert the CD or floppy disks for Windows, and the accessibility options will be added to your system. The next time you start the PC, you'll be able to use the new Accessibility Options Control panel to set up the choices you need.

The Windows Setup screen is the place where you can install Accessibility Options.

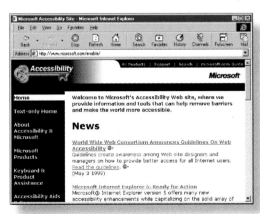

Microsoft's Accessibility site is packed with instructions that make using Windows easier.

The Internet

Tesco **can deliver groceries direct to your home.**

Jargon buster

● **Chat room** An area on the Net where messages you type are relayed to other people immediately, so you can have a conversation in real time.

● **IRC** Internet Relay Chat. The most commonly used type of chat system on the Net, although there are also chat rooms on some Web pages.

● **ISP** Internet service provider. The company that provides your Internet connection. Many now make no charge, so all you will have to pay for is the telephone call.

● **Mailing list** An e-mail address that passes a copy of your message on to all the other subscribers for them to read when they collect their mail.

Once you are online no disability can stop you getting as much from the Internet as anyone else.

The Internet is a great leveller, so it is not surprising to find that many disabled people have made much use of the World Wide Web. It can provide a social forum, via chat rooms or mailing lists, for meeting all kinds of people from all around the world.

Get in touch

As well as allowing social interaction, the Internet can be a useful tool in many other ways. For example, most of the major charities and organisations working with those who have disabilities have Web sites, with lists of suppliers and professionals who can help with your requirements. If you think that your disability means you can't use the computer in any of the ways covered here, you'll be able to find plenty more information on the Web. Look at the Web site for an organisation concerned with your own disability and you'll be able to find contact information and, on some sites, recommendations for products that can help you.

Medical information can be very valuable too, and there's plenty of it online, from explanation of diagnoses to support groups where you can

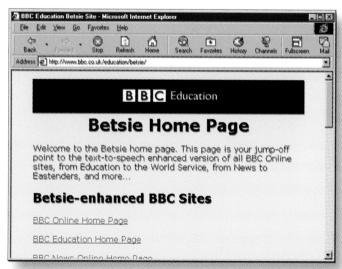

Betsie **helps make Web sites easier for people with screen readers.**

exchange information or find out about new drugs that may be worth discussing with your doctor. You should find pages detailing treatments from the viewpoint of those who have tried them, and those who devised them, and you could share your own hints and tips with other users in discussion forums.

Shop from home

On a more mundane level, how about some help with the shopping? Try visiting a supermarket site, such as Tesco at www.tesco.co.uk. Most of the major supermarket chains have a home-shopping service that lets you choose your groceries and delivers them to your door. Apart from groceries, you can buy almost anything via the Internet – clothes, books, music, gifts. Online shopping is on the up and up, and an ever-increasing variety of consumer needs can be satisfied without having to leave the house.

Setting a standard for all

The World Wide Web is essentially a visual medium, but that doesn't mean that the visually impaired are forgotten. Many major Web sites, including the BBC's news pages at news.bbc.co.uk and the RNIB at www.rnib.org.uk have special sites that are designed for access with screen-reading software. And the latest speech-enabled browsers have been designed from the outset to make them easy for people who can't see well.

The W3C, the organisation that sets the standards for the Web, is even insisting in its latest set of regulations that a properly compliant Web page must have a text description of all images on the page, to make them more accessible. Of course, this is not an ideal solution, and there are still many pages that the visually impaired may find hard to use, but the situation is constantly improving.

Ultimately, the Internet can be whatever you want it to be – a library, a community centre, social club, or just a place to relax. All you need to get online is a modem, which could be one of the most enabling investments you ever make.

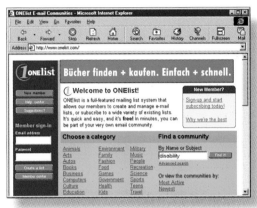

Mailing lists like those at www.onelist.com can be a useful source of support and information.

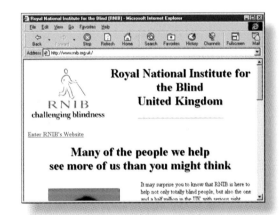

Many charities and support groups, including the RNIB, have a presence on the Internet where you can find valuable information.

In the future

Web tips

● If you are creating a World Wide Web page of your own, make sure that for each image you put on a page, you use the Alt option to specify a meaningful description, so that people using a screen reader can still make sense of the page.

● When you're accessing the Web, if you're visually impaired, turn off images in your browser. You'll save time on the downloads, and access the information you want much more quickly, provided Web sites have been designed to be usable without images.

Jargon buster

Natural language processing A development in computing that enables a computer to make sense of commands and instructions given in ordinary language. Instead of having to remember menu commands like 'file, open' you can simply say something like, 'Open the letter to Dr Jones.'

Thought control

Some thought-control systems work by using a special skull cap with electrodes to monitor the brain's activity, while one involves placing a small glass cone inside the brain, into which nerve endings grow, allowing electrical impulses to be monitored efficiently.

These are completely new methods of doing things and patients have to be trained to control a computer in this way, but systems like these offer real hope that those who have little or no control over their bodies will, if their minds are intact, be able to communicate with the rest of the world.

Advances in technology are of just as much benefit to people with disabilities as to everybody else.

As newer versions of Web browsers are developed, they will include the new standards insisted upon by the W3C, making it much easier for screen readers to make sense of pages.

All talk

As computers become ever more powerful, it's easier to find inexpensive speech recognition software that's efficient and doesn't involve the lengthy learning process that was necessary until recently. The programs are also more reliable, which means that having a cold or a sore throat, for example, shouldn't prevent you from controlling the computer. Natural language processing will make it much easier to learn to use the computer with your voice.

Text recognition, which enables a computer to read a printed page, is becoming much more reliable too, and better at deciphering complicated pages. People with visual problems will be able to put a magazine page, for example, into a scanner and have the computer turn it into text.

And if that text is to be read out loud, you'll be glad that the voices of computers are becoming more natural. Using the power of the latest processor chips, computers are able to work out more about what the text means, putting pauses and an emphasis in appropriate places.

Thought transfer to your PC

Perhaps the most exciting development is in the area of mental control. This is still at the laboratory stage at the moment, but experiments around the world are letting people use the electrical power of their brain to control the pointer on a computer screen. At the University of Tübingen in Germany, a patient of Dr Niels Birbaumer has managed to write a letter using only thoughts to control the computer.

Easy access

With Windows nearly everyone can use a PC, no matter what their level of ability.

Windows has an Accessibility Wizard to help make your computer easier to use. You find it via the Accessibility Options. If these have not been installed, you can do it yourself by using Control Panel's Add/Remove Programs and the Windows Setup tab (see page 177 Watch out! box for full instructions). When the options have been installed, go to Start, Programs, Accessories, Accessibility to find the Wizard.

Using the Accessibility Wizard

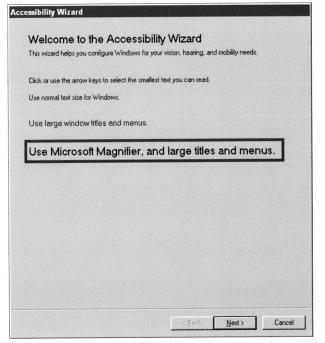

1 There are 21 steps in Windows 98's **Accessibility Wizard** but you may not need to use them all. Since there are far too many steps to cover here, this takes you through the main ones. Besides, the Wizard is incredibly easy to use.

The first few steps let you decide how big things appear on your screen. You can increase the size of the font used in title bars, menus and other areas, switch to a lower screen resolution to make everything appear bigger, increase the size of onscreen buttons and icons to make them easier to see and even change the mouse pointer to a more visible one.

Windows 95 Accessibility

Windows 95 users don't have the Accessibility Wizard and have to set the accessibility features themselves. It's a straightforward process, however. The Accessibility Properties dialogue box has five tabs for keyboard, sound, display, mouse and general settings, and each option is clearly explained and simple to follow.

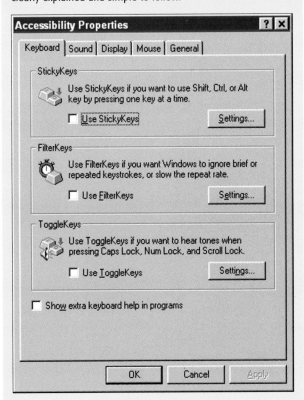

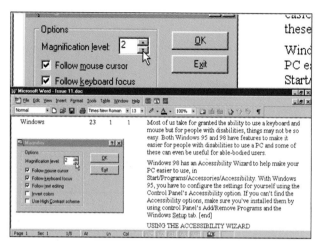

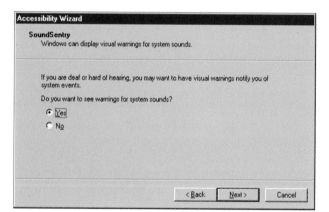

2 People with severe sight problems also have the option to use the **Microsoft Magnifier**. This turns the mouse pointer into a magnifying lens. Everything it points to is magnified and displayed on another part of the screen. You can alter the amount of magnification and even change to a high-contrast colour scheme to make everything stand out.

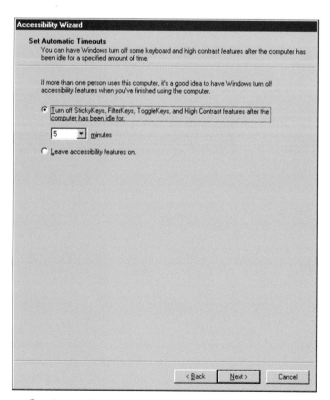

3 The Wizard can help you if you have hearing problems. You can opt to use **onscreen warnings** instead of system sounds and you can activate the built-in sound and speech captions of programs like Microsoft Encarta.

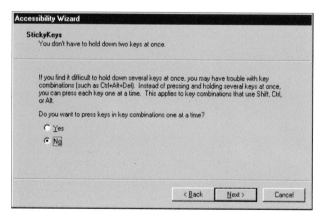

4 If you have difficulty using a normal keyboard and mouse, the Wizard can help. **StickyKeys** is useful if you can't press several keys at once. With StickyKeys turned on, you can use key combinations that involve Ctrl, Alt and Del by pressing each key in turn. So to save a file using Ctrl+S, you can press the Ctrl key once and then the S key. The Wizard can also help if you have a tendency to press several keys at once accidentally.

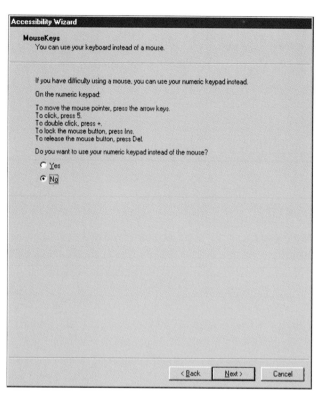

5 People who find it difficult to use a **mouse** can use the keyboard instead. The arrow keys move the mouse pointer, and other keys work as the mouse buttons. If you can use a mouse, you can set the speed of its double-click and set how fast the pointer moves.

6 If more than one person uses your PC, you can set the Accessibility features to turn off after a certain amount of inactivity. You can also save your **Accessibility settings** and load them each time you log into Windows using your own username. This means that people with different accessibility needs can all get the most out of the computer.

Glossary
A Jargon-busting Guide

Active desktop
Active Desktop brings your PC and the Web closer together. When Active Desktop is enabled you can take content from the Web – such as share prices, news pages and images – and use them on your desktop. To update the information you just need to go online.

ActiveX
Technology developed by Microsoft to share information between applications. ActiveX controls can be embedded in Web pages for animation and other interactive effects.

Active window
The part of the screen currently being used, also known as the window that is 'in focus'. When active, the title bar (the top strip of the window) will usually be a different colour from that of inactive windows.

Adapter card
Printed circuit board that plugs into a PC expansion bus to communicate with other bits of hardware. A display adapter, for example, enables the PC to display text and images on the monitor.

AGP
Stands for Accelerated Graphics Port. This is a new type of interface designed for the new breed of super-fast 3D graphics cards. It's great for games players.

Analogue
A signal that varies continuously rather than being composed of discrete steps. Sound waves and clocks with hands are analogue. Clocks with LED displays are digital. A PC performs digitally, so it uses digital-to-analogue conversion (DAC) to produce sounds, display graphics and communicate along phone lines. Analogue-to-digital (ADC) converts analogue signals, such as recorded sound, into digits by 'sampling' the waveform thousands of times a second and storing snapshots of the amplitudes as numbers.

Anti-aliasing
A technique to reduce the jagged appearance of images on screen, which is particularly noticeable when low-resolution pictures are magnified. In anti-aliasing, pixels at the edge of an image or text are given a shade of the relevant colour to give a smoother look.

Anti-virus software
Software that scans for and removes viruses on your PC. Most anti-virus software can be set to check the PC each time you switch on and can also be used to check e-mail or downloaded programs for infected files.

Applet
Refers to small programs, such as the Windows Calculator. Sometimes used to denote programs that can be run only from within other programs. Also refers to programs embedded in a Web page.

Application
A program that produces useful output, such as a word processor, spreadsheet or drawing program, rather than a utility that serves to maintain or run the PC itself.

Archive
To copy and store data away from the computer. Usually means removing data that's no longer current from the computer's hard disk (or extracting dated information from an application, such as e-mails received more than three months ago) in the same way as a library archive holds old periodicals.

ASCII
Stands for the American Standard Code for Information Interchange. A US computing standard that details a set of numbers to represent the characters on a keyboard. It is used by almost all computers and software.

Associate
To link a filename extension – the three letters after the dot in a filename – to a program. For example, the .xls filename extension is associated with Excel. If you double-click on the file it will load the application. If you double-click on a file that is not associated with any program a dialogue box will open asking you which application you want to use to open the file.

Asterisk
This is used as a wild card in filenames, where it can represent one or more letters. Typing C*.txt into the Find File box will find every TXT file starting with the letter C.

Attribute
Each file or folder on a disk can be marked (flagged) with one of four attributes, which reflect their special status. Archive files have been changed since the last back-up; Hidden files don't appear in file listings; Read-Only files can't be changed; and System files are hidden and can't be moved. In practice, these settings can be overridden.

Autoexec.bat
One of two special text files that control the startup process of a computer. Not always necessary with Windows 95 or 98. (See Config.sys.)

AVI
Stands for Audio Video Interleaved. A standard file format for mixed digital video and audio files.

Backslash (\)
A symbol used by DOS and Windows to separate files and folders from the folders or drives that they are in. For example, C:\Windows\Help\Calc.hlp denotes the help file for the calculator (calc) which is inside the Help folder, which is itself in the Windows folder on the C: drive. Folders are sometimes referred to as directories.

Bad sector
A physical fault on the surface of a floppy, or hard disk. Software such as Windows ScanDisk finds bad sectors and marks them off-limits, so that the operating system won't try to write to, or read from them.

Baud rate
The speed at which a modem transmits data. The baud rate is the number of changes that occur in an electrical signal every second. This isn't the same as the number of bits per second transmitted (another, more accurate measurement of modem speed). As modems can compress data there are several bits transmitted in every baud.

Bay
The space inside a PC's case where you fit a CD-ROM, floppy, tape back-up, or hard disk drive. Blanking plates are used to cover spare bays.

BBS
Stands for bulletin board system. An electronic messaging and file download system available free or by subscription. Online services that also offer Internet access are taking over, but there are still many BBSs, including those maintained by hardware and software companies for downloading drivers and upgrades.

Benchmark
A score of how well or quickly a PC, other hardware, or a program performs. Test centres use a set of specially designed tests to evaluate the performance of various components.

BIOS
Stands for Basic Input/Output System. This is a set of essential instructions that manage the basic functions in your PC. The BIOS is stored in read-only memory (ROM) so that it starts when the computer turns on. It tests the hardware at start up, launches the operating system and controls the screen, keyboard and disk drives.

Bit/Byte
A bit is the smallest unit of information handled by a computer. Short for BInary digiT, a bit can have one of just two values: 0 or 1. The value of a bit represents a simple choice, such as on or off, true or false. By itself a bit means little, but a group of eight bits makes up a byte – which can represent one letter, digit, or other character.

Bits per second (bps)
A common way of describing the speed of a link between two PCs or a PC and a printer. It measures how many bits of data can be sent every second.

Bitmap/.bmp
Images are made up of tiny dots (pixels). If you zoom in close to a bitmap image, you'll see the dots grow. Compare this with a vector image, where shapes are calculated mathematically, so they appear sharp however much you zoom in. Files that store bitmap image data are given the filename extension .bmp.

Bookmark
Web site or document marked so you can jump to it, by name, from a bookmark list. Also used by browsers to keep a record of your favourite Web sites.

Boot
To start up your computer. When your PC boots up it carries out a sequence of instructions stored on the BIOS and loads the main operating system. A cold boot starts up the computer from scratch by turning on the power switch. A warm boot is when you restart the computer (without having first turned it off by using the power switch).

Browser
A program used for viewing Web pages – both on the

Internet and on your PC. It can also display images, play sounds and video clips, and run animations or small programs. In addition most browsers let you send and receive e-mail and link up with newsgroups.

Buffer

A holding area in memory used for temporary storage of information. For instance, a print buffer can store data waiting to be printed so that you can carry on working with that application on something else.

Bug

An error in a program that means it does not work properly.

Bus

Sets of cables that connect parts of a PC – such as the processor and memory – and allow them to transfer information. There are three main buses: the data bus carries data around the PC, the address bus carries the memory location for the data, and the control bus carries a set of control and time signals to make sure all the components are working together.

Cache

Pronounced 'cash', this is a storage area where frequently used data is kept. The information can be accessed quicker from the cache than it can from other areas. Web pages can also be cached so that when you want to look at them again they can be loaded from the computer instead of having to access the Internet.

Capture

In Windows, you can save the current screen as an image (capture it) by pressing the Print Screen key. The image can then be pasted into a document or paint program. To capture just the active window and not the whole desktop, press Alt and Print Screen.

Cartridge

A container that holds either ink (for inkjets) or toner (for lasers) that is used in printers. It will need to be replaced or refilled occasionally.

Cascading menus

When you point to an item in a main menu out pops a sub-menu, or cascading menu, with further options to choose.

Case-sensitive

Software that can detect the difference between lowercase (small) and uppercase (capital) letters. You're likely to find this in the Find and Replace function in some word processors. Searching for

'School' won't find 'school'. Most passwords are case-sensitive so be aware that typing in 'John' will not be the same as 'john'.

CD (CD–ROM)

In the PC world, CD–ROMs (Compact Disc–Read Only Memory) can be used to store up to 650MB of data. But CD–ROMs cannot be altered. For that you need CD–R (Recordable) discs, although you can only record on them once. CD–RW (re-writable) discs can be re-recorded. You can delete and re-record information on the same discs so CD–RW drives are good for back-ups.

Chat room

An area of the Internet where messages you type are seen by other people immediately so you can have a 'conversation' in real time. A Chat Room is a program that allows several people to chat at the same time.

Child

A small window that appears inside a main window, often used to display options. For example, if you want to change a font, the options are all displayed in a child window.

CMYK

This stands for cyan, magenta, yellow and key (black), the four colours used in an inkjet printer to make up any other colour.

Code

Instructions to the computer are written in code. Source code is written by a programmer in a programming language. This is converted into machine code which consists of numerical instructions that the computer can recognise and act upon.

Compatibility

Compatibility is a measure of how well computers, or software programs, can work with each other. The easier they can communicate with each other, share information or run the same programs, the more compatible they are.

Compression

A method of reducing the size of a file by squashing the data it contains. Compression programs employ a number of clever tricks to do this and the results can be impressive, with some files being squeezed to less than a tenth of their original size. To use the files or programs they normally need to be decompressed first.

Config.sys

One of two special text files that tells the computer what configuration to use for DOS systems (the old operating

system used to run computers before Windows and which certain games still need to run). The other special startup file is Autoexec.bat. It is not necessary to have a Config.sys file. Without one, DOS will set itself up with basic defaults.

Configure

To adjust software or hardware to suit your particular needs. For example, you can configure Windows so that it displays a different colour background or so that it uses a larger font that's easier to read.

Context-sensitive help

This will display help about the specific thing you are trying to do. For example, in Word, if you are using the Find and Replace function and press the F1 key (this is almost always the Help key) the software should display advice on how to use the find and replace function.

Control panel

This is a collection of icons that allow you to configure the basic functions of Windows and your computer. Among them are controls to define the fonts that are installed on your computer, the display settings, the type of printer that's installed, plus a mass of other options.

Conversion

Changing (converting) from one type of program to another. For example, Word will change a file from the format used in some other word-processing programs into something it can read.

Cookie

A small text file sent by a Web server to your machine when you go to some Internet sites. It identifies you and stores information about your preferences. Cookies are meant to be used when you revisit a site, but other sites can, theoretically, gather information about you by analysing them.

Corrupt

Where data is accidentally changed or destroyed. It can be a software problem or can be caused by a sudden power surge damaging the hard drive. Some utilities programs (such as Norton's Utilities) try to recover the data from a corrupted file.

CPU or processor

This is the central processing unit, the brains of your PC. It is an electronic device – an integrated circuit board or chip – that contains millions and millions of tiny electronic components that carry out basic arithmetic and control functions. The speed of the

processor is measured in Megahertz (MHz). The bigger the number the faster the PC.

Crash

This is what happens when your PC goes wrong and freezes up. A crash can be caused by all sorts of problems with the software, but it normally occurs because the PC has got itself into a muddle or the software you are using has bugs in it.

Ctrl-Alt-Del

Also known as the three-finger salute. Pressing these three keys together helps you get out of a crash. Press them once and it brings up a close box showing the programs that are running. You can then try closing the program that may have frozen the computer. Pressing Ctrl-Alt-Del twice will restart the computer.

DAT

Stands for Digital Audio Tape, a small tape cassette used to store music or PC data. If you use a DAT for music, it provides the same quality as a compact disc. DATs are most often used to provide a back-up for computer data.

Data/Data transfer rate

Data is a general term for anything the computer processes – it could be numbers, words or images. The data transfer rate is the speed at which data can be read from the hard disk and transferred to the processor. On a good drive this is about 5MB a second.

Dedicated

This signifies a PC, printer, program, or even phone line that is used for one particular job only. If you have a network, you might find that you do a lot of printing or that you need to store a large number of files. In this case it would make sense to set aside one PC for printing or storage. It would not be used for anything else.

Default

The choices automatically made by a program if you do not specify an alternative. For example, if you run a word processor and start typing a letter, it will use the default typeface (e.g. Arial) and the default paper size and margins. You can always change these settings later.

Defragmentation

When a file is saved to disk, your PC does not always save it in a single area. If the disk is full, it might have to split the file and save it in sections in different places. This makes it slower to retrieve the file. Defragmentation utilities will reorganise your hard disk so that all the parts of a file are stored next to each other.

Device/Device driver
Device is a general term for the parts that make up a computer system – such as a printer, serial, disk drive and modem. The software that controls each of these different parts is called a device driver, or more commonly just driver. (See driver.)

Dialogue box
A message window that asks you to do something, such as press a button. It is called a dialogue box because it's the closest there is to a conversation between the computer and the user. It's usually used for choosing options, such as creating a name for saving files.

Dial-up connection
This term covers the whole process of connecting to another computer over a telephone line, such as to your Internet service provider. To do this you need a modem and the dial-up software that's supplied with Windows.

Digital/Digitise
Digital means that numbers, rather than a continuously changing signal, represent information. To digitise something is to convert an analogue signal, such as speech or sound, into a numeric form that can be processed by the computer. For example, a soundcard contains an analogue-to-digital converter to convert the sound signal from a microphone into numbers representing the volume and tone.

DIP Switch
Sliding switch which can be moved to one of two positions – open or closed – to set options on a circuit board.

Direct cable connection
A utility or small program supplied free with Windows that allows you to link two computers together using a cable plugged into the serial (or parallel) port on each PC. The two computers can then exchange files or share printers.

DirectX
Needed to play some games. The software lets applications have direct access to the computer's sound and graphics hardware in order to improve performance.

Disable
To stop something from happening. For instance, you can disable (prevent) people on a network from sharing files on your machine or having access to printers.

DLL (dynamic-link library)
A DLL is a program file that's stored on disk and loaded only as and when an application needs it. That means it doesn't use up any memory until it is needed. Large applications, such as a complex word processor, might use several DLLs: one to carry out the spell check; one to manage printing a letter; and a third for formatting the text. DLL files have the extension .dll. The same DLL might be used by several programs so be careful before deleting any.

DMA
Stands for Direct Memory Access. This is a fast method of accessing the contents of memory chips. Normally, if a video card wants to read data from the main memory, it has to go via the central processor. The central processor accesses the memory location and passes the data back to the video card. With DMA the video card retrieves the data directly from the memory.

Domain/Domain name
(1) In Windows 95 and 98 a network can have groups of users or resources. For convenience, these are referred to as domains. (2) Domain is also used to identify sections of the Internet, each of which has a domain name. The domain name is part of the site name (or URL) and ends with the TLD (top-level domain) category. Some you'll encounter frequently are .com (commercial), .co.uk (UK commercial), .ac.uk (UK academic).

Dongle
(1) A physical device – such as a key – which has to be attached to the computer for a particular software program to run on that machine. (2) It can also be a physical lock to keep a computer secure (such as locking the front of a cabinet which has the PC inside it).

DOS
The standard operating system before Windows. DOS – which stands for Disk Operating System – was just a piece of software that managed the storage of files on the disk. It kept track of where the files were, how big they were, and when they were created. It also provided time and date functions and the ability to start other software programs. DOS was controlled through typed-in commands. (MS-DOS just stands for Microsoft Disk Operating System.)

Dots per inch (dpi)
The number of dots that a printer can print on an inch of paper (or on a screen – the number of dots displayed per inch). The greater the number of dots, the smaller each must be and the finer the resolution. Most laser printers print at 600 dpi but the better ones can have a resolution of 1200 dpi.

Download
When you download a file from the Web you are transferring a copy of a file from a computer on the Internet (the remote computer) to your computer (the local one). This can be done either by using a modem or a network. When you send files from your computer to one on the Internet it is called uploading.

Drag and drop
A feature of Windows which means you can move a file, image or piece of text from one place on screen by picking it up with the cursor, dragging it to where you want it and dropping it into place.

Drill down
To start at the top of a menu or directory and work your way down through sub-menus and directories until you find the file or command you want.

Driver
A special piece of software that sits between Windows and a particular device, such as a printer or disk drive. It translates the instructions from Windows into a form that the device can understand. Some drivers come with Windows but most new devices come with drivers supplied by the manufacturer. They need to be loaded before the device will work properly. Drivers are regularly updated as bugs appear or new functions become possible.

DVD
Stands for Digital Video Disk (or Digital Versatile Disk). It's a relatively new CD format that even in its basic form can be used to store as much data as seven ordinary CD–ROMs (4.7GB). Double-sided DVDs can store 17MB. The main attraction of DVD is to distribute feature films and sophisticated interactive multimedia titles. Films are encoded for each country to prevent piracy and to view them you need an appropriate MPEG 2 decoder. DVD drives can also be used to read ordinary CD–ROMs.

Dynamic
Generally, it is used to mean something that changes immediately it is needed, such

as a Web page where the information is updated in real-time.

E-mail
Electronic mail – messages and files that are sent from one computer to another through the Internet.

E-mail address
Like the address on a letter it's a unique location where users receive their e-mail. The address is usually in the form of yourname@domainname – for example yourname@isp.co.uk.

Emoticon
Emotional Icons, better known as smileys. Created by pressing keyboard characters they look like faces displaying a particular emotion. So J is I'm smiling at a joke while L is I'm sad.

Encryption/Decryption
Encryption is the conversion of data into a secret code. Files are encrypted using a password and must be unscrambled (decoded) using the same password (also known as a key). Decryption is taking a message or file that has been coded (encrypted) and changing it back into its original form.

.exe
The filename extension – short for executable – that indicates that a file is a program and can be run by double-clicking on it.

Expansion card
A circuit board that can be plugged in to expand the functionality of your PC. For example, if you want to connect your PC to a network, you will need a network card that controls the way signals are sent over the network cable. You can fit several expansion cards to a PC by plugging them into empty expansion slots.

Explorer
A program that's supplied with Windows 95/98 that lets you manage all the files stored on a disk. With Explorer (officially called Windows Explorer) you can copy files, move files from one folder to another, create new folders, and rename or delete files and folders.

Export
To move information from one program to another. Generally, this will involve converting a file from one format to another format so that it can be read by a different program. For example, if you have written a letter in Microsoft Word and want to give it to a friend who uses Word Perfect for Windows, you need to export the Word document to a Word Perfect format file using the File/Save As option in Word.

Extension
The three-letter code at the end of a filename that generally indicates the type or format of the file. A filename might be Partyinvite with the extension .doc. This shows the file is a document. Similarly, .bmp means a bitmap file, and so on.

FAQ
Stands for Frequently Asked Questions. A FAQ (pronounced fak) is a document that answers questions on specific topics. FAQs are frequently posted on the Internet to save technical support staff having to deal with the same questions over and over again.

FAT
When you open a file, the operating system looks through the file allocation table (FAT) to find out where the file is stored. The FAT is hidden, so you cannot see it. But without it you cannot retrieve any of the information on your disk. Sometimes the FAT gets corrupted. To remedy this problem, run ScanDisk or another disk recovery program.

Fatal error
Often shown by the blue screen of death, a fatal error causes the system or program to crash – with no hope of recovery.

File format
The way data is stored in a file. For example, every document created in Word for Windows is stored as a Word file with special codes to tell Word how the margins are set up, the fonts that are used, and whether images are included.

Filter
Filters work in several programs so as to pick out the bits of information you want from those you don't. For instance, an e-mail filter will stop messages from certain addresses getting through. In graphics programs, filters can be used to add special effects.

Firewall
A firewall is a security device to protect networks (and individual PCs) from outside threats such as hackers. Instead of each computer linking directly to the Internet, they have to go through a separate server (proxy server) which decides which messages or files it is safe to let through.

Flag
A flag is a marker or signal that something's important or needs some follow-up action. For example, in Outlook Express you can flag a message that comes in to show it needs an urgent reply.

Flame
Red-hot passions can be aroused by messages in e-mail forums or other online chat rooms. To flame is to send rude or insulting e-mails to someone whose opinion you don't agree with. Those who do this are called flamers.

Flicker
Images on screen flicker (appear to move) when the picture is not being refreshed often enough or quickly enough. Most screen displays need to be refreshed at 50–60 times per second in order to appear flicker-free.

Font
A set of characters all of the same style (such as italic), weight (such as bold) and typeface (design). For example, labels in Windows are normally displayed in a font called Helvetica or Arial. Fonts are used by computers for their screen displays and by printers for producing printed pages. Windows has TrueType fonts that can be printed and displayed in almost any size, and printer fonts that can only be printed in predefined sizes.

Footprint
The area covered by a piece of equipment, such as a PC or printer. Notebooks need to be small and light enough to carry around so they will have a smaller footprint (that is take up less space) than desktop PCs.

Forum
Forums covering particular areas of interest (such as cookery, computing, chess, etc) are set up by newsgroups or online services. In the forums, you can post messages and get replies as well as find files, downloads and other related material.

Freeware
Computer software that is given away free of charge and often made available on the Web or through newsgroups.

FTP
This stands for File Transfer Protocol and is the way of moving files backwards and forwards across the Web. Using an FTP program – such as Terrapin or CuteFTP – you can take the files, pictures, and text for your Web pages and 'upload' them, via an FTP server, to your Web space.

Function key – F keys
PCs have at least 12 function keys at the top of the keyboard. These are keys that are linked to specific tasks, such as refreshing the screen. However, the keys may have different uses according to different applications, although most use the F1 key to display help information.

GIF file
Stands for Graphics Interface Format. Indicated by the file extension .gif, it is a commonly used format for storing images and bitmapped colour graphics. It was originally developed for the CompuServe online system, but is now one of the most popular formats for images stored on the Internet.

Giga/Gigabyte (GB)
Giga before something means one billion (which, US style, is 1,000 million not a million million as it is in the UK). So the latest PCs with a processor speed of 1 Gigahertz (1GHz) go through 1,000 million cycles a second. A gigabyte (1GB) is 1,000 megabytes. The storage capacity of most hard drives today is measured in gigabytes.

Graphics card
A graphics card produces the picture you see on your screen. It is also known as a graphics adapter, graphics accelerator, video adapter or display adapter. Most cards have special processors to boost performance and have their own memory in which to cache (store) the display. Some graphics cards are best for 2D work (standard applications) while others have been specially designed for 3D effects in games and multimedia titles. Although combined 2D/3D accelerated graphics cards appear to offer the best of both worlds, they may not be quite as fast as cards dedicated to either 2D or 3D.

GUI
Stands for Graphical User Interface. This is a way of representing files, functions and folders with little images called icons. With a GUI such as Windows you can point and click on an icon, using the mouse, rather than typing in the filename, thereby making it easier to use a PC.

Hacker
Originally, this meant someone who loved messing around with computers. Now it's the name for people who try to break into computer systems illegally.

Handshaking
A series of signals that are sent between two communication devices – such as two modems linked by telephone – to establish the way in which they should send and receive data.

Hardware
Any physical unit – hard disk, monitor, mouse, printer, electronic circuit – that is part of a computer system.

Helper applications
Programs, such as sound or movie players, that are launched by the browser to play multimedia content downloaded from the Web. They are different from plug-ins because they are not part of the browser and can be run as stand-alone programs (e.g. RealPlayer).

Heuristics
Heuristic programs are ones that learn from what's happened in the past. For example, heuristic scanning (also known as rule-based scanning) is where the scanning program compares files or programs with the virus files it knows, and decides the probability of them being infected.

Hierarchical file system
A way of storing and organising files on a disk so that each file or folder is located within other folders. The main directory (folder) for the disk is called the root. The 'route' to get from there to a particular file or folder is called the path.

Hit
Originally the way traffic to a Web site was measured. The number of hits was an indication of how popular a site was. Downloading a file from a Web page is a hit, but as each page can contain lots of files (such as picture files) it can take quite a few hits to download a full page. Now the number of visits (that is individual users) to a Web site is used as a better measure of how busy a site is.

Home page
A home page can be the first page you see when you log on to the Internet or the start page on any Web site.

Hot swapping
Means you can connect peripherals such as modems or CD–ROM drives to the computer and work with them immediately, without having to switch off the PC or restart.

HTML
HyperText Markup Language, or HTML, is the special markup code used for creating Web pages and saying how they should look. It's also used for creating hypertext links (see hyperlinks). A Web page has .html as the file extension. There are software programs, such as FrontPage, which are HTML editors that will help you set up and change Web pages.

Hyperlinks

Also known as hypertext links or hotlinks. Click on these to move to different parts of the page or to other Web pages. The link is usually underlined or in a different colour to make it stand out from the text around it. Pictures can also be links. When the cursor passes over a link it changes from an arrow to a pointing hand.

HTTP

This is the method – protocol – by which Web pages are moved around the Internet. If you look in the address bar of your browser, http is usually seen as the first part of any Web address, e.g. http://www.msn.com.

HyperTerminal

A program included with Windows that enables you to dial up another computer, using a modem, and transfer files. It's not for accessing the Internet. It's more useful for accessing bulletin boards.

Illegal operation

This is when a program does something that the computer thinks it shouldn't. Examples of illegal operations include protection faults where a program tries to use a protected block of memory used by another program or Windows itself, and exceptions, which are error conditions trapped by software. Stack faults occur when a program fills up the amount of space reserved for temporary data storage.

Image map

A photo or a drawing on a Web site that you can click on to link to different parts of the Web page or site.

Initialise

To set up a disk or tape for use. Usually, this includes testing the surface of the storage medium for faults, writing a startup file and setting up an index for file information.

Inoculation

Used by anti-virus programs to check for suspicious changes in files. Programs are inoculated – that is protected against virus infection – by recording characteristic information about them. This information is compared each time the program is run. If there are any significant changes, the file may be corrupt or infected.

I/O

Stands for Input/Output, that is, as it suggests, information that comes in and goes out of your computer. I/O cards control the data flow to and from devices such as your hard drive and mouse.

IRC

Stands for Internet Relay Chat. This allows Internet users to chat with others online, in real-time. Through an IRC server, you can join various chat groups. Text you type is sent via the server to all other users in that group or channel. Generally, groups are dedicated to particular topics which are usually reflected in their name.

IRQ conflict

Arises when two peripheral devices use the same number IRQ (Interrupt Request). The interrupt is a request for attention from the central processor. If two devices share the same interrupt – say the mouse and the modem – the processor may react to the wrong device and the system won't work properly.

ISA

Stands for Industry Standard Architecture, a design standard that enabled expansion cards to be plugged into 16 bit expansion slots (known as ISA slots) on PCs. Now replaced with PCI.

ISDN

Stands for Integrated Services Digital Network. This is a standard way of transmitting digital data over a telephone network at high speed – much faster than normal modems.

ISP

Stands for Internet Service Provider. A company that offers users a connection to the Internet.

Java/JavaScript

Java is a programming language used extensively on the World Wide Web. Small Java programs called Java applets are downloaded from a Web site and run on your computer by a Java-compatible Web browser, such as Netscape Navigator or Microsoft Internet Explorer. The use of Java enables more interactive content than is possible through HTML.

JPEG

A standard you may come across if you use graphic images. JPEG is a complex way of storing images in a compressed format so they take up much less disk space. The file extension is .jpg.

Jumpers

A small plug or wire on a device that can be moved to alter the way the device is configured.

Kilobyte (KB)

A measure of the capacity of a storage device or size of a file. Usually written as KB, a kilobyte is equal to 1,024 bytes (210 in binary notation).

KHz

A measure of the frequency of a sound. One KHz (or kilohertz) is equal to 1,000 cycles per second. The higher the number, the higher pitched the sound. You will see KHz mentioned in the specification of a soundcard. This can define two separate functions. The first is the range of frequencies the soundcard can output. The second is the frequency at which the soundcard takes samples of a sound when recording it onto your disk. A soundcard looks at the level of a sound thousands of times each second and so builds up a picture of it. The more times it takes a sample, the more accurate the recording.

LAN

Stands for Local Area Network. This is a way of connecting several computers together within an office or building so that you can exchange files or messages with another user on another computer that is connected to the network. A wide area network is similar to a LAN, but links computers that are miles apart, even those in different countries.

LCD screen

Portable computers do not have room for a bulky monitor. Instead, they often use an LCD (Liquid Crystal Display) screen. There are three types of LCD screen available: monochrome, DSTN (Double Super Twisted Nematic) colour and, at the top of the range, TFT (Thin Film Transistor) colour. A TFT screen is capable of displaying clear, bright and sharp images with tens of thousands of different colours. However, TFT screens are expensive to manufacture and they require a lot of electrical power to run.

Macro

A series of commands or operations that enable you to automate common tasks in various programs, such as Word or Excel.

Media player

A utility program supplied free with Windows that allows you to run multimedia files including sound or video files.

Megabyte (MB or Mbyte)

A measure of the data capacity of storage devices, including hard drives, that is equal to 1,048,576 bytes (220 in binary notation). Megabytes are also used as the measure of the storage capacity of main memory (RAM).

Memory

Generally, this means some device where information can be stored and retrieved. In practice, it usually refers to the fast electronic components known as RAM, or Random Access Memory, that stores data and is connected directly to the processor. Electronic memory chips remember data only for as long as electricity is supplied.

Memory expansion

This means adding more electronic memory chips to your computer. Your PC needs memory to run software programs and Windows needs as much memory as possible. Many top-end PCs today come with 128MB of RAM.

MHz

A measure of the frequency of a timing signal that's equal to one million cycles per second. The higher the MHz (megahertz) number, the faster the clock that's generating the signal. This normally refers to the main clock that sets the timing signal for the processor chip in your PC. The faster the timing signal, the faster the processor will run.

Minimise

To shrink an application window down to an icon. Minimising an application allows you to run several applications at the same time.

Modem

The name comes from MOdulator/DEModulator. A modem is a device that converts electronic signals from your PC into sound signals that can be transmitted over a phone line. To receive information the modem works in reverse and converts the sound signals back into digital electronic signals. Modems are also used to connect to the Internet. They can be internal or external. External modems are plugged into your serial or USB port. A modem's speed is measured in bits per second (bps) and the top models currently transfer data at 56Kbps (56,000 bits per second), which is roughly equivalent to three pages of A4 text a second.

Motherboard

The main printed circuit inside your PC. It usually has the major components, such as the processor and memory, together with connections for expansion boards.

MPEG

Stands for Moving Pictures Expert Group. A set of standards for compressing audio and video files.

Multi-tasking

The ability of Windows to run several programs at once. You could be typing a letter in a word processing program while sending an e-mail. In fact, the processor handles each program one at a time but does so quickly enough to make it appear they are running concurrently.

Newsgroups

One of the features of the Internet. They are free-for-all discussion forums.

OCR

Stands for Optical Character Recognition. This is software that takes a scanned text image and converts it into ordinary text. The scanned text can then be loaded into a word processing program – such as Word – for editing.

OEM

Stands for Original Equipment Manufacturer. A company that produces equipment, such as a computer, using basic parts made by other companies. Only the biggest computer companies make everything themselves.

Orientation

The way in which a piece of paper is held. Portrait orientation is with the longer edge vertical, and landscape orientation is with the longer edge horizontal.

Pages per minute (ppm)

The number of standard A4 text pages a printer can print out each minute. With colour printers there are usually two speeds – one for colour printing and one for black and white.

Parallel port

The socket at the back of your PC that lets you connect it to a printer. A parallel port sends data to the printer over eight parallel wires. Some other devices, such as ZIP drives, can connect through the parallel port.

Partition

A way of dividing a hard disk into chunks. Each partition is treated by the operating system as though it is a separate drive. For instance, if you buy a large 16GB hard disk, you may find it convenient to split it into four 4GB partitions called C:, D:, E:, and F:.

Patch

A small software program, often accessible as a piece of code that can be downloaded over the Web, which is issued by manufacturers to correct a bug that is causing persistent problems in a larger program.

PCI

Stands for Peripheral Component Interconnect. A high-speed connection on the motherboard of your PC that can be used by components that need to exchange large chunks of information fast. PCI is a faster way of transferring information than a 16 bit ISA expansion slot.

PDA

Stands for Personal Digital Assistant. This is a general term for any small, electronic personal organiser, as is the term palmtop computer.

PDF

Stands for Portable Document Format. Many hardware and software manuals are now distributed in electronic format, invariably Adobe Acrobat .pdf. This can only be opened and printed using a reader program which can be downloaded for free from the Adobe Web site.

Peer-to-peer network

A simple network in which no single computer is in control. Each acts as a server to the others in the network and shares their resources.

Peripheral

Any add-on item that connects to your computer, such as a printer or Zip drive.

Pixel

The smallest single unit on a display, or on a printer, the colour or brightness of which can be controlled. A monitor normally has a resolution of 72 pixels per inch, whereas a laser printer has a resolution of 300 to 600 pixels (also called dots) per inch.

Plug and play

A development that is a combination of hardware and software, designed to make PCs far easier to upgrade. The way it works is complex, but the result is simple. Plug in a peripheral and when you reboot, Windows will automatically configure it to work with your system.

Port

A physical connector for linking input and output devices to the computer.

PPP

Stands for Point-to-Point Protocol. A set of commands that allows a PC to use the TCP/IP protocol over a phone connection. Normally, TCP/IP will work only over a network, but the PPP system fools it into working over a phone line.

Protocol

A set of codes and signals that allows two different PCs to communicate. A simple protocol ensures that data is correctly transferred from a PC to a printer along a printer cable. Other protocols ensure that a PC can communicate via the Internet or over a network. A protocol is like a spoken language. If you cannot get two PCs to exchange information, it's likely that they are using different protocols.

QuickTime

A video system originally used on Apple computers but also available for PCs. It is commonly used by interactive multimedia software such as encyclopaedias. The player for QuickTime is free and is usually bundled along with programs that require it.

RAM

Stands for Random Access Memory. This memory allows access to any location, in any order. The memory chips in your PC are RAM – any location can be accessed by specifying its address. Magnetic tape – used for long-term storage – is not random access; you must read through all locations before you reach the one you want. RAM is short-term only. While the PC is switched on, it can store part of the operating system and run applications and other work, but all the contents will be lost when the PC is switched off. The more RAM a PC has the faster it will be.

RAM drive

An area of memory made to look and act like a disk drive. It has its own drive letter and you can create and store files on it.

ROM

Stands for Read Only Memory. This is a memory device that has had data written onto it at the time of manufacture. You cannot store your own information in ROM. It's contents can only be read, for example a CD–ROM.

Refresh rate

Measures how many times a second the picture on a monitor is updated in order to maintain a constant flicker-free image. The image on the screen is visible because tiny dots of phosphor shine but the glow lasts a few tenths of a second only. The dots have to be hit by an electron picture beam to get them to glow again. This process is repeated 60 to 70 times per second.

Registry

A database at the heart of Windows which contains information about every program stored on the disk and the users, networks and preferences. You'll never see the registry, but it's worth knowing it's there in case you see an error message such as Object Not Found in Registry. This means a program has not been correctly installed.

Remote access

To use your PC from another location, via a phone link. You need two PCs, each with a modem, and special remote access software. This allows you to dial one PC and access the files and folders on its hard disk as if you were there.

Resolution

Measure of the number of pixels that are displayed on your screen. The more pixels per given area, the sharper the image and the higher the resolution.

Rich text format (RTF)

A way of storing a document that includes all the commands that describe the page, type, font and formatting. The RTF format allows formatted pages to be exchanged between different word processors.

Safe mode

A special operating mode of Windows 95 or 98, that is selected if Windows detects a problem when starting. Safe mode does not load many of the (potentially troublesome) drivers, to enable you to try to identify the problem and fix it. When you first install Windows 95 or 98, you should create a startup disk that contains the configuration details for your PC. If nothing else works, Windows will ask you to insert this disk and will copy the initial settings over.

SCSI

Stands for Small Computer System Interface (pronounced scuzzy). This is a high-speed parallel interface standard. Originally used with Apple Macintosh computers, it now appears in a lot of PCs.

Serial port

A port to which you can connect serial devices such as a mouse or modem. Through it, data is sent and received one bit at a time, over a single wire. Data in a PC is usually transferred around the computer in parallel form eight or 16 bits wide. However, if you want to use a modem, for instance, you need to send it the data so that it can be converted into sound signals that can be sent one at a time over a telephone line.

Server

A dedicated computer that provides a function to a

network, such as storing images or printing data.

Shareware
Software which is available free for you to sample. If you keep it, you are expected to pay a fee to the writer. Shareware is often confused with public-domain software which is completely free.

Shockwave
A programming language designed to bring animation to Web pages. To view its effects you need a plug in, otherwise some Web pages you visit won't display properly.

Software
Any program, or group of programs, that tells the hardware how it should perform, including operating systems, applications and utility programs.

Soundcard
An add-on device that plugs into an expansion slot inside your PC and generates analogue sound signals. Soundcards are used to play back music and sound effects, such as from a Wav or Midi file, or CD–ROM. A wavetable card is most realistic; it has samples of real instruments used to create music, rather than a synthesiser.

Status bar
A line at the top or bottom of a screen which gives information about the task currently being worked on, such as the position of the cursor, the number of lines, filename, time and so on.

Swap file
A hidden file stored on the hard disk that Windows uses to hold parts of programs and data files that don't fit in memory. Windows moves data between the swap file and memory as needed. The swap file is a form of virtual memory.

TCP/IP
Stands for transmission control protocol/internet protocol. This is the network protocol used to send information over the Internet. It describes how information must be packaged and addressed so that it reaches the right destination and the computer can understand it.

Terminate and stay resident (TSR)
A program which loads itself into main memory and stays there even when the user exits it. It is then immediately available at the press of a hotkey. Commonly used for utilities and for drivers such as a CD–ROM driver. However, TSRs often cause difficulties

when installing new programs. To see which TSRs are running, press Ctrl-Alt-Del and close all the programs you can.

Thumbnail
A miniature graphical representation of an image. Used by graphic designers as a quick and convenient method of viewing the contents of graphics or DTP files without opening them.

Touch screen
A computer display that has a grid of infra-red transmitters and receivers positioned on either side of the screen, which is used to control the cursor. When you want to make a selection or to move the cursor, you point to the screen, breaking two of the beams, and this gives the exact position of your finger.

TWAIN
Stands for Technology Without An Interesting Name. It is the standard way for scanners to communicate with a PC. All scanners come with a TWAIN driver, which makes them compatible with any TWAIN-supporting software.

Upgrade
To improve the performance or specification of your computer by adding more RAM, a larger hard disk or another kind of improvement. Software can also be upgraded from an old version to a more recent one.

URL
Stands for Uniform Resource Locator. A URL is the technical name for an Internet address. For example, the URL of the Microsoft home page is http://www.microsoft.com.

USB
Stands for Universal Serial Bus. This is a recent standard for connecting peripherals, such as scanners, printers, cameras and mice. You can add up to 127 devices through a single port. USB also supports hot plugging, that is, connecting or disconnecting devices without switching off the PC.

Utility program
Utility programs, or 'utilities', help you get more out of your PC. They provide file management capabilities, such as sorting, copying, comparing, listing and searching, as well as diagnostic and measurement routines that check the health and performance of the system.

Vapourware
Products which exist in name and marketing hype only and are never likely to appear!

Virtual memory
Neat trick to give your PC more memory than it physically has. Free space on your hard drive is used as a temporary storage area and information is swapped in and out of memory as needed.

WAP
Stands for Wireless Application Protocol. WAP mobile phones can view simple Web pages to look at e-mail, check share prices, or get the latest news.

WAV
This is the format that Windows uses for storing most sound files. They can be recognised by the .wav extension.

WYSIWYG
Stands for What You See Is What You Get. The user sees a document exactly as it will appear in the final version. An example is a word processing or DTP program where the display on screen is the same as the image or text that will be printed, including graphics and special fonts.

Zip file
A file format used to save disk space. A single Zip file is used as a container for one or more compressed files. These must be expanded to their original size before they can be used. The format was originally devised for use by utilities called PKZip and PKUnzip, but is now so common that virtually all compression and decompression programs can handle the format. Compressed files are shown by the file extension .zip.

Zip Drive
A high-capacity disk drive from Iomega which can store from 100MB to 250MB of data on sturdy, pocket-sized removable disks. Because of their capacity they are useful for backing up day-to-day data.

Index